PELICAN BOOKS
African Affairs

EDITOR: RONALD S

Southern Afri
The New Poli

Basil Davidson is an historian of Africa whose books include *Old Africa Rediscovered* (1959), *Black Mother* (1961), *The African Past* (1964), *Africa in History* (1968, paperback edition 1975), and *The Africans, a Cultural and Social History* (Penguin 1973). He has also long specialized in the study of Portugal's former colonies, Angola, Guinea-Bissau and Mozambique, and has written *The Liberation of Guiné* (Penguin 1969) and *In the Eye of the Storm, Angola's People* (Penguin 1974). He has been visiting professor at universities in Africa, the U.S.A. and Britain, and is an honorary fellow of the Centre of West African Studies, University of Birmingham.

Joe Slovo practised as a barrister in Johannesburg (1951–63) and has appeared as a defence counsel in numerous political and civil rights trials. In 1956 he was arrested on an allegation of High Treason – whilst acting as one of the defence counsel for the other accused – and charged with 156 other political activists in a trial which was to last for four years and which ended in acquittals. He was detained under the emergency regulations which followed the Sharpeville shootings in 1961 and left South Africa in 1963. Since then he has been a full-time functionary of the liberation movement.

Anthony R. Wilkinson was born and educated in Rhodesia. He studied Politics and History at University College, Swansea (1967–70) and then returned to Rhodesia for a few months. Since 1972 he has been engaged in research for a doctoral thesis on *Insurgency and Counter-Insurgency: The Dimensions of the Conflict in Rhodesia* in the Department of International Relations at the London School of Economics and Political Science. During 1975 he was a Research Associate at the International Institute for Strategic Studies in London. Anthony R. Wilkinson is the author of several Adelphi Papers, including *Insurgency in Rhodesia, 1957–1973: An Account and Assessment* and several articles on contemporary Southern African affairs.

Contents

PART THREE

From Rhodesia to Zimbabwe
Anthony R. Wilkinson

List of Tables and Text Figures

Foreword

Some time ago, I received a copy of the paper on guerrilla warfare in Rhodesia, written by Anthony Wilkinson for the International Institute for Strategic Studies. It was a paper that underlined how vitally involved was the course of guerrilla warfare in Rhodesia with developments in Portugal's African empire and in the Republic of South Africa. I accordingly proposed to Mr Wilkinson that he contribute to a book which would include related studies, and he readily agreed. I then invited Basil Davidson, whose interest in African history has never assumed that history is shut up in the past, to contribute the section on Portugal's African empire; and, to write on South Africa, Joe Slovo, who had himself been closely concerned in the decision by the African National Congress and its allies to undertake armed struggle there.

From the outset, there was no design that the three contributors should collaborate. For an effective collaboration demands a sufficient correspondence of outlook. Here, then, are three separate views: but of what is essentially a single subject.

They are far from being always in conflict. There is no disposition to invest armed struggle with glamour. All war is ugly. And this is war. Indeed, each contributor in his own way makes it plain that those who set out to wage such war, did so not lightly, but only after long attempts to secure change by other means had unmistakably failed. Moreover, as each contributor makes no less plain, the violence of the revolutionary is a response to the violence of the régime, whose establishment was not due to measures of peaceful persuasion, and whose survival has never relied on the force of its claim to benevolence.

In the course of conflict, inevitably, the violence of the régime becomes more intense, widespread and overt; and in the process, advances the very challenge that it is directed to defeat. For, if the régime cannot isolate and crush that challenge virtually as it emerges, violence against it must increasingly involve its environment; driving those who are still cautious, still undecided, but who are punished or threatened nonetheless, to join the challenge themselves. The point is thus reached where whatever the régime chooses to do must weaken its hold. If it reduces the scale of its violence, it facilitates the advance of the challenge; and if it does not, it fortifies that challenge with expanding popular support. Those search-and-destroy missions, upon which counter-insurgency has so often come to depend, strike at the props of the régime itself.

This presupposes, however, that the revolutionary movement does not squander its opportunities; above all, because the leadership comes to believe that it must command a blind obedience from the led. The success of armed struggle does not require an infallibility of judgement; mistakes, like reverses, cannot be altogether avoided. It does require a creative relationship between the leaders and the led; a continual democracy of learning that alone can translate mistakes into a reinvigoration of purpose. And to this process, indeed, there must never be an end. For success merely transforms the terms of struggle. To make a revolution is the prelude to making it work. And the revolution that succeeds only to discard that democracy of learning, on the pretext that the leaders now need to protect the led from themselves, is a revolution that simultaneously becomes its own executioner.

Meanwhile, for some, the phase of armed struggle has barely begun. Such beginnings are particularly difficult. For the challenge is most vulnerable when it is still emerging. And how much more difficult the beginning must be, when it confronts not the forces of a distant metropolis, itself backward and poor; nor those of a settler population relatively so small that it has already needed to solicit assistance from outside; but those of a rich industrial state, whose régime can rely on the adherence of a considerable community. South Africa is, in important respects, a special case.

Yet the South African régime has been revealing distinct signs of alarm at its own vulnerability. More than ever, with the eruption of strikes through successive layers of political repression, it recognizes that the major source of its material strength, in industrial development, must constitute a major weakness, in the dependence of this development on black labour. In the ideological dog-days of Dr Verwoerd, official diviners claimed to see in 'apartheid' the possibilities of reducing such dependence. But with gathering suggestions that these possibilities might involve some sacrifice by the white community, the diviners found the ranks of their faithful thinning fast. The number of blacks summoned to serve the promotion of white privilege has continued to mount.

Nor does the régime consider South Africa to be so far a special case as to permit indifference to the changes taking place in the rest of the continent. Even as the contributions to this book were being prepared, events were re-shaping the material. The long-lived Portuguese dictatorship fell at last to a disaffection within the armed forces that owed much of its impulse to the momentum of the African challenge; and the new Portugal set about the formal surrender of the imperial mission. The implications for the survival of the settler régime in Rhodesia and for their own security were not lost upon the rulers of South Africa, who became correspondingly concerned to achieve a helpful understanding with those same black governments and movements abroad that they had once so execrated and threatened.

They are not without pressures to exert. They can make life so much easier for those willing to accommodate themselves, and so much more difficult for those who refuse. The gifts they bear, of grants and low-interest loans for economic development, of goods and markets, glitter more brightly alongside the darkening prospects of trade and aid elsewhere. And their threats, of subversion and sabotage and direct military chastisement, are no less effective for being held, just far enough to remain still partly in sight, behind their backs. Prosperity and peace, of a kind: it may seem an agreeable proposition. But the price to be paid is high. For it means abandoning not only the cause of the subjugated in South Africa, in fact, if not in form: the present commanders of white supremacy pride themselves on being realists and will know how to ignore the ritual of protest and complaint. It means abandoning also the cause of something better than the old future for Africa.

So often in the past, men have risen against their rulers to achieve freedom not only for themselves, but for others, for all. And when after freeing themselves, they found the achievement of freedom by others a rather less absorbing concern, it is because they have meanwhile been turning their own new freedom into an old servitude with a different name. So many of those who set out to free themselves in other parts of Africa, attached the achievement of that freedom to the cause of a free South Africa. Just as South Africa was for them the supreme symbol of their subjugation, so it became the supreme symbol of their commitment to a new society, a new culture of freedom; not only in the individual territories wrested from imperial repression but across a continent united for a new history. And now, there are those jealously sovereign states, sanctifying frontiers drawn by European predators to define their respective domains; those élites scarcely less remote from the multitude than their imperial predecessors were; those prisons crowded with agitators and troublemakers. What is new?

To be sure, that is not all. There are régimes which continue to keep one hand within reach of the commitment, while the other gropes for the passage of retreat. And Mr Davidson makes out an eloquent case for our recognizing that a new politics has emerged at last, from the course of armed struggle against Portuguese power. It may well be the beginning of that elusive new society, that new history for Africa. At least it seems to encourage a renewal of hope. And that in itself is momentous.

So many have simply ceased to believe in the possibility of a different Africa. They have accommodated themselves to the reality that the past dictates. Yet the men who defeated the Portuguese empire believed in a different reality; believed that the dictatorship of the past is an illusion which only hopelessness confuses with the real. If that different reality is not now denied by the very régimes that develop from it, it must excite among other Africans a search to make it their reality as well. And it is inconceivable that, within this different reality, there will be room to accommodate white supremacy.

Ronald Segal
April 1975

Acknowledgements

From Rhodesia to Zimbabwe by Anthony R. Wilkinson is an expanded version of Adelphi Paper No. 100, published by the International Institute for Strategic Studies in Autumn 1973.

Part One:

The Politics of Armed Struggle: National Liberation in the African Colonies of Portugal

Basil Davidson

What has to be achieved is that people themselves discover the need for armed struggle. As for guns, those you can always find . . .

Nguyen Van Tien

Introduction

A lot has been written about guerrilla warfare over the past dozen years; and that, unhappily, includes a lot of nonsense. There were even occasions when a luridly romanticized figure of 'the man with the gun' could be presented, just because he had a gun, as offering 'all the answers' to an audience both wide and international: only to reveal, amid cries of foreseeable disillusionment or disgust, that really he had no answers or none worth listening to.

And yet the history of these years has also shown that 'the man with the gun' could have, and in certain notable cases probably has had, unique and effective answers to political problems. In an obsessively ego-boosting world, moreover, it has even been that these answers were often of a kind that was singularly pure and unself-seeking, answers that jaded and abused peoples could accept with a sense of moral renewal, answers that could promise a creative peace attainable by no other means.

What happens when guerrilla action is not a sordid or deplorable adventure: when it stems from a serious and useful programme, capable of directing violence to controlled and constructive ends? How does that come about? What sort of people bring it into being?

To these particular questions the answers here come out of Africa. That may be unexpected, even surprising: Africa hasn't had much of a reputation for doing much that is new, or for doing it with much success. All the same, the facts about these answers are not in dispute. The facts are only little known or not known at all.

The heritage of the colonial period in Africa was often a hard one. Some of the toughest of its problems lay in the persistence of régimes of racist dictatorship in South Africa and Namibia,

Zimbabwe and the Portuguese colonies of Guinea-Bissau and the Cape Verde Islands, Angola with the islands of São Tomé and Principe, and Mozambique.

Peaceful change was tried by Africans of these territories, but was found impossible. Men saw that only a constructive use of violence – more accurately, of counter-violence to the violence of their racist rulers – could achieve the change that needed to be made. Otherwise things would stay as they were for the great majority of people, or things would get worse.

This chapter is about a constructive use of counter-violence in the colonies of Portugal. These countries were extremely distant and obscure when the politics of armed struggle began there early in the 1960s. They are less unknown to the world today. All the same, many alert and well-informed persons might still find it hard to place these countries on the map, or to say anything much about the fifteen or sixteen million Africans who live in them.

Yet it remains that the people of these colonies wrote an altogether remarkable story of liberating struggle during the 1960s and early 1970s. This story has much to tell that is of a moral and political interest reaching far outside the boundaries of these territories, or even of the wide continent of Africa itself.

1 A Decisive Success

'Our armed forces,' said General Costa Gomes, 'have reached the limits of neuro-psychological exhaustion.' That is what the Portuguese Chief of Staff and afterwards President of Portugal had to tell the press in the Mozambican capital of Lourenço Marques (since re-named Maputo) on 11 May 1974.

Put a little more bluntly, Portugal's soldiers and airmen had had enough. They did not therefore run away from the Africans they had been fighting for so long: in Angola since February 1961, in Guinea-Bissau since January 1963, and in Mozambique since September 1964. But they decided to end their wars. They took it on the chin. They accepted their defeat.

That led directly to the Portuguese officers' *coup d'état* of 25 April 1974, which overthrew the dictatorship established in Portugal forty-eight years earlier. Decolonizing had become the only way to end these wars that were ruining the Portuguese, these wars that Portugal could not win. So the dictatorship was overthrown because it would not decolonize. The world then saw that the African liberation movements had done more than free their own peoples: they had also given the Portuguese their chance to free themselves. It was a decisive victory over misery and oppression in Europe as well as in Africa; and it was a military victory.

'If you don't now make a firm peace, or if you try to stop the peaceful withdrawal of our forces,' the commandant of a major Portuguese military base in Guinea-Bissau told his general during the second week of August 1974, in the hearing of a friend of mine: 'then I and all my men will declare ourselves prisoners-of-war of the P.A.I.G.C.'[1]

I got to know this commandant. He was not demoralized and he was certainly no coward. But he had made up his mind, even if rather late in the day (yet better late than never), that peaceful withdrawal had become the only sensible and patriotic policy for the Portuguese to follow.

Like others of his kind, he had little interest in politics. As a professional soldier, he had gone to the wars along with the rest; and year after year he had carried out his orders. These orders had certainly killed or wounded far more civilians, including women and children, than guerrillas; but this commandant had continued to obey them. Now he could see convincing reasons for disobeying them. In this he was like a large number of Portugal's professional soldiers, and a still larger number of Portugal's conscripts. The generals might want the wars to continue, but the generals sat safely in the rear. By the beginning of 1974 their orders for offensive action were less and less obeyed. In the end they were not obeyed at all.

A military success, then; and of large dimensions. The armed forces of the Portuguese dictatorship had fought hard; they had also fought with every means at their disposal. For years this dictatorship had spent almost half of Portugal's annual budget on the support of its armed forces in Africa. By 1968 these forces totalled some 130,000 metropolitan troops in all arms, not counting other tens of thousands levied in the territories themselves.[2] These were by far the largest armies ever raised in Portuguese history: by ratio of population sizes, they were about six times larger than the largest United States military force maintained in South Vietnam.

And they were not alone in their effort. On the contrary, they were well and continuously supplied by their allies of the North Atlantic Treaty Organization with bombers and helicopters, napalm and fragmentation bombs, sophisticated aiming-sights and other products of the latest technology, as well as money and diplomatic support. Almost every major power in the Western world, as well as the government of South Africa, helped the war effort of the Lisbon dictatorship. It could not be said that the dictatorship had failed through lack of aid and encouragement from its friends.

The men and women who outfaced and outfought this huge machinery of repression had begun as handfuls of guerrillas, poorly armed, scantily trained. They had followed the tactics of guerrilla warfare, learning as they went along but applying what they knew with skill and courage. They had suffered many setbacks, several disasters, painful losses, years of living at the end of their nerves and bodily strength. They had kept on, had got better at their work, reinforced their gains. By 1974 they were far from having reached the limits of exhaustion, whether 'neuro-psychological' or not. They were prepared for more years of warfare, even for as many more years as their victory might require.[3]

It may be questioned if the world had previously seen a success to compare with this one. Enormous modern armies, of a general toughness and tenacity never in doubt until near the end, were outpaced and outmatched by fighters who came from populations whose technological level, whose initial command of any aspect of 'modern science', whose 'starting point' of literacy or any other educational preparation, were always far lower than had been the case, for example, in Cuba or Vietnam. In technological terms, these were very 'backward' populations. And yet they were able to win.

The essential reason why they were able to win lay outside the military field. Successful guerrilla warfare is always and above all political warfare; and so it was in these wars, abundantly and often brilliantly. The men and women who led these struggles were certainly effective in their military tactics and strategies. But they excelled in their politics.

They gave to their politics of national liberation a dynamism and expanding reality that carried their resistance from its early ripples, which were almost nothing, to a tide that nothing could stop. It is their politics that are really interesting. Their politics explain what must otherwise remain mysterious.

That is what the Portuguese side of these wars also showed. For the essence of the Lisbon *coup d'état* which overthrew the old dictatorship was precisely that the politics of national liberation had won Portuguese hearts and minds as well. There is copious evidence for this, whether in the *coup* itself or in its major consequences throughout the rest of 1974. Many examples might be offered of this 'transfer' to the Portuguese of the African politics of liberation. One, at least, may be useful here.

On 29 July 1974, in the still colonial capital of Bissau, the territorial assembly of the Guinea-Bissau section of the Portuguese Armed Forces Movement, (MFA), the movement of young officers who had carried through the *coup* of 25 April, met in convocation and acclaimed a new statement of their views and aims.

This Guinea-Bissau section of the MFA had taken a lead before; and evidence even suggests that the whole movement first took shape among officers serving in Guinea-Bissau. In advance of other territorial groupings of the MFA, moreover, the group in Guinea had extended itself right down the ranks, and had become an 'army movement' with a potentially and even to some extent a really democratic structure.[4] Now, on 29 July, its territorial assembly went a long step further towards fructifying the twin hopes sown by the *coup*, those of 'Decolonization and Democratization'.

'The colonized peoples and the people of Portugal,' ran this memorable declaration, 'are allies. The struggle for national liberation has contributed powerfully to the overthrow of fascism and, in large degree, has lain at the base of the Armed Forces Movement whose officers have learned in Africa the horrors of a war without prospect (*sem finalidade*), and have therefore understood the roots of the evils which afflict the society of Portugal . . .'[5] What could be a clearer demonstration of the power and influence exercised by the politics of national liberation?

Or where, from another angle, could one better see the full impact and persuasive meaning of the *political* principles of the national liberation movements? Of political principles such as that enunciated by Luis Cabral, assistant secretary-general of the PAIGC and president of the independent state of Guinea-Bissau, during August 1974: 'We have fought this war without hatred for the Portuguese people, and we are ending it without hatred.'[6]

And as for Guinea-Bissau, so also for the Cape Verde islands and for Mozambique and potentially for Angola and its offshore islands of São Tomé and Principe. 'In the course of its struggle,' ran Article 19 of the agreement signed on 7 September 1974, between the Mozambican movement of national liberation and the government of Portugal, 'FRELIMO has always distinguished between the Portuguese people and the Portuguese state, and will develop its efforts to build a fraternal and harmonious co-operation between Portugal and Mozambique.'[7] Portugal had gained at home from this African success; but she could also gain in Africa.

So the political victory was larger even than the military victory to which it had also given rise. This political victory for the Africans was one that could become a political victory for the Portuguese as well. History has not often shown us anything like that.

Yet this was a success that for years had seemed a vision so remote as to be barely thinkable. When the PAIGC was founded secretly in 1956, eighteen years before Portugal withdrew, its entire membership consisted of six persons. When the MPLA of Angola was similarly launched in the same year its numbers were not much larger, and in any case were desperately few. And when in 1962 FRELIMO took shape from a scatter of little nationalist groupings, its formation did not even occur in Mozambique but in neighbouring Tanganyika (Tanzania). Yet these were the movements that would thrust Portugal's armies to 'the limits of neuro-psychological exhaustion', and would then make peace on their own terms.

How did it happen? The full answer is one of tortuous complexity and ravelled detail; much of it has still to be revealed. Yet one can at least untangle its main threads, and see where these came from and how they were spun, and who it was that had the spinning of them.

To do this, one needs to cast back a little in time.

2 The Colonial Background

A British historian of the Africans has justly observed that 'all the European empires in Africa were empires of race . . .'[1] Much became specific about the Portuguese colonial system and ethos, but essentially they were no different from those of the British or the French or other European rulers of the continent. The language of aims and intentions might vary from the floridly paternalist to the frankly brutal; generally, in practice, it came down to pretty much the same thing.

'What are we doing in the Congo?' asked a Belgian Minister of Colonies in 1920, and answered himself: 'We have a dual aim there. To spread civilization. To develop markets for Belgium, and Belgium's economy.'[2] Speaking for the British imperial system somewhat earlier, Lord Milner had struck a more elevated note. 'Imperialism as a political doctrine,' he explained, 'has often been represented as something tawdry and superficial. In reality it has all the depth and comprehensiveness of a religious faith. Its significance is moral even more than material . . .'[3]

Yet a disrespectful eye would have noticed that it was all one in the end. The dispossession of the Africans of South Africa, where Lord Milner laboured at the altars of his faith, was more sordidly pursued even than in the Belgian Congo. The French imperialists, for their part, made no bones about the material profits they were chasing in Africa, and regarded men like Milner as characteristic English hypocrites.

Not so, however, the Portuguese; or at least those Portuguese concerned with Portugal's 'African mission'. They were great Milnerites. Seldom can a country's spokesmen have vanished so completely into the clouds and mists of rhetorical exaggeration. Even during the old Republic, before 1926, the language generally in use about 'Portugal in Africa' made Lord Milner's seem earth-bound by comparison. The men of the dictatorship soared still higher into the skies of the unreal.

Thus we find Franco Nogueira, as the dictatorship's foreign minister in 1966, explaining to an audience in the United States that 'we alone, before anyone else, brought to Africa the notion of human rights and racial equality': and this at a time when the overwhelming majority of all Africans in the Portuguese colonies were not only legally and practically bereft of the most elementary civil rights, but had been subject for many decades to a régime of discrimination that automatically denied them the least hope or possibility of racial equality. Portugal might be criticized, continued Nogueira: but 'we reply that our African provinces are more developed, more progressive in every respect, than any recently independent territory in Africa south of the Sahara, without exception';[4] and this at a time when all three of these 'provinces' were being scorched by the fires of Portuguese napalm and lit up, week after week, by African villages in flames.

What the Portuguese were really able to bring to Africa, as the records patiently explain, was neither civilization nor equality, but first of all the slave trade so as to furnish new plantations in Brazil, and afterwards a localized exploitation of African land and labour whose crudity reflected the feudal or semi-feudal degradation of Portugal itself. Their mariners of the fifteenth century were valiant seamen, but they made their fortunes by looting the cities of coastal Africa and then of India. They drove their keels through unknown oceans, crossed horizons never seen by any European before them, and made landfalls on countries for which Europe did not even have names. But what followed upon these mariners was a system of primitive extraction, not of civilization.

Even this, for an immensely long time, was limited to a few forts and posts along the seaboard of West Africa, near the estuary of the Congo river in Angola or southward for a few hundred miles, and similarly along the coast of Mozambique or inland up the course of the Zambezi river. Even in 1846 the total number of Portuguese in the 'kingdoms of Angola and Benguela' was only 1,832, and 1,466 of these were in the capital of Luanda; no more than six Europeans lived in the Angolan 'backlands' east of the coast. Nor was it much different in Mozambique. And when the true colonial period began for the Portuguese, in the second half of the nineteenth century, its basis in primitive extraction did not change. It only expanded.[5]

It expanded after the 1870s, and consistently during later times, in two ways. First, it expropriated African land in favour of Portuguese and other European immigrant settlers, both in Angola and Mozambique though not in Guinea-Bissau where rural settlement of Europeans was never practised. Secondly, it expropriated African labour. This labour expropriation took a variety of forms. Outright slavery within these countries gave way to masked substitutes, later known as 'contract labour'. These provided labour at dirt-cheap rates of pay, or none at all, for administrative as well as settler needs. Another form of land-and-labour coercion, much used in the later decades of the system, obliged African peasants to grow export crops at prices fixed by Portuguese purchasing companies. From the African point of view it is scarcely exaggeration to say that the system evolved from one of outright slavery to one of conditional slavery, and that it so remained until the great upheavals of the last few years.[6]

In all this, the great difference from other colonial territories was one of degree rather than of principle. The guiding principle in all these territories, or at least in all those where white settlement occurred, can perhaps be seen most easily in labour legislation. Though varying much in detail, this legislation was universally based upon the principle that Africans could not be said to be working unless they worked for wages: in other words, unless they worked for Europeans, since wage-paid labour was practically unknown among Africans until the colonial period was well advanced.[7] This attitude responded to the general colonial difficulty of inducing Africans to quit their villages, where they worked for themselves (though not for cash wages), and to go to work for Europeans. Two solutions were found. In each case they were invariably glossed with the same excuse: to make Africans work for wages – that is, to supply labour to settlers – was the right and proper way to bring Africans what were known, again universally, as 'the blessings of civilization'.

One of these solutions, deriving from attitudes of slavery, was to round up Africans by force, take them to their 'places of work', and make sure that they worked there. All the colonial powers used this method. Not a single road or railway or other 'public work' of the early colonial period was built or laid or raised without directly forced labour, even if this was not always admitted to be such. In that respect the Portuguese were no worse than any of the others; and perhaps they were even better, if only because they built fewer roads, railways or other 'public works'.

The second solution was to impose on individual Africans a personal tax which had to be paid in cash, with imprisonment and convict labour as the penalty for failure to pay. Although quantities of coin were beginning to circulate in coastal territories before the end of the nineteenth century, the majority of rural Africans possessed none or very little. So they had to earn the coins they needed for tax payments, and there was only one way of doing this: going to work for Europeans at whatever rates of pay the Europeans cared to give them.

As befitted the economically most advanced of the colonial powers, Britain was the first to apply this second 'solution' on any scale, and the earliest definition of its method and attendant advantages seems to have been provided, again very fittingly, by Cecil Rhodes when Prime Minister of the Cape Colony of South Africa. His Glen Grey Act of 1894, though not in itself a great success, was in many ways to become a model. It enacted that African males should pay a 'labour tax' of ten shillings a year – perhaps £5 or $11.50 in the values of 1974 – unless they could prove that during three months of the previous year they had been 'in service or employment beyond the borders of the district'. The design was that large numbers of rural Africans would thereby be forced to leave their villages and take employment on white farms. This would increase the labour supply and so lower the level of wages.

'You will,' Rhodes explained to the Cape Assembly, 'thereby

remove [the natives] from [their] life of sloth and laziness, you will teach them the dignity of labour and make them contribute to the prosperity of the State, and make them give some return for our wise and good government.'[8] They were words of a kind that Portuguese colonial legislators were often to repeat in the years which then lay ahead.

The point of these few observations is not to offer a potted sketch of colonial realities, but to indicate the nature of the similarities as well as differences that had to be faced by people living under one colonial rule or another. They received the same 'blessings' as their neighbours, but those in Portugal's colonies received them in forms and quantities special to the Portuguese. For the Portuguese, being themselves a poor and much abused people governed rigidly from above, were generally reduced to sketching a caricature of the great imperial mission. They too talked incessantly of high principles. But in practice they used coercion, whether directly or indirectly, on a scale that never ceased to grow until the 1960s; and they thus used it long after other Powers had reached a point where they could rely for supplies of labour on the 'machinery of the market': on economic patterns, that is, whose coercions were inherent to a way of life pinned ever increasingly, and 'automatically', to the earning of wages or the need for cash.

One needs to insist upon this long-continuing Portuguese use of primitive forms of coercion because it became one of the major factors in shaping the rise of popular resistance after the Second World War. Of course there were other formative factors. The general crudity of a poorly-paid and often demoralized administration was one of them. The consistent repression of public protest or criticism was another. The direct impoverishment of rural Africans, whether by the obligation to grow export-crops or in other ways, was a third. The much lower wages paid to urban Africans, in comparison with those paid to urban whites, was a fourth. The rise of nationalism elsewhere in Africa was a factor of another kind. Ghana became independent in 1957, Guinea in 1958, Senegal and the Belgian Congo in 1960, Tanganyika in 1961; and the example of all these neighbours taught new lessons. And there were, as we shall see, other and more intimately shaping factors of a political nature. Yet the burden of forced labour was an all-pervasive weight. Resentment of it goes a long way towards explaining the mass response that the liberation movements were able to evoke.

3 Portugal in Africa: A Special Case?

Portugal was not a 'special case' among the colonizing Powers by any essential difference of policy or principle. But Portugal clearly became such a case by reason of her peculiar political backwardness and economic poverty. The difference was never very great in what was intended, for the 'basic texts' of the Portuguese will be found to have said the same as those of richer powers: the difference appeared in the application. Crude, spasmodic and confused, the latter formed the arena in which the politics of national liberation had to struggle for survival and success.

It might be thought that Portugal's subjugation to a fascist-style dictatorship, quite early in the main colonial period, would have made a large difference to the Africans of these territories. When beginning to study Portuguese colonialism twenty years ago, I used to think so. Certainly the dictatorship's methods of repression and coercion became generally far more severe and painful, not to say downright stupid, than those of colonial governments emanating from parliamentary democracies. Yet it seems doubtful if the advent of the dictatorship made life significantly worse for the majority of colonized Africans. What was chiefly done, within these perspectives, was to transfer to the Portuguese themselves a totalitarian rule already practised towards Africans. A people which had enslaved another duly forged its own chains.

This is another point of historical importance, for it helps to explain the developmental continuity of African protest and resistance. These peoples did not find themselves, after 1926 with the coming of the dictatorship, moved suddenly from liberal enlightenment to the dark night of arbitrary rule. The darkness was already upon them. It became darker still, at least after the 1930s; but that was all. This is why later forms of African protest and resistance grew organically from earlier forms.

A continuity of colonial theory and practice can be seen in every large aspect of the system. Most easily, perhaps, it can be seen in the work of the man who was Portugal's major system-builder in Africa, Norton de Matos. Appointed to govern Angola shortly before the First World War, he set about modernizing the 'labour situation', by this time so near to a revival of the outright slavery of the nineteenth century as to threaten an international scandal. Norton's method was to extend the contractual system of recruiting labour. By the end of his governorship, in 1915, he had at least published a series of regulations designed to limit and reduce the element of direct coercion.

In vain, however. Norton returned to Angola in 1921, again under the parliamentary republic but this time as High Commissioner, a post equivalent to Governor-General. He found that his earlier decrees had gone for nothing. 'A veritable leprosy of corruption now covered almost everything that touched on native labour, and it cost me much in my first two years [1921–2] to cauterize and suppress the disease.'[1] He began to publish more regulations. They had little long-term effect.

But in other ways Norton left his mark. He completed the conquest of Angola, suppressed the last remnants of the authority of chiefs in the eastern interior, and carried through a transformation from military rule to civilian administration backed by troops and police. No less important for what was to come later, he also laid the foundations for the system of racist discrimination and virtual *apartheid* over which the governors of the dictatorship (1926–74) were to preside.

These foundations were twofold. First, they underpinned a pattern of direct rule through nominated 'chiefs' whose subservience had to be complete, and duly became so. Secondly, they provided for a rigid segregation of the population into defined categories. What emerged had in practice no real difference from the South African system save for one comparatively unimportant exception. Persons of mixed origin – mestiço or mulatto in the jargon of administration – could assimilate themselves to whites, as in South Africa they could not (unless they were able to conceal their origin). To that extent it was true, and remained true, that Portuguese 'colour prejudice' was less emphatic than in South Africa. But this worked in favour only of an insignificantly small number of blacks who were able to achieve the wealth or status required for such assimilation. The vast majority of blacks remained beyond the pale. Counted as *indígenas*, natives, they were the mere objects of administration, just as in South Africa. They formed rather more than ninety-nine per cent of the black populations.

Norton's decree 137 of 1921 became a key document. It applied only to Angola, but comparable regulations would afterwards erect parallel situations in Mozambique, and to a lesser degree in the relatively settler-free Guinea-Bissau. Pursuing a familiar policy of divide-and-rule, Norton set about dividing large ethnic groupings into a number of smaller ones, mainly through the method of establishing village settlements 'under the direct chiefship of native *regedores* ['chiefs']' selected by the administration and regarded as convenient tools.

[This] concentration of native peoples is to be done by tribes, chiefships and families subordinate to the same *seculo* ['sub-chief'] . . . All the natives of the Province of Angola are to be regrouped in places chosen for the founding of native settlements. From the date of promulgation of this decree, no native may build his hut within a perimeter reserved for the founding of urban residential centres for Europeans or civilized natives [assimilated persons], nor may these last build huts in places destined for native peoples.[2]

It may go without saying that no such neat pattern ever evolved from this early version of South Africa's Group Areas Act and its like. The thing was simply beyond Portugal's power of application. Yet efforts were made to apply it. They denied all the high-flown promises of 'racial equality', but these promises continued to be made, especially whenever a new influx of settlers called for the expropriation of more African land.

A brave old American missionary, eye-witness to Portuguese administration since the early years of the century, is one of those who have described the scene. Writing of 1943 in one of the relatively populous central-western districts, Dr Merlin Ennis noted in his journal that the local administrators

> made large concentrations. People were not given an opportunity to move with any convenience, nor were they consulted as to the desirability of the sites, but their villages were destroyed ruthlessly . . .
>
> This was done with the usual ferocity. Old and well-established villages with good, well-built houses, schoolhouses, orchards, gardens, irrigation ditches, had their houses torn down and the people themselves were herded into inconvenient and insanitary sites.[3]

Twenty years later the same process was repeated during the liberation struggle, but on a much larger scale. This time the aim was primarily to 'deny the population to terrorist infection'. With that in mind, the Portuguese army drove tens of thousands of rural Africans into army-guarded camps and settlements: just as, at the same time, the South African authorities were driving 'their Africans' into new sites dictated by the laws of *apartheid*. In this and in other ways the administrative attitudes of the parliamentary republic were carried on under the dictatorship.

There were local variations from territory to territory, but all the three major Portuguese colonies were governed by the same general rules. All knew forced labour in the direct sense. All knew it also in the indirect sense: in the obligation, that is, to grow export crops for European buyers. The man who succeeded Salazar as dictator of Portugal, Marcello Caetano, defined the system when a professor of Lisbon University. 'The natives of Africa,' he taught in a course of lectures given during 1952–3, 'must be directed and organized by Europeans . . . The blacks must be seen as productive elements organized, or to be organized, in an economy directed by whites.'[4] This was the reality behind the paternalist verbiage.

It followed that 'the natives' could be allowed only the narrowest scope for self-expression or self-defence. The parliamentary republic had been sure of this, as the work of Norton and his like had repeatedly proved. The dictatorship was still more sure. After all, the scope for self-expression or self-defence barely existed, after 1926, for the mass of Portuguese themselves. How much less could the dictatorship allow any such scope to 'natives'?

A more detailed record would bear out this general account of the circumstances in which the liberation struggle had somehow to shape itself. The numbers of assimilated blacks and 'mulattoes' became a little larger. But they were still insignificantly small; while their social status, if anything, tended to fall in relation to the growing numbers of white settlers who wanted urban jobs. Colour discrimination grew, no matter what the laws might say. Even the lucky few, struggling to understand their situation so as to find out how to improve it, saw themselves enveloped in the general ignorance that bedevilled the Portuguese themselves and encouraged the mystifications of Lusitanian mythology.

The rest of the Africans of these territories, more than ninety-nine per cent,[5] were in practice without any means of self-defence, let alone of self-enlightenment. At best they were regarded as 'productive elements organized or to be organized in an economy directed by whites'; at worst, as faceless savages. There were courageous Portuguese who saw this and protested. They made no difference. They lost their jobs or were packed away in jails.

It was a difficult heritage for the Africans of the 1960s: certainly, more difficult than that of many other colonized peoples. A consistent denial of all legal means for acquiring political information on one hand, and the administrative promotion of 'tribal differences' on the other, stood squarely across the path to unity of resistance. A few blacks and 'mulattoes' might acquire a modern education, but for this they had to pay the price of ceasing to be Africans. Where other Africans could use their education to inspect the stratagems of nationalism in Europe, and exploit the possibilities of reformist pressure from the 'mother countries', those of the Portuguese empire had no such opportunities. They found it difficult to learn even about events in neighbouring African countries.

When the national movements began to emerge, they had accordingly to find their way out of an extreme isolation. 'Perhaps it is too soon,' wrote Amílcar Cabral, one of the most memorable and influential of those who made that difficult journey,

'to write the history of the liberation of the Portuguese territories. But those who will one day write it will have to recall a fact of characteristic influence on the development of these struggles, whether in their internal dynamic or in their relation with the outside world: the *wall of silence* built around our peoples by Portuguese colonialism . . .'[6]

This wall of silence proved very hard to pierce.

4 Towards a Strategy of Nationalism

Whether here or elsewhere, the roots of nationalism lay in a striving for the means of self-defence against an imposed inferiority: in a struggle for equality of opportunity and livelihood. They flowered in an attempt to win advantage from the arguments and ethos of European nationalism, specifically the mature bourgeois-nationalism of the imperialist period: to use the language of the rights of man in Africa as this had been used in Europe, and so devise stratagems for progress and reform that were modelled on European stratagems in Europe. To the extent that this attempt has now succeeded it has accordingly done so at the cost of accepting the European nationalist model, even while history may suggest that this model has exhausted its potential for constructive change.

Such strivings, for a long time, were the work of a very few men, and still fewer women, who were able to acquire the modern education that could 'explain Europe'. The bulk of the colonized populations remained within their own historical frameworks of belief and behaviour. These, too, they sought to use in their self-defence. They fought the invaders in many stiff battles. After they were defeated they rose in countless rebellions that were duly put down in what became known as 'campaigns of pacification'. They tried other methods of self-defence: religious, cultural, even economic. Much of this they did within the ideas and attitudes of Africa's own history, of the heritage that they had received from their own past. Not until after the Second World War, and in the Portuguese colonies not until the late 1950s, did the ideas of nationalism, the ideas of the 'European heritage', begin to mean anything to the vast majority of these colonized peoples.

Before that time, the privileged few who could seek for a

strategy of self-defence in the ideas of European nationalism were largely severed from the mass of their fellow-countrymen. They wished to defend their people as well as themselves, but at the same time their own positions of relative privilege rested on accepting the superiority of the civilization represented by their conquerors. What they wanted or were obliged to want, or at least were obliged to appear to want if they were to have any success, was to achieve the freedoms that would enable Africans to be 'raised to the level of Europeans'. They were bound, in short, to argue the African case in terms of the values and suppositions of their European rulers.

The argument was thus conducted according to the varying attitudes of those rulers. In the French colonies the dominant principle was assimilation to French culture. For a long time, therefore, 'French African' nationalists pressed not for independence but for citizenship, while the French rulers, for their part, were happy to reinforce the argument at least to the extent of making possession of the French language a 'civilizing must'. In the British colonies, or rather in those where the absence of white settlers left an eventual African independence as a theoretical possibility for some time in the future, the argument was conducted in terms closer to those of nationalism. But from early days, especially in West Africa, there was a vivid accent on the values and virtues of Africa's own cultures. To this extent the early nationalists, who also preached the virtues of the European model as a means of African progress, had to be in contradiction with themselves.

A good example is that of a talented publicist of the Gold Coast (Ghana), Attoh Ahuma, in the years before the First World War. Like others before him, Ahuma argued that Africans should remain true to their own traditions, languages, cultures. But at the same time he saw their future in terms of Europe's civilization. 'Let us help one another,' he wrote in a well-known passage, 'to find a way out of Darkest Africa. The impenetrable forest around us is not darker than the dark primeval forest of the human mind uncultured. We must emerge from the savage backwoods . . .' But the 'savage backwoods' were precisely the place where Africa's own civilizations had taken shape.

The early nationalists of the Portuguese colonies were involved in the same contradiction. Unlike their successors, those who spoke and wrote during the years of the nineteenth century enjoyed a fairly wide freedom of expression. They founded newspapers in the colonial capitals. They thundered against Portuguese misrule. They called for far-reaching reforms. But they did all this in terms of a future which would 'civilize Africa' by European means. They accepted the goals of Europe's 'civilizing mission' even while rejecting the means that were used. If the *preto boçal*, the 'bush black', was to have any worthwhile future, they thought that he would have to be assimilated to a civilization which could not conceivably be of his own making. They were courageous men, and their dilemma was an understandable one. They saw the damaging gulf between the 'bush black' and the technologies that came from Europe. It was also a gulf between themselves and the masses. But they knew no way of getting across it, except by way of the European world.

Then came Norton de Matos' severities, the end of the parliamentary republic with its relative liberalism, and the installation of an authoritarian dictatorship which intended that the gulf should remain, and, if possible, be widened. There were several consequences. The break between the masses and the educated few who protested, or wished to protest, became practically complete. Such protest as remained possible had increasingly to be made within the narrow limits of a Portuguese civilization now in deepening decay. The 'wall of silence' became higher than before, harder to climb over: less and less was heard from the world beyond it. Even those who got to Portugal found a wall of silence there as well. Any news worth hearing had to be gleaned from democratic groups who worked in secret and faced a continuing persecution.

Protest continued. Individuals raised their solitary voices before being shut away in prisons. Rural communities rose in new revolts. And the whole picture, when it can be put together, will show that news did in fact get through the wall of silence, stimulating new ideas, giving rise to new hopes. Eduardo Mondlane, the pioneer of Mozambican nationalism who was to be assassinated in 1969, could recall how reports of Fascist Italy's invasion of Ethiopia in 1935 penetrated to remote Mozambican villages and lit new fires of belief in an eventual African liberation. Others have spoken of similar influences. Yet all such news was dulled by distance and obscured by the repression.

5 1945 and After: Bridging the Gulf

Four chief stages mark the long and testing route that led from the helplessness of the 1930s and early 1940s to the birth of movements of unity and struggle, and onward from there to the armed resistances which eventually brought down the dictatorship itself.

The first stage saw the emergence after 1945 of a new group of political thinkers among the educated few. These men and women, some of whom were afterwards to win a world-wide reputation, proved capable of evolving new strategies for a situation clearly much changed from that of the years before 1945. Intellectually, they were gifted persons, some of them outstandingly so. Yet intellectual distinction was not their only asset.

In strong contrast to earlier nationalists, they were able to step beyond the conceptual boundaries of their rulers' thought. Thanks to a realist and at times a Marxist formation acquired by clandestine contacts in Portugal and Africa, they could make their analysis and inferences while standing outside – or, according to their individual quality and experience, more or less outside – the ideas and categories of bourgeois nationalism and its Portuguese variant. In short, they were in a position to escape at last from the old contradiction between 'Europeanized intellectual' and 'bush black'. They could set about bridging the gulf between the few who were educated in the realities and possibilities of the modern world, and the many who were not.

This could not be easy. It proved extremely difficult. But these pioneers began. Around the middle of the 1950s, in a more or less perilous clandestinity, they formed new nationalist groupings or would-be groupings – of 'nationalists without a nation', as one of them would wryly recall long afterwards.

Several of these groupings managed to survive. Two or three proved effective.

A second stage opened late in the 1950s when the colonial administrations, enormously alarmed by the advances of African nationalism in neighbouring territories, set their police to tracking down and destroying these embryonic movements. This stage culminated in the repressive outrages that are familiar to such operations. The years 1959–60 saw several large-scale police shootings of African civilians who were responding in one way or another to nationalist calls for protest or demonstration.

These shootings and their like were a spur towards developing the next stage, centred around the years 1959–60. Hitherto the nationalist groupings, or at least those capable of serious purpose, had clung even if faintly to the hope that various forms of illegal but peaceful pressure could still induce the dictatorship to concede reforms. Exactly what such reforms might achieve was probably not clearly seen, or so the evidence suggests; and yet the pathway to reform could still appear as the only practicable way ahead.

Now this road was closed. In a thousand acts of repression the dictatorship showed that no reforms would be conceded. Thus deprived of any 'reformist option', these nationalists were left with no active choice but armed revolt. Colonial violence must duly evoke its answer in a counter-violence.

The fourth stage, and the one with which we are concerned here, saw the unfolding of the political and military potentials in this counter-violence with all their ambiguity of positive and negative factors and reactions. The positive factors could promote a unity of consciousness and struggle, and project a sense of nationhood where none existed. But the negative factors could obstruct the process. As events in Portugal would show in their own way during 1974, the positive factors outweighed those that were negative; but the latter remained an important aspect of the 1960s and early 1970s, especially in Angola.

The great successes eventually achieved, and obvious even to the most incredulous observers during 1974, can be said to have derived from two developmental trends. The first was concerned with the effort of the leaders of the genuine movements – for other movements appeared that were nothing of the kind – to bridge the gulf between themselves as a 'new élite of a new kind', and a sufficient mass of Africans: sufficient, that is, to set in motion and sustain and constantly enlarge a unity of consciousness and struggle.

The second trend was essential to the first. It was to shift these movements from the ideas of a merely reformist nationalism to ideas and aims that would imply and gradually define a change in the nature of society. This meant going beyond all question of reforming 'what existed', whether of colonial autocracy and repression, or of 'traditional' institutions such as polygamy and rule by elders; and to aim at the building of new attitudes and structures such as could liberate a new society from the trammels of the past.

The movements thus acquired a revolutionary character. But this, one should note, was not in the least a gratuitous grafting-on of revolutionary doctrine 'from outside'; nor had it anything to do with the slogans of 'guerrilla romanticism'. To some degree it was the product of a Marxist analysis by leaders. But the crucial point, beyond any such influence, lay in the fact that this shift from reform to revolution was vital to success.

Successful movements have to win mass support. But that is only their first task. If they stay content with this they will soon be defeated. Having won mass support, they must go on to win *mass participation*: that is, the voluntary, active and increasingly responsible self-commitment of a widening multitude of individuals to the *practice* of unity and struggle. Only this can enable such movements to survive, develop, and succeed.

The reason why this is so is twofold. Only if mass support is transformed into mass participation, whether 'at the base' or 'at the top' or in the ranks between, will leaders lose their élitist situation, and the gulf be well and truly bridged between the few and the many. And only if this happens will the movement prove able to withstand the enemy's repression and its own tendencies to organizational weakness or internal conflict.

Once this transformation comes about – as, in these cases, it did come about – then other developments follow. Mass participation takes shape across the whole field of action. Far more than in the military field, where the liberation army may be able to absorb only a few thousand full-time fighters, mass participation now means active individual membership of elected political committees, and the shouldering of numerous responsibilities which derive from the effort, in liberated areas, to build new structures for a new society.

That is why these movements became revolutionary. No doubt their best leaders always wanted this, saw it as a necessary justification for the pains and sufferings of armed resistance to an extremely repressive enemy, and planned for this result. The fact remains that the shift from reform to revolution was indispensable to a growing unity of consciousness and struggle. Whether in the measure of their success or the measure of their failure, all the examples prove this.

This is also why these movements were able in their liberated areas to develop and realize a revolutionary programme of consistent social change from the roots of their reality. Mass participation ensured this, too: no people, and certainly no peasant people, are going to accept the price of armed struggle for the sake of a programme that they do not carry through themselves. Revolutions are made at home; otherwise they fail.

Quite a few outside commentators, some merely frivolous, preferred to see things differently. They looked at the provenance of arms and ammunition or of technical training, and assigned this or that movement's ideas and loyalties to Moscow or Peking or some other fancied foreign 'centre of subversion'. They had failed to understand the vital mechanisms in play. Or else, perhaps, they were the victims of a familiar ethno-centrism, and could not believe that Africans were capable of evolving revolutionary programmes of their own.

The dictatorship's generals suffered from both forms of blindness. General Kaulza de Arriaga is a good case in point. Appointed as commander in Mozambique during 1970, he arrived with the conviction, as he hastened to explain, that he would end the war within a few months. When he was finally sacked by Lisbon in 1973, his army had not won the war but had reached, instead, 'the limits of neuro-psychological exhaustion'. But this was the same general who had advised the

Portuguese officers' corps, in a contribution to 'Lessons of Strategy in the High Command Course' written during 1966–7, that: 'Subversion is a war above all of intelligence. One needs to have a high level of intelligence in order to conduct it. Not everyone can do this. The Blacks do not have a high level of intelligence. On the contrary, they are the least intelligent of the world's peoples.' At least he was given the chance to learn better.

Certainly, the new leaderships were careful students of revolutionary examples. Yet none of their studies could have helped them much, as they themselves have carefully explained to any who would listen, unless the movements they led could realize their own native potential, could grow from their own roots, could build upon their own reality. As all the records eloquently show, the extent to which this happened was to be the crucial indicator of success or failure against the colonial system and the society to which that system had given rise.

Only three movements can be found to have met this challenge. These were the PAIGC of Guinea-Bissau and the Cape Verde Islands, FRELIMO of Mozambique, and, with some special handicaps of its situation, the MPLA of Angola. All the others, whether as splinters from these movements or as rivals from the start, failed to move from mass support to mass participation; most of them failed even to win mass support. None of these others, in consequence, could even begin to promote that wide unity of consciousness and struggle out of which a people's liberation must be born.

Each of the three genuine movements was, therefore, necessarily involved with an autonomous and complex process of democratization. This process was made more difficult, but also more original, by the nature of existing class formations. These were blurred in their social and ideological boundaries, indistinct, immature. But they were still the matrix there to be reshaped.

One such formation encompassed a great variety of rural people who might be said to constitute a peasant class only by ignoring their many internal tensions and stratifications. This class had to be the main vehicle of struggle because ninety per cent of these peoples belonged to it; but its components could become that only if its tensions and stratifications were analysed and understood.

A second class was less differentiated within itself but still far from homogeneous or socially coherent. Its components were a majority of 'urbanized Africans'. Many still had village roots, and all of them were in any case, save for a few localized exceptions (such as dockers), quite different from a working-class in the European or American sense of the term. They too could be won for the struggle, but only if their internal characteristics were similarly analysed and understood. The care with which this was done may be seen in many published documents: in none so clearly, perhaps, as in the writings of the founder of the PAIGC, Amílcar Cabral. Here, for example, he is discussing the characteristics of that section of the 'urban class' which may be defined as a petty bourgeoisie:

> As for the Africans, the petty bourgeoisíe [of Guinea-Bissau, but the same applied broadly to Angola and Mozambique] can be divided into three sub-groups as regards the national liberation struggle.
>
> First, there is the petty bourgeoisie which is heavily committed to and compromised with colonialism: this includes most of the higher officials and some members of the liberal professions.
>
> Second, there is the group which we perhaps incorrectly call the revolutionary petty-bourgeoisie: this is the petty-bourgeoisie which is nationalist and which was the source of the idea of the national liberation struggle in Guinea-Bissau.
>
> In between lies the part of the petty-bourgeoisie which has never been able to make up its mind between the national liberation struggle and the Portuguese.
>
> Next come the wage-earners, whom you can compare roughly with the proletariat in European societies, although they are not exactly the same thing. Among them, too, there is a majority committed to the struggle, but, again, many members of this group were not easy to mobilize – wage-earners who had an extremely petty-bourgeois mentality and whose only aim was to defend the little they had already acquired . . .[1]

Armed with this kind of detailed analysis, the movements were able to evolve a 'strategy for mobilization': that is, for the winning of a mass support such as could develop into mass participation. And, with that, the initial few could progressively cease to be 'nationalists without a nation', could get out of their initially élitist isolation, could stop 'substituting their voice for the people's voice', and more and more could speak as the delegated representatives of a people with a voice of its own.

But who were the initial few? They emerged, as Cabral described in the same essay, from an urban 'petty bourgeoisie' definable more by its usual employments than by any class consciousness. These were the lower and sometimes middle employees of the colonial administrations; the handful of African or mestiço clerks who worked for the Portuguese commercial monopolies; the occasional student who managed to obtain higher education and become a doctor or a lawyer (or, as in Cabral's case, an agronomist); and others who were shop assistants, warehousemen, male nurses in hospitals mainly for Europeans, occasional truck-drivers, a few privileged crane-men in the docks, even labourers of various types, as well as 'rootless' youths without any employment at all.

It appears that the deciding factor among them all was that they worked for Europeans or alongside Europeans, and were subject to constant discrimination from the level of wages to the level of personal insult. The importance of this experience, again in Cabral's words, is that 'it allows comparison: this is the key stimulant required for the awakening of consciousness':

> As far as Guinea-Bissau is concerned, the idea of the national liberation struggle was born not abroad but in our own country, in a milieu where people were subjected to close and incessant exploitation: this may be true, but so far as the struggle is concerned it must be realised that it is not the degree of suffering and hardship involved which matters. Even extreme suffering does not in itself necessarily produce the *prise de conscience* required for the national liberation struggle.
>
> In Guinea-Bissau the peasants are subjected [he was talking in 1964] to a kind of exploitation equivalent to slavery; but even if you try and explain to them that they are being exploited and robbed, it is difficult to convince them by means of an unexperienced explanation of a technico-economic kind that they are the most exploited people. Whereas it is easier to convince the workers and the peoples in the towns who earn, say, 10 escudos a day for a job in which a European earns between 30 and 50 that they are being subjected to massive exploitation and injustice, because they can see it for themselves.[2]

This was also true of Angola and Mozambique. In 1970 the fighting units of FRELIMO made good their hold on the northern part of the important District of Tete. Months later they were firmly across the Zambezi river. Months later again they were active in the adjoining southward district, Manica e Sofala. By 1974, on the eve of the *coup*, they were pushing into southern Mozambique. Among their senior commanders was a man of thirty named Sebastião Mabote, one of many participants 'at the base' who had risen to leadership since 1964. One day in 1968, while commanding units briefed to guard the second congress of FRELIMO, held in the District of Niassa in northern Mozambique, he sat on a tree stump and talked about his life. The 'key stimulant' had proved effective for him too:

> I worked as a typist in a lawyer's office. His name was Saraiva. He presided over a juvenile court and had a private practice. I was in charge of the private side of his work and I earned 600 escudos a month. But alongside me there was a white girl working, and she didn't know the job, so that most of the work fell on me. But they paid her 3,200 escudos a month, more than five times what they paid me.
>
> But the injustice wasn't only in the money. It was also in the way they treated me. All the same, they wanted me to accept *assimilado* status. My father was against that; so was I. Why? Because I knew the real situation of the assimilados. I saw that the assimilado and the indígena (native) were really in the same situation . . .[3]

Mabote began to argue against this discrimination, was labelled subversive, tracked by the police, persecuted in various ways: all this took him to FRELIMO.

Others have told their own stories of the 'comparison'. 'To take my own case,' Cabral said in a rare moment of talking about himself,

> as a member of the petty-bourgeois group which launched the struggle in Guinea-Bissau. I was an agronomist working under a European who everybody knew was one of the biggest fools in the country. I could have taught him his job with my eyes shut, but he was the boss. This is something which counts for a lot: this is the confrontation which really matters . . .[4]

The 'key stimulant' and other factors of the same kind, such as the absence of any possible reformism within the Portuguese context, urged these men and women to action. But what kind of action? They had to find their way: to each other as well as to the masses who could alone make action effective, and therefore worth-while. It wasn't a simple problem. It couldn't be solved by any mere act of will. It needed time, opportunity, and courage to make use of the opportunity.

This was the task of the little groupings formed during the 1950s. They gathered membership from students who came from Europe, as well as from others who had completed their studies. These brought a wider understanding of the political possibilities. Sometimes they brought the experience of political struggle in Portugal itself. Others joined with only a local background, and with much less formal education. For these, the chance contact with Portuguese dissidents, whether Communist or not, was often important. 'I worked for a pharmacist in Bissau,' one of the most effective of the early commanders of the PAIGC said of himself, 'and his wife was a Communist. She talked to me, she explained her point of view, she helped me.'[5]

They worked gradually towards a clarity of aim; and those who survived the attentions of the Portuguese political police (the PIDE, the dictatorship's Gestapo) were to form the core of the great movements that were to follow. What is perhaps most interesting about these early groups is that those who became effective as leaders all reached the same general conclusions on theory and practice. Their principal merit, to adapt some words of Cabral's in a memorial address dedicated to the honour of Eduardo Mondlane, the assassinated Mozambican leader, 'did not lie in (their decision) to struggle for the freedom of (their) people. (Their) principal merit lay in being able to merge (themselves) with the reality of their country, to identify with their people:'[6] in other words, to bridge that gulf between the few and the many, and to evoke the mass participation which was to carry these movements to success.

Yet they often came to their parallel conclusions from very different starting points. Some came from a Marxist approach to the analysis of reality: Cabral himself, Marcelino dos Santos (vice-president of FRELIMO), Agostinho Neto (president of MPLA). Others came from far less sophisticated intellectual beginnings. Samora Machel (president of FRELIMO) is an outstanding example of those who had to fight their way to clarity of theory and practice through the merest cracks in the 'wall of silence'. There were many like Samora, though few so brilliantly effective. And then there is the very striking case of Eduardo Mondlane, whose formation was anything but Marxist: whose training, on the contrary, was that of an orthodox American sociologist. And yet Mondlane also arrived at the same conclusions as the others, and became the architect not only of FRELIMO's development from a group of exiles to a people's movement, but the steersman through some of FRELIMO's most difficult years.[7]

These movements were thus the product of a cultural convergence. Against the background of their reality, of their immediate and actual personalities, the leaders moved towards the people: above all towards the peasants, the rural populations, the despised 'bush blacks' of earlier times. This needed a strenuous personal effort. Europe-educated leaders had to learn or re-learn their native languages, adapt their life-styles, take themselves through a process of self-analysis that could be painful, driving as it must against a weight of prejudice and habit. 'Behind me,' remarked the Angolan leader, Mario de Andrade, when visiting the liberated areas of Guinea-Bissau some years ago, 'I have several generations of "shod feet" ': of forebears, that is, whose positions were those of relative privilege within the colonial situation.

Such men had to achieve a reconversion of attitudes, modes of behaviour, personal ambitions and expectations; and the gruelling nature of forest life was not the greatest of their difficulties. Others had to overcome corresponding obstacles or complexes, whether of inferiority or superiority. None of them was in the position of the old nationalist leaderships of the reformist period in the British and French empires. These could assume the leadership of movements of mass support that seldom or never moved from acclamation to participation. Such men were free to travel around their countries and make promises of reformist gains. They could be content to register their mass support while remaining an élite, while not building with anything but words the crucial bridge between the few and the many.

The leaders of these movements in 'Portuguese Africa' had no such scope, even if they had wished for it. They had to build that bridge. Otherwise there was nobody to listen to them, or, at least, nobody who would believe what they said. Yet once they began building it they found that the people would also begin building from their side. Convergence developed. Ideas began to go both ways. There began a process of mutual acculturation: of the leaders to the cultures of the rural populations, of the latter to the ideas of the leaders.

6 The Line of March – and Diversions

Anyone who should doubt this fact of convergence might reflect upon that large majority of the leaderships of all three movements who were to emerge from the rural populations, from the masses, from the 'grass roots'. Or there is the copious evidence of what happened in areas liberated from colonial control during the 1960s. All sorts of ordinary people could there be found at work within new structures and organizations built by their movements. And if it had been otherwise, in fact, these movements could not have survived, much less succeeded.

Again it is Cabral who has provided key definitions. He took up the theme of this process of mutual acculturation during his Syracuse lecture in honour of Mondlane:

> The armed struggle for liberation, launched in response to the aggression of the colonialist oppressor, turns out to be a painful but efficient instrument for developing the cultural level both of the leadership strata in the liberation movement and of the various social groups who participate in the struggle.
>
> The leaders of the liberation movement, drawn generally from the petty-bourgeoisie (intellectuals, clerks) or urban working groups (workers, drivers, other wage-earners), have to live day by day with various peasant strata in the heart of rural populations. They come to know the people better. They discover at the grass roots the richness of the people's cultural values (whether philosophic or political, artistic, social or moral). They acquire a clearer understanding of the economic realities of their country, and of the problems, sufferings and hopes of the masses of their people.
>
> Not without a certain astonishment, the leaders come to realise the richness of spirit, the capacity for reasoned discussion and clear exposition of ideas, the facility for understanding and assimilating concepts on the part of populations who yesterday were forgotten, or else despised as incompetent by the colonizer and even by some nationals.

The leaders thus enrich their culture: they develop personally, free themselves from complexes, reinforce their ability to serve the movement in the service of the people.

That is one aspect of the process. But there is a second, just as important:

On their side, the working masses and in particular the peasants, who are generally illiterate and have never moved beyond the boundaries of their village or their region, lose, in contact with other groups, the complexes which constrained them in their relations with different ethnic and social groupings. They realize their crucial role in the struggle. They break the bonds of their village universe. They integrate themselves progressively in their country and in the world. They acquire an infinite amount of new knowledge that is useful to their immediate and future action within the framework of the struggle. They strengthen their political consciousness by assimilating the principles of national and social revolution postulated by the struggle. And so they become more able to play their decisive role of providing the principal force of the liberation movement.

All this being so, 'the armed struggle therefore implies a veritable forced march along the road to cultural progress'.

No such march, it should perhaps go without saying, could be made without failures and futilities. The record of these painful but efficient years provided many examples of leaders who failed to build their bridge and march across it, and who, having failed, were lost in self-isolation, withdrawal from the struggle, or defection to the colonial power. Fearful betrayals occurred, unforgettable assassinations, fruitless diversions. Trusted leaders collapsed into opportunism; and whole groups replied by retreating into one or other form of 'tribalism'. Puppet 'movements' mushroomed under one diversionary impulse or another, sometimes in the name of 'anti-communism', sometimes in that of 'revolutionary purity', and thrust their distractions on the scene.

These splinter or diversionary groupings have been sufficiently described elsewhere;[1] but a few words about them may be useful here. Most were 'movements' in nothing but name and achieved their notoriety, when they had any, only through the direct or indirect agency of this or that foreign backer or hopeful foreign beneficiary. One or two, such as COREMO in relation to Mozambique or UNITA in relation to Angola, were able to develop a fitful guerrilla action in brief moments, but never came within sight of developing a broad unity of consciousness and struggle. They soon vanished from the scene, or else they grew content with a token existence: with the 'mountain-topism'[2] of a presence tolerated by the Portuguese army because this presence was usefully divisive on the African side. And from that position they duly embarked, as in the evident Angolan case of UNITA,[3] on a secret alliance with the Portuguese army. A few, such as FLING in relation to Guinea-Bissau or MOLIMO in relation to Mozambique, were never more than little claques of exiles whose ineffectiveness was total. Only one of these rival formations could enter a serious claim to be a movement that mattered. This was the FNLA in relation to Angola.

The FNLA appeared in the capital of Zaire, Kinshasa (then Léopoldville, capital of the former Belgian Congo), in March 1962.[4] It was the product of a union between two exile groupings of Angolans. The more important of these, the UPA (Union of Angola's Peoples, originally Union of North Angola's Peoples), had been formed during the 1950s and had prometed a disastrous rising among the Kongo of the São Salvador region, and other local peoples, during March 1961. This had led to a ferocious military repression from which the UPA (and then FNLA) proved quite unable to protect the population, with the resultant flight of hundreds of thousands of village people out of northern Angola into Congo (Zaire). Thereafter the FNLA was able to maintain under its control a small area south of Bembe, but proved incapable either of extending this area or of winning adherents outside the Kongo ethnic group.

The FNLA accordingly failed either to become a serious threat to colonial control or to contribute towards a broad unity of struggle. Waiting to see which way the cat would jump, its leaders – and above all its chief leader, Holden Roberto – remained in Kinshasa, where they appear to have achieved a considerable personal comfort. The probability is that the FNLA would then have vanished from serious politics but for one strong card of Holden's. He was a personal relative of President Ssese-Seko Mobutu, the military ruler of Zaire, and he was also Mobutu's trusted political henchman. Promoted by the CIA,[5] Mobutu now saw his own political interest, and presumably that of his external allies, in obstructing the MPLA so that he would be able, when the time came, to have his own place behind Holden's at the negotiating table.

All through the 1960s, accordingly, Mobutu worked very deliberately against the MPLA, and, after assuming dictatorial powers in Zaire during 1965, saw to it that the MPLA should be entirely barred from any access to northern and north-western Angola by way of the long Zairean frontier. There seems little doubt that in doing this he contributed directly towards the various difficulties of the MPLA after 1972. Certainly, he made it practically impossible for Angola's only effective national movement to develop its struggle in the colonial heartlands west of the Cuanza river.

The result of all this was that although the FNLA could in no real sense be regarded as a national movement, unless of the Kongo ethnic grouping as a separate nation, it remained of political and diplomatic importance. So the FNLA has to be considered in a somewhat different light from the stooges or would-be rivals mentioned above. Perhaps the most generous way of regarding it, with its political progenitor the UPA, is as a reformist and élitist movement of the old type.

These were among the African distractions on the pathway of those genuine movements which developed out of reformist nationalism into the revolutionary nationalism whose outlines have been sketched here, and which were able, because they did so develop, to make headway against African distractions as well as colonial repression. They went on their way. Badly wrecked after its premature rising in Luanda during February 1961, and then by the hostility of the Congo (Zaire) authorities in Léopoldville (Kinshasa) where its surviving leaders had taken refuge, the MPLA was able to rebuild a fighting movement from a base in Brazzaville (People's Republic of Congo) during 1963–4, and then from a base in Zambia during 1965–6. Between 1968 and 1972 it was able to root itself into the loyalties of the scattered peoples of the eastern region of Angola, and, despite an extremely hostile terrain, to unfold there a long and successful fight against the Portuguese.

The PAIGC embarked upon its internal mobilization in 1959, and then, having patiently won mass support that was already developing into mass participation, launched its armed struggle in January 1963. This went well from the start, because of long preparation and a very effective leadership, and also to a lesser extent from a characteristic miscalculation of the Portuguese army command. That command was convinced that the PAIGC consisted merely of 'incursive bands' coming in from the neighbouring Republic of Guinea (former French Guinea). It therefore concentrated on guarding the country's frontiers, and was ill placed to take care of what went on at its rear inside the country. By 1966, in any case, the PAIGC had secured a firm strategic initiative in large areas of the country. By 1968 it had clearly won the war on the mainland, even if the Portuguese were not yet ready to admit the fact.

FRELIMO began training its first fighting groups in Algeria during 1963. These were committed to the northern districts in September 1964. They did well in Cabo Delgado and Niassa, but failed elsewhere. They held on stubbornly to their gains, extended them, widened their movement, improved their methods. Towards the end of the 1960s they were ready for new advances. These came on all their fronts, but were most spectacular in the strategically crucial district of Tete, lying between Rhodesia and Malawi. By 1972 they had clearly passed the point where any Portuguese effort could hope to stop them.

The strategies of a revolutionary nationalism, worked out through harsh years and applied with courage, were now seen to be mature. A sceptical outside world awoke to the undeniable evidence that something very new had entered the African scene.

7 Guerrilla Warfare

This entry on the scene was inseparable from armed struggle: from what is often, and often misleadingly, called 'guerrilla warfare'; and I put in the quotation marks because this kind of warfare, as we shall see, is not always what it may seem to be, at least when conducted so as to be able to succeed. To begin with, in any case, one should note that armed struggle in itself cannot offer any guarantee of success, no matter how courageously endured and fought. As many Latin American cases have revealed, armed struggle can just as well become a guarantee of failure.

Courage is not enough; and violence has no inherent virtue even when it is not, as it mostly is, an unmitigated evil. If violence must sometimes become the midwife of a new society it still requires that the infant is ready to be born and that its parents are well prepared to rear it. This may appear terribly obvious in the second half of the 1970s, with so many disastrous 'graspings of the guerrilla rifle' in the history of the last twenty years. But just because of those disasters, and their contrast with the great successes, the point may still be worth some emphasis.

Its truth can be seen from another angle: from that of the actual techniques of guerrilla warfare. There may no longer be any need to enlarge upon the success with which the Africans of the Portuguese territories mastered these techniques. Yet this success could only be a secondary reason, if a weighty one, for their defeat of the dictatorship. For they invented nothing new in the practice of such warfare. They adapted the experience of others, even of others who had ended in defeat. If mere success in 'guerrilla battles' were the real test of success, then the Boer commandos of 1899 and after – to offer a remote example – would have prevailed over the British Army of that time. If the

Greeks who fought the Nazi army of occupation during the Second World War had been able to profit from their military successes – to adduce a more recent example – then they would have governed Greece after the war was over. Without the right political strategies, no quantity of skill and courage can make much difference to the outcome. Short-term guerrilla gains will still end in defeat. And this is what emerged, time and again, from the 'Portuguese African' scene.

The leaders of these movements have had rather little to say about their military techniques and tactics. Understandably. First, because this was the relatively 'easy part' of their struggle: easy, that is, in the sense that what had to be attempted was always pretty clear. Secondly, because security advised silence. Generally, though, it can be said that they followed a pattern familiar from other and well-documented wars of liberation since the late 1920s, whether in one part of the world or another.

This pattern falls into a succession of military phases, and these, by all the evidence, seem scarcely open to anything save local variation for scale and circumstance. All these phases call for courage but also for cunning; determination but also for a cool head. They are messed up by individualist acts of bravado, but they rely greatly on individual heroism.

After due political work among the people so as to explain what they are up to, and why, a few men and women begin the struggle. For that they need a little military training, though not much, and at least a small supply of elementary firearms. They launch the first minor attacks, and the element of surprise masks their initial weakness. They prove 'it can be done': invariably, as it appears, to populations which greatly doubt if it can. Osvaldo Vieira has described the first action of the PAIGC in northern Guinea-Bissau: 'We had three weapons. There were ten of us. We ambushed three of their vehicles and killed seven of them. We captured eight weapons ...' It takes a lot of qualities to do as much. But 'before that the peasants did not believe us. After, it was different.'

Those qualities are wasted unless the necessary political preparation is complete. Such actions are useful only if they lead the way from mass support to participation, and thus to other and bigger actions. But when that happens the initial few gather volunteers, lead slightly larger units, make more attacks.

This is the beginning of the 'guerrilla phase' proper; this is partisan warfare. It has a dual objective. One part is to raise morale by hitting relatively small and easy targets, such as police posts or isolated army trucks, and to exploit these small successes so as to increase the number of fighters. The other part is to establish the first small outlines of a liberated area: of an area which the liberation fighters will eventually control.

With time, effort, and unfailing courage, the units multiply in number, though little in individual size. They reach the point where neighbouring units can combine in slightly larger actions. This is still guerrilla warfare: the warfare, largely, of part-time fighters who otherwise work in their villages and wait, beguiling the boredom of this kind of life, and likely to be wondering, as often as not, how it is all going to turn out.

Two great dangers besiege this phase. They cannot be avoided, and are overcome only by good leadership. The first of these dangers lies in the invariable counter-offensive by the army of occupation, the enemy's army, an offensive waged by men who are confident of success (their awakening comes later), and who possess superior weapon power. This first major period of enemy offensive must be countered by the ceaseless evasive action of guerrilla units, but also – and this is what is really difficult – by a determined effort to save from enemy reprisals at least a substantial part of the supporting civilian population. This protection will be only partial, and grim reprisals will be suffered by civilians. But only if the attempt is made, and is at least partly successful, will the guerrilla units survive with the sort of civilian backing that will continue to move, no matter what the cost, from support to participation.

The second danger comes into view with a further unfolding of this guerrilla phase. All the known examples display it. Guerrilla commanders are men of great daring and self-confidence; they could not otherwise survive this early phase. But they are also likely to be young and politically inexperienced. Success can go to their heads. They can become local heroes whose personal ambition and prestige set them at odds with the movement's unity and progress. At best they may ignore the essentially political nature of their struggle, and develop a 'military commandism' which can turn them into petty dictators. At worst they may retreat into 'mountain-topism', and eventual sell-out to the enemy.

Criticising military weaknesses in the PAIGC during 1965, Cabral spoke of wastage, lack of initiative in attack, 'and even a certain demobilization which has not been fought and eliminated . . .'

> And with all this, as a proof of insufficient political work among our armed forces, there has appeared a certain attitude (*mania*) of 'militarism' which has caused some fighters and even some leaders to forget the fact that we are *armed militants* and not *militarists* . . .[1]

But with these dangers sufficiently overcome – and it appears unlikely that they are ever entirely overcome – there then opens a new phase. This consists in the transformation of a certain number of volunteers from many purely local units into the core of a regular army. That is when guerrillas cease to be guerrillas, and become soldiers. Now they accept a stiff discipline, though still within a markedly democratic style of command. They go where they are ordered and fight when they are told. They acquire new military skills and better weapons. They embark on larger actions of assault and ambush.

The danger of military commandism remains, but is reduced now to a matter of political discipline at levels of well-integrated organization. That is why effective 'guerrilla-type' armies incorporate full-time political workers who are also soldiers; these are known as 'political commissars' or by some comparable label. They are there to ensure that the army remains a political army and puts political factors always first, whether in relation to the enemy, to the civilian population, or to attitudes and habits within its own ranks.

At this stage, better outside supplies of weapons and ammunition must be assured. There may be local conditions which enable some of the necessary supplies to come from inside the country: from the ranks of a demoralized local army supporting an army of occupation, as happened most notably in China and in Yugoslavia. The armies of the liberation movements in 'Portuguese Africa' were also able to win a small supply in this manner, chiefly from peasant militias armed by the Portuguese during the late 1960s. But generally there is an absolute need, as in 'Portuguese Africa', for supply from outside the country, whether of strike weapons such as mortars (and thus of mortar ammunition) or, later, of still more sophisticated weapons such as missile launchers, missiles, and light artillery. None of these can be captured from the enemy except on the rarest of occasions. And of course there must be facilities, whether 'outside' or 'inside', for training men to handle and sight such weapons.

Without this kind of outside supply – and Cuba, insofar as it was an exception, only proves the rule – no movement of armed struggle can go on growing and developing. It will stagnate, and in stagnating will become demoralized, increasingly inactive, finally useless. Much nonsense was written in the early 1970s by commentators who praised the UNITA 'movement' in eastern Angola for being, as they claimed, independent of outside supply and yet capable of continued expansion. The upshot showed that no such expansion had occurred; nor, in the circumstances of Angola, could it have occurred. To suppose otherwise was to indulge in romanticism or political manoeuvre.

But if the problems of succeeding in this new phase are overcome, then the whole tactical position changes. The enemy now finds himself in the classical dilemma repeatedly produced by the liberation armies in 'Portuguese Africa':

In order to dominate a given zone, the enemy is obliged to disperse his forces. In dispersing his forces, he weakens himself and we can defeat him. Then in order to defend himself against us, he has to concentrate his forces. When he does that, we can occupy the zones that he leaves free and work in them politically so as to hinder his return there.[2]

The Portuguese commanders tried two ways of resolving this dilemma after it began to be acute for them in the mid-1960s They multiplied their bombing raids. And they redoubled their efforts to corral rural populations inside the barbed wire of defended camps, precisely so as to prevent the liberation movements from taking advantage of zones left free of Portuguese army control.

This corralling tactic, coupled with helicoptered 'search and destroy' raids by commando units, was borrowed from the Americans in South Vietnam, who had themselves developed it from British experiments in Malaya. It gave rise to pain and suffering for the populations thus driven from their homes and forced under Portuguese army control; but it failed. In Malaya it had succeeded because the guerrillas there were mostly Chinese who, for one reason or another lying outside the scope of this survey, had not been able to win the mass of Malayan peasants for their cause. It failed in South Vietnam for the contrary reason: the Viet Cong, like the Viet Minh, had won peasant support and had transformed this into peasant participation. Its failure in 'Portuguese Africa' was generally due to the same reason as in Vietnam. The peasants were in favour of the liberation movements. Their sufferings in the camps tended only to make them more so.

By 1970 it was evident in Guinea-Bissau and Mozambique that PAIGC and FRELIMO had developed their phase of regular warfare, by highly mobile 'guerrilla' tactics, to the point where they had grasped a strategic initiative which the Portuguese could not regain. Thereafter it could only be a matter of time, and, as we shall see, the deployment of new weapons. The same was true for the MPLA in the eastern districts of Angola, but with the decisive difference that these districts were very thinly populated, and were geographically so wide and ecologically hostile as to make a sure progression towards the west, towards the main centres of population, too difficult. Thus held to the eastern districts, the MPLA was unable to exploit the strategic initiative which it had seized in them. There developed a certain stagnation. Stagnating movements of armed struggle are movements heading for internal trouble. Only in 1975, during a 'second war of liberation' against invading forces, could this stagnation begin to be fully overcome by the MPLA.

Such was the outline of these wars. The three territories all displayed many local variations, but all were variations on the same pattern. A few conclusions of general application may now be possible.

To begin with, as one may perhaps usefully insist again, a

successful war of liberation can never stem from military adventure, no matter how sincerely motivated, but only from the political exploitation of a general situation which is felt by the mass of people to be hatefully and obviously unjust. The 'big words' about freedom and independence will achieve nothing if the 'little words' about local grievance and oppression are not persuasive first.

Secondly, this political exploitation will fail unless it can also pass from the gathering of sympathy to the mobilization of active volunteers. It is one thing to want change. It is quite another to fight for it or work for it when all the odds still seem unfavourable. Yet without a steady stream of new volunteers, the most courageous band of pioneers will soon find itself in isolation and defeat.

Thirdly, this move from sympathy to action will not take place, again by all the evidence that we have, unless the right arguments are found. But the finding of these right arguments depends only in part on a right analysis of the *general* situation. Far more, it also depends on the most intimate knowledge of local habits, languages, hopes, fears, expectations, interests. There can be no question, as some have argued *in vacuo* (and disastrously), of 'extending the revolt' by mere optimism or exhortation. Peasants are not optimistic people. They will not be moved by exhortation. They will follow only leaders who prove that they closely understand and share the peasants' own lives: in the beginning, no doubt, they will follow only those who come from the peasants' own ranks.

Here one of the pioneers of the PAIGC is talking of the years of political mobilization which preceded the launching of armed struggle:

> Our procedure was to speak in a village and then go out into the bush to spend the night. It was the only way we had of making ourselves and the party known. Little by little, party sympathizers among the village people would come out into the bush bringing us meals. Later on, we were able to call out the villagers – or at least some of them – and talk with them, explain the meaning of our struggle, and ask their help . . . Believe me, mobilization is a much, much harder thing than armed struggle itself . . .[3]

But this mobilization is also vital. 'Without it, nothing of lasting value can be done. This political preparation is the toughest, most daunting, but also most important aspect of the whole campaign of national liberation.'[4]

Fourthly, in line with the development of the *resultant* political and military struggle – the two aspects becoming inseparable – the organization of this type of movement has to be such that the fact and influence of *widening participation* becomes, and remains, a dominant and conscious process. Its promotion has to govern and develop further from every major act of policy.

In 1972, for instance, the PAIGC organized a general election by universal adult suffrage throughout its liberated areas. The aim was to elect regional assemblies which would in turn elect a national assembly such as could form the democratic foundation for an independent state, as well as providing for the beginning of a separation of powers between party and state. But the aim was also, and very consciously, to widen political participation in the governing structures of the future state: to take the populations of the liberated areas through another exercise in political education so as to show, once again, that *povo na manda na su cabeça*, that 'people have to do things for themselves'. So it was that weeks and even months were spent in holding meetings to explain the meaning of elections and assemblies; in drawing up an electoral register; in appointing those who would supervise the balloting; in discussing what factors had influenced the selection of candidates: factors of local balance between villages, of choice between men and women, of this or that other local matter.

Fifthly, and again following from all this, the development and further growth of participation must not be allowed to rob the revolutionary vanguard of its leading role, nor separate that vanguard either from its long-term objectives or from its organic posture of leading from the grass roots, albeit with an accepted authority. Otherwise the vanguard will move in one direction, or in several, while the people go off in another.

Each of the first four rules emphasises the primacy of the *politics* of armed struggle. The fifth rule does so too, but in ways that are especially hard to meet: only the most resolute practice of internal democracy can satisfy the crucial demands of this fifth rule. That is why the most successful advances of the 1960s and early 1970s were invariably preceded, among these movements, by internal campaigns of ardent discussion and detailed explanation, often in prolonged conferences where real or incipient conflicts, whether political or personal, could be brought into the open and decided by a visible majority. And it is also why periods of setback were those when internal discussion had lapsed or failed.[5]

Other such conclusions might be drawn from the record of the three movements, and tested against these movements' relative success, or against the failure of other movements conducted in a different way. Another implication of these 'rules', for example, is that the pace and progress of military action whether in terms of intensity, weaponry or type of objective, must not outstrip the capacity of mass participation to absorb and understand their point and purpose. Otherwise there will be 'overheating', just as surely as the reverse, military idleness, will lead to disbandment. A further implication is that the structure of the movement has to be constantly reviewed and overhauled so that the internal mediation of power remains a genuine interplay between those who give orders and those who carry them out. Much else might be said; but these five 'rules' and their implications are evidently of an iron necessity. They must be met substantially, or the end will be disaster.

But if they are met, as each of the three movements in 'Portuguese Africa' met them in the measure of its political and military success, then the struggle develops a meaning and momentum of its own. It acquires its own expanding dynamism. It leads towards original ways of solving what former attitudes and institutions, whether of a 'traditional' type or of a colonial type, cannot solve. There takes place a crucial and irreversible 'forced march on the road to cultural progress' by a mass of individuals who, developing together as they work or fight, come to form a new community, begin to shape a new society:

(For) consider these features inherent in an armed liberation struggle: the practice of democracy, of criticism and self-criticism, the increasing responsibility of populations for the direction of their own lives, literacy work, the creation of schools and health services, the training of cadres who come from peasant and worker backgrounds, and many other achievements.

When we consider these features, we see that the armed liberation struggle is not only a product of culture. It is also a *determinant of culture*. And this, beyond all doubt, is the prime compensation to the people for the effort and sacrifice that are the price of their war . . .[6]

Cabral was speaking here, one should note, in the specific terms that he invariably preferred. Other peoples might well be able to liberate themselves without armed struggle. Generally, the qualified leaders of these movements have been careful to make it clear that they do not regard armed struggle as the only instrument of liberation, but that each people, analysing its own situation, considering its own circumstances, must decide for itself what manner of liberating instrument it will use. The key will lie, in any case, in the successful arousing of a new political consciousness and the participation which this can achieve.

Armed struggle, in the Portuguese colonies, proved to be the only effective instrument when all efforts at peaceful pressure had yielded nothing save increased repression. It was an extremely difficult instrument to use. But once forced to accept this challenge of armed struggle, the peoples of 'Portuguese Africa' discovered how to turn their great initial weakness into a new and sufficient strength. The best way to see how this was done is to turn to the lessons of the liberated areas.

8 Practising What You Preach

Over the double gateway into the municipal gardens of the colonial capital of Bissau there was flown during August 1974 a banner with a strange device: strange, at any rate, while Portuguese troops were still on guard along the wall of that same park. 'Under the leadership of the PAIGC,' affirmed this banner, 'we are going to build a new society.'

An improbably large ambition, it might appear, in any circumstances. Here it could seem all the less realistic for its being proclaimed, on the whole, to a boulevard kept void of any audience by the dour and drenching rains of August. But the claim was made; and I mention this banner because I happened to see it there myself. Other such claims were being made by FRELIMO banners in Lourenço Marques and Beira, chief cities of Mozambique, or fluttered in the streets by African supporters of the MPLA in Luanda, the capital of Angola. Was this more than a gesture of demagogy?

Demagogy it may have seemed to many of the inhabitants of those cities and to similarly uninstructed foreigners chancing to be there. But in truth it rested on the central reality of the liberation wars. That is to say, it rested on the structures and institutions of a new society already in place throughout large areas sufficiently cleared of enemy control, and sufficiently guarded against raids by enemy troops. The task was no longer to fashion and launch those structures and institutions: the task of 1974 was to extend them to areas and towns now released by colonial withdrawal. The banner in the Bissau municipal gardens, flying even before the Portuguese army had departed, did not express a pious hope. It defined a practical programme whose early stages were complete.

There are two large questions here. In these circumstances,

what does 'a new society' mean? And, again in these circumstances, what is a 'liberated area'?

The second is simple to answer. When guerrillas begin their armed struggle in rural areas,[1] form their first small groups, launch their early attacks, survive the ensuing military repression, and gradually expand their influence and effectiveness, they do not yet have a liberated area. What they have is a contested area. Neither side exercises any general control of security in this contested area: each side fights to obtain that. The occupying power will claim that its forces are in command there, and have only to meet occasional incursions by guerrilla bands from outside the area. On their side, the guerrillas may quite probably make the contrary claim. Both claims belong to the realm of propaganda.

But when guerrilla units move into the next large phase and produce a mobile force of full-time fighters; and when this force in any given area becomes strong enough to induce the enemy to disperse his own force among a number of fixed garrisons in defended camps; and when these camps are continuously and effectively besieged so that their garrisons can raid outside them only by fighting their way out of them, then the zone or area in question is rightly called a liberated area.

For it meets two conditions essential to the work of social and political renovation. First, the military situation of this contested area which has become a liberated area is such that the movement of liberation can generally defend it except against helicoptered ground-raids or aerial bombardment. Both of these are necessarily localized or, as to ground-raids, sporadic. They can be very destructive. But they do not materially change the military situation.[2]

Secondly, this situation is one that can be held over a long period of time, or even, in fortunate cases, until the war is won. And even if its control of security is temporarily lost to major military offensives by the occupying power, this can happen only after due warning, given by more or less obvious enemy preparations. The forces of the liberation movement can then protect the civilian population in large measure, either by fighting off attacks or by having time to move civilians from one area to another. When the enemy offensive peters out, the situation can be restored to what it was before.

Genuinely liberated areas are always surrounded by widening contested areas as the dynamics of guerrilla expansion push the armed struggle outward into new zones.

This pattern in Mozambique, Guinea-Bissau, and Angola was demonstrated repeatedly during the 1960s and early 1970s. In the Mozambican districts of Cabo Delgado and Niassa, for example, the early units of FRELIMO established a number of contested areas after 1964; after about 1967, FRELIMO could rightly claim to have transformed these into liberated areas. The same sequence occurred in Tete district after 1968 and 1971; while further south the contested areas of Manica e Sofala were on their way towards becoming liberated areas when the Portuguese army decided to withdraw. If most of the eastern districts of Angola remained as contested areas after 1965, some of them had taken the next step by 1970, although the peculiarly hostile circumstances of that particular struggle made these liberated areas small and fragile and, as it turned out, of relatively brief duration. In Guinea-Bissau the establishment of genuinely liberated areas began as early as 1964, and the process continuously expanded from that date.

What happened in these liberated areas? They were the product of the move from support to participation, of the process of mutual acculturation between movement and masses. Because of this, these areas became notably different from the rest of the country. This was true in two senses, one negative and the other positive. Negatively, colonial power had been swept from the scene and, with it, the facts of colonial rule. All taxes were abolished there: a major change in the Portuguese context, since the Portuguese had taxed just about everything remotely taxable, even down to village wakes for the dead. All Portuguese traders had likewise vanished,[3] or, at least, all trade within a colonial framework. The forced cultivation of this or that cash-crop had likewise ceased; and so, of course, had forced labour.

But the interest lies in the positive factor. The colonial system being removed, what other system should replace it?

All the qualified leaders of liberation from the Portuguese colonial system have stressed the validity of Africa's 'traditional cultures'. The term is a useful one, but is not intended to suggest that these cultures were somehow static, or, as it were, produced entire and rounded to completion from the lap of the gods and ancestors. When the colonial period began, these cultures were the product of 'tradition' but even more of historical development. They were the end-result of centuries of internal growth and evolution from foundations by then extremely old. What the liberation leaders were insisting on was that this development, broken off and stopped by colonial rule, must now be renewed and continued. The revolutions they had in mind were no kind of importation from outside, but, as Amílcar Cabral especially liked to say, the re-launching of the processes of Africa's own history.

This was not, he also said, in any major sense some kind of 'return to the source' of cultural origins. That return was a need felt only by a colonial petty-bourgeoisie which had become 'culturally uprooted, alienated or more or less assimilated', and which thereby sought an identity denied by its colonial situation. But 'the masses have no need to assert or reassert their identity, which they have never confused nor would have known how to confuse with that of the colonial power'. Once freed from the constricting shell of that power, they can selectively extend a culture they have preserved: they can 'make history'.[4]

But this development, this 'making of history', means what it implies: purposive change, selective transformation, cultural reconception. 'A lot of people think that to defend Africa's culture, to resist culturally in Africa, we have to defend the negative things in our culture. But this is not what we think ...'[5] A system to replace the colonial system could not be a reversion to 'what existed before', even if that were possible. Far from it: 'our cultural resistance consists in the following: while we scrap colonial culture and the negative aspects of our own culture, whether in our character or in our environment, we have to create a new culture, also based on our own traditions but respecting everything that the world today has conquered for the service of mankind.'[6]

The same thought was expressed in another way by Agostinho Neto, the Angolan leader. 'We are trying to free and modernize our people by a dual revolution: against their traditional structures which can no longer serve them, and against colonial rule.'[7] And the same basic idea was again reflected in the Mozambican Marcelino dos Santos's counter-posing of bourgeois nationalism, reformist nationalism, to what he defined as revolutionary nationalism.[8] Or consider how Samora Machel, president of FRELIMO after the loss of Mondlane in 1969 and afterwards president of Mozambique, put the same underlying thoughts:

When we took up arms to defeat the old order, we felt the obscure need to create a new society, strong, healthy and prosperous, in which all men free from all exploitation would co-operate for the progress of all.

In the course of the struggle, in the tough fight we have had to wage against reactionary elements, we came to understand our objective more clearly. We felt especially that the struggle to create new structures would fall within the creation of a new mentality.

Creating an attitude of solidarity between people to enable them to carry out collective work presupposes the elimination of individualism. Developing a healthy and revolutionary mentality, which promotes the liberation of women and the creation of a new generation with a collective feeling of responsibility, requires the destruction of inherited corrupt ideas and tastes.

In order to lay the foundations of a prosperous and advanced economy, science has to overcome superstition. To unite all Mozambicans, transcending traditions and different languages, requires that the tribe must die in our consciousness so that the nation may be born.[9]

The task was thus altogether different from 'a mere Africanization of the existing colonial structures'[10] within which neither the tribe had died nor the nation had come to birth. It was as different from any such neo-colonial exercise, any such taking over of 'what existed', as it was different from a reversion to the structures of the pre-colonial period. The task was to *develop* indigenous structures (cultures, concepts, patterns of behaviour, and the rest), and thereby to modernize them: to transform them, that is, into the framework of a society 'capable of respecting everything that the world today has conquered for the service of mankind'. But this task, in the nature of the circumstances of the liberation struggle, in the nature of the absolutely over-riding need for *participation*, had to be carried out for the people of the liberated areas by those people themselves, individually and collectively. The revolutionary party should lead, must lead: but as an initiating influence, as a critic and commentator 'from within', as an attentive chairman of the great debate.

In this same perspective the revolutionary party had another duty and a very practical one. This was to ensure that the effort and sacrifice spent in winning and holding a liberated area should be seen and known to have its recompense, as soon and effectively as possible, in positive gains that everyone could share. These gains were the elementary schools, forest clinics, and other social services that were launched and staffed and supplied in the measure of the possible.

It may be easy to overlook the value of such gains to populations never given them by the colonial system, save in the scantiest measure. Nobody who spent any length of time in these liberated areas would be likely to make that mistake. One day in 1972, far into the southern liberated areas of Guinea-Bissau and across the coastal creeks of remote Como, I picked up the patients' register of a forest clinic of the PAIGC and counted up the names for the previous two months: they came to more than 600. No clinic had ever existed there before.

Yet these clinics and schools were more than mere additions to 'traditional culture' freed from colonial power. They were instruments of cultural progress. Their creation and their conduct invoked new responses, new attitudes. Village girls volunteered for training and became nurses. Village leaders volunteered for the responsibilities of running schools and clinics, supplying the teachers with food, ensuring that recalcitrant parents were persuaded to sacrifice the labour of their children so that the children could go to school. Village militias were involved in protecting these gains, sacrificing their time (and sometimes their lives) in doing so.

A dual process developed, projecting a model of its own. Rural populations were called on to govern themselves in new ways.

Elective committees for individual villages or groups of hamlets took the place of 'rule by elders', or 'rule by chiefs', just as they also took the place of rule by the nearest Portuguese official and his police. These committees found themselves concerned with a whole range of social and cultural activities, such as those just mentioned but many more besides: the gathering of information about the enemy, the supply of food and other necessities by voluntary contribution to the fighting forces and its non-military services, the maintenance of canoe transport, the participation in a new trading system, and again much else. They were renewing their independence of pre-colonial times. But they were also modernizing it.

One may still object: yes, but how far was all this really different from 'the mere Africanization of the existing colonial structures'? How far was it more than an improvization which, after independence, would revert to another form of neo-colonial dependence upon élites who, in their turn, would become dependent on dominating foreign partners?

No one can guarantee the future; and the finally convincing answers will become available, no doubt, only in the years ahead. For themselves, the liberation movements would probably reply now as they replied in 1974 on the eve of their triumph: that the problems they had set out to solve could not conceivably be solved by the mere coming of independence. All that this independence could offer was a wider opportunity to solve them. The process was launched; now it would be necessary to take it further. 'We are entering a new phase: less harsh, more difficult. Only if the peasants are able to transform themselves into people living thoroughly within the modern world, only if they modernize themselves, shall we have the guarantee of success.'[11]

What might be said at this stage was that the new structures of self-rule in liberated areas, together with their new institutions of social and cultural modernization, had begun to project a society which was already quite different from a neo-colonial one. These new structures existed and they worked: so much was discovered in 1974 even by the most disbelieving of observers. They were not just patterns of organization, much less sociological abstractions. In the measure that they existed and worked they were the product of a specific level of political understanding, in its time and circumstance a revolutionary understanding, among populations for whom the practical democratization of daily life now became a conscious experience. For this understanding was no kind of incidental factor in the situation, no mere accretion by way of 'political indoctrination': on the contrary, it was an integral maker of the triumphs registered in 1974.

Would this new society resist the 'natural' trend among leaders to revert to petit-bourgeois ideas and ambitions, and move off into corruption and decay? Formulating the question back in 1966, at a time when left-wing opinion up and down the world was still inclined to be patronisingly superior about 'African initiatives' (or, like right-wing opinion, merely ignorant of them), Cabral maintained to an international audience that the leaders of national liberation, being chiefly petit-bourgeois in origin, could follow two possible paths. These leaders could 'betray the revolution, or they could commit suicide as a class': and this is 'the dilemma of the petty bourgeoisie in the general framework of the national liberation struggle'.[12] It was a formula that many of the orthodox disliked, for it was not 'in the books'. All the same, it went to the heart of the matter. Subsequent betrayals by individuals or groups would amply make that point.

On the other hand, the degree in which these leaderships of petit-bourgeois origin could and really did 'commit suicide as a class' in building their bridge to the masses, and in becoming united with the masses, was what could be seen and measured in the liberated areas of the 1960s and early 1970s. Naturally, the degree varied. But wherever liberated areas were made and held for long periods of internal reconstruction, one could even say that the 'suicide' became a matter of course: no real reconstruction was possible without it. For there arose, around the leaders of petit-bourgeois origin, a complex structure of new leadership which was petty-bourgeois neither in its origins nor in its development.

Embraced and pressured in this way, the challenge of 'petit-bourgeois suicide' became widely accepted. The exceptions proved this, for wherever they occurred the outcome was political dissension, strife, betrayal, or disaster. At the same time, this wider leadership of peasant origin was also in process of becoming a leadership imbued with the ideas and objectives of a society opposed to the servitudes of African 'tradition' as well as to those of colonial rule, and therefore to the servitudes that emerge in a neo-colonial situation.

A process, of course: it takes time for people to practise what they preach; a lot of time. Knowing this was one of the reasons why the leaders of these movements were in no particular hurry to complete their armed struggle during the 1960s. How many diligent cadres served the cause, but still kept their eye on future chances for personal career and privilege? How many valiant fighters spoke warmly of the equality of women, for example, but still held firmly to the exploitation of their own wife or wives? How many said one thing, but still thought another? How far, on the other side, had this rural population revolutionized itself?

In the end, with success in the phase of armed struggle, the answers would evidently turn upon the degree in which the fruits of liberation could be realized by new modes of production, above all of rural production: in the raising of a predominantly rural society to the level of a new economic system. This could only be a harvest of the future. None of the leaders of these movements, so far as I know, ever allowed himself or herself to suggest that they were, as yet, 'building socialism'. All were far too conscious of the real levels of productive force on which they stood. What they did allow themselves to claim, though prudently, was that the politics of armed struggle could and would carry their peoples to a point where new modes of production, a new economic system, non-capitalist and potentially socialist, became possible as well as desirable.

In the immediate present, meanwhile, the politics of armed struggle had carried these peoples to a point where they could enter on their independence with the sovereign gain of possessing, already, the foundations of a social and political system they had founded for themselves: and one, besides, which implied the further objective of a new economic system. At least in

Guinea-Bissau and Mozambique during 1974, they had no need to take over any of the structures and institutions of colonial rule, and thereby assume, willingly or not, a neo-colonial heritage. On the contrary, it was their own society they could bring to independence, a society forged and tempered by long sacrifice and effort. Like others before them, they came with national flags and anthems. But, unlike others, they were also able to arrive with new and tried standards of practical democracy, equipped with the practical means of teaching and extending these even down to new textbooks for their schools, and armoured by the practical lessons they had had to learn. Whatever their problems in the future, it was already a large achievement. For colonized Africa, it was also a new achievement.

9 The End of the Beginning

Various strands wove into the rope that finally choked the dictatorship on 25 April 1974, and dragged open prison doors and pulled down systems of repression, drawing forth a different future, whether in Portugal or Africa.

The military successes of the movements were the chief strand, though created by underlying political successes. These did more than defeat the dictatorship in Africa. They defeated it in Portugal as well. Unflinching African resistance caused the dictatorship to wreck itself by recklessly throwing blood and money into its wars, until its true nature was revealed even to orthodox army officers who, like those in Guinea-Bissau, came to understand 'the roots of the evils which afflict the society of Portugal'.

Then it was that Portuguese dissidence, kept alive clandestinely by brave men and women through decades of repression, broke into the open at all levels. The jails of the dictatorship now filled with many who had previously said nothing, or obeyed. Avoidance of military service became a national and a patriotic theme. And so massive in its numbers had the mainly illegal immigration of Portuguese workers and peasants already grown, whether to escape conscription for military service in Africa or deepening poverty at home, that the official census for 1970 could even show a slightly smaller total population than in 1960. The Paris region had acquired the third largest concentration of Portuguese after Lisbon and Oporto.

The ruin and misery made by the wars had long been marked by critics at home. These had been silenced or ignored. But they were also marked by patrons of the dictatorship abroad, and some of these, whether in Washington or London or elsewhere among Portugal's official allies, became more difficult to ignore.

What these allied patrons said in public was little enough and designedly tactful; but it appears that they said rather more, and more sharply, in private. The records on that are still closed; but the hints were many.

At least by 1970 Marcello Caetano, now Oliveira Salazar's successor in running the dictatorship, was having to listen to advice which called for some kind of 'forward policy', in Africa though not in Portugal, capable of achieving by political manoeuvre what military effort had failed to deliver: that is, the undermining of the liberation movements. His response came in 1971, and it was legalized in 1972. It took the form of verbal changes in the constitution of Portugal. These allowed that the 'overseas provinces' might look forward to some kind of identity of their own, and might even in due course be permitted to call themselves 'autonomous states'.

The changes were minimal. All real authority, in financial or military or administrative matters, was to remain in Lisbon. If the advisory legislatures of the 'overseas provinces' were slightly enlarged, and allowed even for the emergence in these legislatures of a black majority, their powers were scarcely widened from the purely decorative nature they had possessed before. As a means of undermining militant African nationalism, these were gestures that came, at best, some twenty years too late. Even so, they were hotly condemned by the 'ultras' of the dictatorship's more extremist wing, men such as former Foreign Minister Franco Nogueira and veteran commanders such as General Deslandes. On the African scene itself, they made no practical difference of any kind.

Perhaps Caetano saw things as they really were, although his subsequent statements from exile in Brazil cannot encourage one to think so. In any case, there were others who did. Among these was a cavalry officer past sixty years old who had shouldered his way slowly up the ranks of command through decades of inactive service, but whose personal influence was enhanced by a close connexion with the Champalimaud banking group in Lisbon. During the Second World War this man was one of those Portuguese officers whom Hitler's generals had welcomed on tours of inspection in occupied areas of the Soviet Union; he is even said to have visited the German Sixth Army during the early stages of its vain attempt to take Stalingrad. After 1961, nearing the age of fifty, he secured his first operational command in action against the nationalists in Angola. In 1968 he was appointed, then a brigadier, to the combined position of governor and commander-in-chief in Guinea-Bissau. Soon afterwards he achieved general's rank.

This was António Sebastião Ribeiro de Spínola, a man with a turn of mind that was rare in the upper ranks of the dictatorship. His strictly authoritarian views, in other words, did not altogether muddle his understanding of reality. He arrived in Bissau in the wake of a defeated predecessor, General Arnaldo Schultz, and came rapidly to the conclusion, as his actions and writings amply show, that he could not hope to win by military means. By 1969, accordingly, Spínola had embarked on political warfare in the form of what he called a 'better Guinea' programme, designed to undercut the position of the PAIGC This programme was coupled with various enterprises in subversion, including a commando raid on Conakry, the capital of neighbouring (ex-French) Guinea. The raid failed in two of its principal objectives, which were to kill or capture Amílcar Cabral and the PAIGC's staunchest ally, President Sékou Touré of Guinea.[1] Two years later, Spínola's police agents fomented and launched a conspiracy in Conakry which did succeed, most lamentably, in murdering Amilcar Cabral.

Only a desperate need to meet the military challenge of the PAIGC could explain such conspiracies. But outwardly, of course, Spínola maintained that all was well. Those who wished to swallow his propaganda duly did so: sometimes they swallowed it hook, line, and sinker. Thus Brigadier W. F. K. Thompson, military correspondent of the London *Daily Telegraph*, could blithely tell his readers as late as November 1970 that: 'Militarily, the rebel movement is of no consequence.'[2] Other such judgements were scarcely less inept.

Spínola himself, however, was no more fooled about realities in Guinea-Bissau than were his sorely harassed garrisons. Talking to a South African journalist, a few months after Brigadier Thompson's unhappy exercise in reassurance,

Spínola confided his real trend of thought. His explanation was characteristically opaque, and yet clear enough. Things had long since passed the point where military repression could end 'the conflict'. Military repression must be supplemented by political manoeuvre. This must recognize that 'mistakes had been made which brought about a psychological climate favourable to the development of subversion'. But it was not too late 'to eliminate' these mistakes by 'an anti-reactionary counter-revolution'.

This strange objective – surely one of the oddest contradictions in terms devised by authoritarian rulers in modern times – would have to 'meet the legitimate ambitions of the people'; 'promote social justice and equality of all citizens'; and 'build up as quickly as possible economic and social progress'.

None of this would retain much interest for us were it not for what Spínola went on to say. He proceeded to explain a plan for Portugal as well; and this was the plan, or the scenario if you prefer, that was to prelude his part in the developments of 1974. His prospective 'anti-reactionary counter-revolution' which would rob the PAIGC of their political initiative in Guinea-Bissau – and, by implication, rob FRELIMO of theirs in Mozambique and the MPLA of theirs in Angola – was impossible, he explained, without considerable changes in Portugal itself:

> To support a social counter-revolution in a developing region implies the setting-up of dynamic, solid and efficient structures and to meet these needs the homeland (Portugal) is still encumbered with a slow-moving, obsolescent bureaucracy . . . If we wish to operate the social counter-revolution which will ensure our survival as a great nation, *we must reform the structures on the home front* . . .[3]

In March 1973 the PAIGC began shooting down Spínola's bombers with ground-to-air missiles. In July the decisively important fortress-camp of Guileje was levelled to the ground, and its garrison destroyed, in a few hours of artillery and mortar bombardment to which Spínola could now make no reply. In September he threw in his hand, and resigned from his command and governorship.

And then the scenario unfolded.[4] Though thoroughly beaten in the military field, as well as in his politics, Spínola was welcomed home by Caetano as a conquering hero. A few months later he published a book with discreet official backing. This told the Portuguese that the wars were lost and must be brought to an end. The extremists of the régime, notably General Kaulza de Arriaga – he who had gone to Mozambique to end the war in a few months, only to be sacked in 1973 for his failure – responded with an effort to unseat both Caetano and Spínola. Forewarned by a senior officer in whom Arriaga had confided, Caetano and Spínola moved first. But then, leaping past Caetano and overtaking Spínola, a widely-placed group of junior officers banded together in an Armed Forces Movement, formed about a year earlier in semi-clandestinity, made their *coup d'état* of 25 April.

What followed upon that is too complex a story for telling here, though all of it was closely linked to the wars in Africa, which continued to dominate the scene. Briefly, the 'changes in structure' proposed by Spínola, and to some extent agreed with Caetano, were rapidly and irreversibly outdated by the *coup* and its democratic consequences. Invited to head the new régime, Spínola had to accept or watch the tide of change sweep past him. Temporizing, he accepted.

His aim was to limit those democratic consequences and, in Africa, to save for Portuguese domination whatever might still be saved. Up to July he was successful in preventing any Portuguese agreement to African independence. But that was all. And it was not enough.

In mid-July, the Armed Forces Movement took over the government, demanding agreement to African independence as the only way to end the wars. Once again Spínola had to choose between going with the tide or seeing himself rejected. Again he went with the tide, and made his famous speech accepting African independence.[5]

The important point to notice here is that the decisive factor lay in the refusal of the liberation movements to compromise with their objectives. Immediately after the *coup* they were asked by Lisbon to agree to a permanent cease-fire as a prelude to unspecified Portuguese concessions. They refused. This left Spínola with no more cards to play, since his armies in Africa had decided that the wars must end.

The issue was therefore quickly settled for Guinea-Bissau; and also, if not yet officially, for the Cape Verdes as well. Even by August it was becoming apparent that the PAIGC enjoyed overwhelming support in the islands, and that nothing save military repression could prevent the islands from advancing to their independence, and then, if they should so decide, to the federation with Guinea-Bissau long advocated by the PAIGC. Independence for the islands duly came on 5 July 1975, after a general election which gave a landslide victory to the PAIGC.

The issue was likewise settled for Mozambique, and almost as quickly. A brief 'settlers' revolt' in Lourenço Marques put the only remaining 'open question' to the test: would the Republic of South Africa intervene to prevent at least southern Mozambique from government by FRELIMO? The answer proved to be no: Pretoria quickly made it clear that Portuguese withdrawal would be followed by no military incursions; later on, in Angola, they changed their minds. On 7 September an agreement between the Portuguese government and FRELIMO gave Mozambique a provisional government, with FRELIMO in majority control, until June 1975; and provided that Mozambique would then become independent with a FRELIMO government; and this duly came about under an energetic and successful FRELIMO leadership. On 10 September 1974, Portugal also recognized the independent state of Guinea-Bissau.

Angola was a different case. More white settlers lived there than in Mozambique: perhaps 350,000 compared with 200,000. But that was not the main point of difference. Many of these settlers appeared ready to accept an African independence, as had many of the Mozambican settlers. Part of the difference lay in the turbulence of a strong group of Angolan whites who had still to learn the lesson of lost colonial wars, and continued to think that some kind of minority rule was possible. They might have had less influence on the Angolan scene had it not been for another part of the difference, epitomized in Spínola's appointment during June of the Salazarist general, Silveiro Marques, as Angolan governor. This appointment appears to have been related to President Spínola's continuing effort to 'save Angola for Portugal'; and behind this effort one could also descry the influence of Angola's mining wealth and of the major trans-national corporations, including Gulf Oil and Krupp, already much involved in getting that wealth out of the country.[6]

Apparently thinking themselves thus encouraged (and perhaps they had solid reasons for thinking so), extremist settlers in Luanda went on the rampage and killed many African civilians. Reports began to come through of thousands of settlers being organized as an armed force ready to erupt in favour of a settlers' independence; of a search for white mercenaries in South Africa; and of covert South African support. These reports seemed to have substance, and dark days loomed ahead.

Yet it still appeared true that no coalition of settlers could possibly hold down Angola by any variant of 'unilateral independence', unless this coalition received large military support. The Portuguese army was unwilling or unable to provide that support; so, at this point, was the South African army. Two alternatives remained. One was a continued slide towards chaotic violence. The other was a process of negotiation for transfer of power to the representatives of Angolan African nationalism.

Unlike Spínola and his international backers, the government of Portugal which took over power in mid-July of 1974 wanted to negotiate this transfer of power. Their difficulty – and here was a third part of Angola's difference from Guinea-Bissau or Mozambique – lay in divisions on the African side. Some of these divisions were the fruit of Central African politics; others were related to the history of Western intervention. Thus President Ssese-Seko Mobutu of Zaire was busy pushing the claims of his protegé and partner, Holden Roberto, with the latter's FNLA. On another 'front of diversion' the Luanda settlers now discovered a sudden affection for Jonas Savimbi and his nebulous UNITA.

None of this might have greatly mattered, perhaps, if the MPLA had at that time been the strongly unified movement of 1971. Democratic Portuguese preference was in any case for the MPLA; and this for two reasons. First, the MPLA was manifestly the only movement capable of leading a broad front of African unity of the type created by FRELIMO and the PAIGC. Secondly, the MPLA had never withdrawn from its non-racist principles. In company with its companion movements of Mozambique and Guinea-Bissau, it looked to an independent future in which white citizens should have equality of rights with blacks: no more than equality, but also no less. This counted for much with Portuguese who still had bitter memories of the massacre of several hundred white civilians during the 1961 rising associated with Holden and the UPA (afterwards FNLA). The armed forces government which took over in mid-July clearly wished to negotiate with the MPLA.

But the MPLA was in trouble within itself. This ensued from frustrations that appeared after 1971: chiefly, the frustration deriving from Mobutu's long refusal to allow any access to the Angolan north and north-west, and thereby give the MPLA relatively sure military access to crucial western and west-central districts of Angola. Other disintegrating factors were also present. There had emerged an evident lack of internal discussion about major decisions, such as the decision of 1972 to try to get round Mobutu's hostility by accepting a reconciliation with an otherwise hostile FNLA. This lack of internal discussion may have arisen from an over-stretched leadership; there is a good deal to suggest that it did. But Angola's geography and Mobutu's hostility also made their weighty contribution.

It was followed, in any case, by partial disintegration. This became manifestly latent towards the end of 1972, and erupted early in 1973. A number of unit commanders active in the Mbunda[7] zones immediately west of Zambia broke away under the lead of Daniel Chipenda, and formed what became known as the 'Eastern Rebellion Group'. Many of the fighting men and political workers continued to remain loyal to Neto, but Zambian complicity with Chipenda's defection deepened the split. Much bitterness ensued, and fresh complexities. The split continued. During 1973 the armed struggle paid the price, especially in the Mbunda zone. Then came the *coup d'état* and its consequences, catching the MPLA in disarray. This was slightly worsened in May 1974, when a group of nineteen dissidents, based on Brazzaville in the People's Republic of Congo, issued a manifesto accusing Neto's leadership of 'presidentialism' and other forms of disregard for internal democracy.

This second dissident group, calling itself the 'Active Rebellion Group', contained several talented nationalists and was led by one of their veterans, Father Joaquim Pinto de Andrade; but their grounds for complaint, however well- or ill-founded, were narrowed by the fact that not a few of them had lately withdrawn from active participation in the armed struggle. One among these, the literary critic and former acting president of the MPLA, Mario de Andrade, had an evident reason for complaint at the hands of the leadership associated with Neto, for this had consistently refused to make use of his qualities as publicist and diplomatist. Others seemed to be in a strikingly weak moral position, and their dissidence proved futile.

After mid-July and Spínola's speech of 29 July, when the new Portuguese government of the Armed Forces Movement turned to negotiate with a unified African nationalist movement, the difficulty was to find one. With its officers at odds, the MPLA's ship of state lay stranded on a distant beach; and efforts to relaunch it failed for several months. Meanwhile it became clear that Mobutu and his external allies were working overtime to secure an Angolan provisional government in which the opponents of the MPLA – whether Holden of the FNLA or Savimbi of UNITA, or Chipenda of the 'Eastern Rebellion Group' – would be able to guarantee the kind of 'solution' that would be acceptable to Mobutu and those who backed him, principally the USA.

Yet the star of the MPLA, so often dimmed before, now began to rise again. The summer months of permitted political activity in western and central Angola had revealed powerful African support for the MPLA and for Neto's leadership, especially in the crucial district and capital of Luanda. By October the MPLA and its local allies were openly in control of the sprawling African suburbs around Luanda. An initial delegation from the movement's leadership arrived in Luanda on 8 November to a welcome from immense crowds of jubilant supporters.

The outlook for Angola had now become vastly different from a year earlier. Decolonization was accepted by Lisbon; and this acceptance was decisively confirmed in September by Spínola's induced withdrawal from the presidency of Portugal. The national movement represented by the MPLA had still to repair many deficiencies, but was rapidly gaining, under Neto's determined leadership, a far wider support than ever before. This support was continually increased, after about the middle of 1974, through the action of a network of democratic committees, known as *Poder Popular*, 'People's Power'. At this stage, around the middle of 1974, it began to appear likely that the national movement of Angola would be able to get on top of its many problems, even if not quickly or easily, and launch the country at last upon a course towards peace and reconstruction. For this hope to be realized, however, two conditions were required. One was continued support for the MPLA from the local Portuguese administration and army, so as to discourage dissidence, put down banditry, and allow the nationalists a chance to gain practical experience in new fields of administration. The other was that there should be no foreign-launched attempts at armed intervention against the national movement.

Neither condition was fulfilled. Lisbon shifted away from support for the MPLA, and turned increasingly to a policy of 'holding the ring' between 'the three movements'; this could only widen dissidence and reduce the chances of peace. A 'tripartite' government was thus installed at the outset of 1975 that proved as futile as it was divisive. What Lisbon now hoped, evidently, was to secure in Angola what it had totally failed to get in Mozambique and Guinea-Bissau: a 'government of compromise' convenient to the maintenance of a para-colonial régime.

And it became further evident that others had the same project in mind. By the end of 1974 it was clear that there were powerful foreign interests which saw the future in terms of a repetition of events in the ex-Belgian Congo during 1961: the destruction of the only effective movement of national union (that of Lumumba in the case of the ex-Belgian Congo) as a prelude to the installation of a government which would be more or less completely subservient to the overriding interest of major investors. This operation in the Congo had led to years of inter-ethnic blood-letting and degradation in every field of public life, and eventually to an outright personal dictatorship, that of General Ssese-Seko Mobutu. A similar operation to destroy the MPLA and to instal FNLA or UNITA in Angola could be expected to ride to victory over still larger massacres and confusions. Fortunately for the Angolans, the MPLA was a far stronger and more sophisticated movement than Lumumba's had been able to become. The 'Congo scenario' would be hard to realize here. Much force would be needed.

But much force was duly applied. Partly it was applied by the reinforcement in the far north of the FNLA's 'army' with elements from Mobutu's army and with mercenaries from the Portuguese army. Partly it came by way of an airlift from Zaire and Zambia of war materials and other aid to UNITA's groups isolated in the centre of the country. But above all it came in October 1975 with the northward thrust of South African armoured columns, coming up from Namibia with helicoptered support along with a tail of FNLA and UNITA 'occupying troops'. For weeks and months the tide of war swung back and forth. The agreed date of independence came in the midst of this, 11 November. The last of the Portuguese army and administration crept wretchedly away on the eve of that day. On 11 November the MPLA in Luanda declared the independence of the people's republic of Angola; while FNLA and UNITA proclaimed their own 'independence', in Huambo, under a government which was to have an FNLA prime minister one month and an UNITA prime minister the next, so little did these two essentially élitist and tribalist organizations trust each other.

Towards January 1976 it appeared that the MPLA and its newly-proclaimed republic were slowly gaining the upper hand, and that the dangers of another 'Congo situation' were receding. Diplomatically, they had won the recognition of nearly half the states of independent Africa and, crucially, that of the Federation of Nigeria, which came down firmly for them on 24

November. They now looked to be in a fair way to win recognition from most of the rest, even though the U S State Department was putting strong pressure on its 'friendly states' in order to dissuade them from according recognition. No single state, on the other hand, had yet recognized the FNLA–UNITA government in Huambo (Nova Lisboa), and the chances of any doing so were lessened on 5 January when MPLA units drove the FNLA out of the latter's northern base of Uige (Carmona). Militarily, the new army of the MPLA was also gaining ground in other sectors of this 'second war of liberation', as it was now called. The South African northward push had been halted in November some 200 miles south of Luanda, and the South African government was soon showing signs of regretting its gamble. These military successes were due partly to the improved morale and organization of the army of the MPLA, and partly to the substantial delivery after June 1975 of war supplies by the Soviet Union and of troops by Cuba. By December, these Cuban troops had proved decisive.

Two other developments remain to be noted for the record up to the end of 1975. One was that a large proportion of Portugal's settlers allowed themselves to be panicked into leaving Angola for Portugal, although the MPLA multiplied its efforts to dissuade them: evidently those who panicked them now thought that these mostly very right-wing settlers would be more useful in Portugal than in Angola. At all events, they went in their thousands, and Portugal's self-defeat entered another stage. The second development was that the small south Atlantic islands of Sao Tomé and Príncipe duly achieved their independence. An agreement between Lisbon and the islands' independence movement, Movimento de Libertação de Sã Tomé e Príncipe (MLSTP), was signed in Algiers on 25 November 1974. This provided that a provisional nationalist government should administer the island with Portuguese co-operation until 12 July 1975; and on the latter date independence was proclaimed. How far the MLSTP would share the political ideas and intentions of the mainland movements remained to be seen; but a new chapter in this small territory first occupied by Portugal in the fifteenth century had clearly opened.

10 A New Situation

The final months of 1974 registered in any case an entirely new situation throughout the former or still colonial territories of 'Portuguese Africa', and 1975 confirmed this. Colonial rule was entirely removed from Guinea-Bissau and largely from Mozambique; prospectively removed from the Cape Verde Islands; and manifestly approaching its end in Angola and the Angolan off-shore islands of São Tomé and Príncipe. At the same time it was clear for Guinea-Bissau and Mozambique if not quite yet for Angola that this was decolonization of a new kind in Africa. It supposed the further building of nations on a non-élitist and non-reformist basis. It implied far-reaching social reconstructions.

These liberations linked up with other African attempts at breaking from the structures received by newly-independent countries late in the 1950s or early in the 1960s. They brought a powerful contribution to that new fund of ideas and objectives which had already begun to accumulate in other parties or political movements wherever those inherited structures were under serious question. They helped to throw a sharp light ahead: the light in which Africa's forty-odd states could eventually find their way out of the disabling framework of reformist nationalism, of separatist nationalism, of client nationalism, and begin to unite their resources and their talents.

With a voice more emphatic than anything heard before, these movements not only declared (what was in any case obvious) that Africans could govern themselves, but that Africans could govern themselves in ways that would overcome the handicaps of their colonial or para-colonial heritage. And in affirming this the voice was the reverse of demagogic. Here the facts were not ignored. Independence was a prelude, dearly paid for. But it was only a prelude. The chief work was still to be done.[1]

This was evident from the mood of these movements in 1974. A sense of triumph, yes: but also a sense of renewed effort. Not only in relation to obvious transitional problems, such as the absorption of urban populations only then released from colonial control; the making good of at least the worst of the technical shortages left behind by the Portuguese dictatorship;[2] the creation of national monetary and fiscal systems. But also, and much more, in relation to long-term problems.

They rejected the neo-colonial model. This meant that they rejected their colonial inheritance in the economic field as well as in the political (in so far as the two can be sensibly distinguished from each other). Since 1965, at least, the Portuguese system had moved rapidly to the acceptance of international investment as a means of maximizing the export of minerals and cash crops. Fashionably, this was called 'development'. Unfashionably, it was denounced as 'growth *without* development': as growth of the colonial system without any corresponding development of the colonized peoples.[3]

The liberation movements were well aware of the argument, and thought the critics right. They were against policies of 'growth without development'. They would go on exporting cash crops and minerals, because their economic inheritance gave them no alternative. But they would make sure, if they could, that export growth should not remain the chief regulator of their countries' economies.

They would practise, they explained, policies of widening self-reliance. They would give their whole priority to raising standards of life and levels of productivity among the rural populations which formed the great majority of their peoples. 'What we want to do,' said Luis Cabral, president of Guinea-Bissau, in August 1974, 'is to develop our countries from the villages to the towns, and not the other way round.' This policy should enable them to bring immediate and real gains to the rural populations, using exports as the servant of their policy and not as its master. As time went by, it should also enable them to move towards industrialization by means of capital accumulation from the gains of the rural areas.[4]

It was early to enlarge upon the wider implications. Obviously, the new economies would not be of a capitalist nature: if they were, they would have to revert to policies of 'growth without development'. Obviously, again, these economies would contain many elements of state control of industry and commerce. Wouldn't this therefore become a form of state capitalism? If it did, how could any sure opening to an eventual socialism be retained? The answers were to be given by the degree in which the principles and practices of mass participation could be strengthened and extended. A revolutionary process had opened during the years of armed struggle. This process was in conflict with types of centralizing stagnation associated with the structures of state capitalism. It was out of a further unfolding of the process that a new society could emerge.

Being addicted to modesty and realism, the spokesmen of the movements and of the new states had little to predict about the future. Their confidence lay in what had been achieved; and what had been achieved was a sure and broad foundation for constructive change. Change towards socialism? Yes, but these men and women had studied their world. They were aware that socialism, no matter how one may define it, demands high levels of cultural attainment, much technology, adequate reserves of democratically-controlled capital, and, not least, a large and even very large 'domestic market'.

This is no doubt why it will be found that their few statements on matters of this range and scope were invariably couched in terms of an organic African unity such as the general African situation could not yet be made to yield. Here the long-term problem would not be to resolve conflicts between the peoples of Africa, but between those who ruled them.[5] Essentially, the overcoming of this problem lay in the continued liberation of the Africans: that is, in the further development of reformist nationalism into revolutionary nationalism, into the nationalism which, being non-élitist and therefore non-capitalist, could eventually break through the constricting frameworks of the last three centuries. When this began to happen on a wide scale, the potentials for a wide and real unity might begin to be realized.

Their view, in other words, is to be seen as resolutely historical. Perhaps it was the whole development of their struggles that had given them this long view. They had learned to know the weaknesses and contradictions of an already independent Africa; they had suffered much from these. They had therefore needed to understand the reasons for these weaknesses: that many states, for example, possessed little more than a façade of independence concealing powerful outside interests which opposed the work of liberation. They had learned to analyse the peculiarly semi-colonial condition of Portugal itself, and to see that the Portuguese, like the Africans, were likewise in the grip of stronger interests that controlled them.

And this, again, is why their statements on matters of this kind were couched not only in terms of a necessary African solidarity, but, beyond that, of a world-wide solidarity with anti-imperialist movements of thought and action. To that solidarity they could claim to have made a notable contribution. For it was the success of their politics of armed struggle that had given the Portuguese in Europe the chance of democratic renewal. And when was the last occasion that a major constructive change in Africa had caused a major constructive change in Europe? In terms of political influence, these movements might even claim to have reversed the trend of centuries, right back to the beginnings of the Atlantic slave trade and the origins of Europe's domination of Africa.

For the time being there were transitional problems, with other immediate problems coming across the skyline. The freeing of Mozambique made the settlers' régime in Rhodesia untenable: how would that situation be resolved? How would it be answered? The final outcome in Angola still remained an open question at the end of 1975: even when answered by MPLA and Cuban defeat of South African invading columns, what would threaten next? Not a few of the African states were finding the revolutionary themes of the peoples of the former Portuguese colonies anything but pleasantly digestible: how would they react? Or again, powerful international interests had worked against the liberation of the Portuguese colonies and suffered defeat along with the dictatorship they had buttressed for so long: even after their defeat in Angola, what continuing hostilities could be expected from them? The questions multiplied.

I mention these questions only as a measure of the distance travelled since the politics of armed struggle appeared on the scene. They are the questions of another phase, that of the further liberation of the Africans after 1975, of the further development of international solidarity of thought and action: twin objectives which the liberation movements had long accepted as bone-and-sinew of their own meaning and existence. As it was, the unfolding of political opinions and class interests in 1976 showed at once, though not a bit surprisingly, that the politics of armed struggle, of 'united front' against continued colonial rule, must lose their relative 'simplicity' as soon as that rule was removed. A new phase of internal ideological contention now opened.

This was clear in Guinea-Bissau, where the 'petit bourgeoisie' of lately liberated towns, and above all Bissau, demonstrated a foreseeable (and long foreseen) desire merely to occupy the jobs and privileges vacated by the departed Portuguese. That implied an acceptance of the continuity of existing structures, attitudes and ideas. It cut directly across the policies and intentions of the PAIGC, and, of course, against the radical changes realized by way of new structures in all those areas liberated by the PAIGC during the war. A political campaign had therefore to be launched against this trend.

The same contention was clear in Mozambique. There the leadership of FRELIMO found itself obliged to sack or demote a number of commanders and other militants for corruption, 'militarism', and other manifestations of the same 'petit bourgeois' trend. In December 1975 a minor revolt by such 'reformists' had to be put down, and this, no doubt, was not the end of the matter. But the 'petit bourgeois' trend was perhaps clearest of all in Angola.

By the end of 1975 more than 200,000 Portuguese settlers had fled from Angola, though an exact figure was not to hand. They had fled in a wave of panic which the MPLA, true to its anti-racist principles and foreseeing how many more difficulties this exodus must pile on the infant republic, had tried vainly to oppose. Why did these settlers panic? Some had good reasons for doing so. The majority, it seems, were deliberately panicked by other Portuguese. Did the latter now calculate that these fiercely 'right-wing' settlers would be more useful in Portugal as things then stood: useful, that is, to the cause of counter-revolution? However that may be, they departed in their tens of thousands, abandoning their farms, quitting their skilled urban jobs, leaving vacant whole ranks of responsibility in the public services. This meant that all those supporters of the MPLA, especially in newly-liberated towns, who were ready to be content with an independence which merely evicted the Portuguese, could now hope for relatively privileged jobs inside the structures which the Portuguese system had left behind it. There emerged a 'right-wing trend' which was at once the subject of hot debate. It was not unexpected.[6]

'The chief contradiction' in Angola, said an MPLA militant of Dondo during December 1975, in a fairly characteristic contribution to this debate, was manifestly 'between the Angolan people and international imperialism', including of course the South African troops still fighting against the MPLA in south Angola.

> But this should not allow us to ignore signs of a right-wing trend within our ranks . . . nor the fact that two well-defined ideologies are at work: the ideology of the working class, of revolution, and the ideology of the bourgeoisie . . . Whether we like it or not, a class struggle is going on here . . .[7]

Reporting this speech the MPLA journal, *Vitória Certa*, enlarged upon its meaning with an editorial. This castigated the 'widespread opportunism' that could now be seen among employees of the public services, including members of the MPLA, who were simply on the hunt for personal gain. The same issue gave rise to other cases of the same trend. War-caused shortages of food and money could only reinforce this 'chase for benefits'. At the same time, mirroring this 'right-wing trend' though in a minor way (and mirroring, too, the political conflicts on the left in Portugal, and, no doubt, the Sino-Soviet dispute), there also emerged a 'left-wing trend'. The more extreme members of this second trend now claimed to see the whole MPLA, leadership and all, as no more than 'the instrument of a petit bourgeoisie seeking to become a national bourgeosie', and argued that the MPLA could not carry through 'the revolution'.[8]

Striving meanwhile to win the war for independence by as wide and effective a mobilization as possible, and in the midst of many economic confusions and social disasters, the leadership of the MPLA held firmly to their course. Their speeches and writings at this dramatic time make it plain that they judged the right-wing trend to be the real danger to what they had set themselves to achieve: to win the war, that is, in such a way as to lay the groundwork for an independent country orientated in the direction of socialism. Yet all this vivid debate, with its sudden outburst of discussion about profoundly complex and important issues of policy and development, could point to another gain won in the struggles of these years: no such issues could ever have been discussed before. The years ahead would show the full measure of this gain. Neto's leadership used it now in efforts to reinforce the cause of national unity and social renewal.

Elsewhere, too, the movements now in power embarked on political campaigns of new construction, whether moral or material. In Guinea-Bissau, as in the sister-Republic of the Cape Verde Islands, there opened another phase of political mobilization, this time to continue and extend the building and unfolding of a modern society such as the armed struggle had rendered possible. The same was true of Mozambique, whose government under Samora Machel's vigorous leadership fulfilled in March 1976 another of its promises, and applied sanctions to the settler régime in Zimbabwe. Already a different future stood upon the threshold.

These pages have not tried to read oracles but to elucidate the politics of armed struggle: the politics of the phase in 'Portuguese Africa' that was coming to an end in 1974. This phase has written a crucial chapter in the modern history of the Africans. It is one of long and bitter suffering. But it is also one of large achievement in the annals of creative change. Its influence on the whole outcome for southern Africa will be correspondingly profound.

Notes

Chapter 1: A Decisive Success

1. PAIGC: national liberation movement of Guinea-Bissau and the Cape Verde Islands (*Partido Africano de Independência de Guiné e Cabo Verde*). Now the ruling party of both Republics.

2. For summaries of Portuguese official statistics on war spending, etc., see relevant United Nations documentation, especially A/9023 (Part IV), UNO, New York.

3. The writer made his acquaintance with these movements in the second half of the 1950s, before the wars began. After the wars began he visited the liberated areas of the PAIGC in Guinea-Bissau in 1967 and 1972, of FRELIMO (*Frente de Libertação de Moçambique*) in 1968, and of the MPLA (*Movimento Popular de Libertação de Angola*) in 1970. In August 1974 he again visited the PAIGC in Guinea-Bissau, by now an independent state, and witnessed the early stages of Portuguese withdrawal. During the Second World War he had served as a British officer with the Yugoslav army of national liberation (in 1943–4) and with guerrilla formations in northern Italy from January 1945 until the end of the war in that country.

4. See 'M F A na Guiné', *Boletim Informativo*, No. 1, 1 June 1974, Bissau, for full details of this structural reorganization, together with names of those serving on all relevant commissions.

5. Declaration quoted in full in the MFA – edited newspaper, *Voz da Guiné*, Bissau, 10 August 1974.

6. In an interview with the author.

7. *Le Monde*, Paris, 10 September 1974.

Chapter 2: The Colonial Background

1. C. Fyfe, *Africanus Horton*, Oxford University Press, 1972, p. 154.

2. Louis Franck, in a passage reprinted as preface to *Recueil* of Belgian Congo administrative texts and directives: 4th edition, Brussels, March 1925.

3. Alfred Milner, *The Nation and the Empire*, Constable, 1913, p. xxxii.

4. F. Nogueira, *The Third World*, with foreword by Dean Acheson, Johnson, 1967, pp. 154–5.

5. On the reality of Portuguese attitudes to race, see C. R. Boxer, *Race Relations in the Portuguese Colonial Empire, 1415–1825*, Clarendon Press, 1963. For the history of Angola in this context, see B. Davidson, *In the Eye of the Storm: Angola's People*, Allen Lane, 1972, Penguin, 1975.

6. See, for example, E. Mondlane, *The Struggle for Mozambique*, Penguin, 1969; and a number of relevant essays in Amílcar Cabral, *Unité et Lutte* (Collected Writings), Maspero, Paris, 1974, (2 volumes).

7. I pass over, for simplicity's sake, many reservations that would have to be made on conditions of employment in certain West African territories, where the export-market economy was more advanced than elsewhere in terms of African participation. For a summary of the latter, see A. G. Hopkins, *Economic History of West Africa*, Longman, 1973.

8. *Hansard*, Cape Colony, 1894, pp. 362–9.

Chapter 3: Portugal in Africa: A Special Case?

1. Norton de Matos, *A Província de Angola*, Porto, Portugal, 1926, p. 127.

2. ibid., p. 126.

3. From the journal of Dr Merlin Ennis: copy in the author's possession.

4. M. Caetano, *Os Nativos na Economia Africana*, Coimbra, Portugal, 1954, p. 16.

5. A semi-official analysis of the 1950 census figures by Adriano Moreira showed black *assimilados* in Angola as being about 0.75 per cent of the whole black population. The comparable proportion for Mozambique was smaller still, and for Guinea-Bissau about 0.3 per cent (*As Élites das Provincias Portuguesês de Indigenato*, Junta de Investigações do Ultramar, Lisbon, 1956). By 1960 the proportions were probably a little less exiguous, perhaps by 1 per cent or so; but the 1960 census figures allow no distinctions to be drawn between Whites and Blacks in this respect. For a factual review of Portuguese colonial educational policies and their results, see Eduardo de Sousa Ferreira, *Portuguese Colonialism in Africa* UNESCO, 1974.

6. In a foreword to B. Davidson, *The Liberation of Guiné*, Penguin, 1969, p. 9.

Chapter 5: 1945 and After: Bridging the Gulf

1. Excerpt from one of the crucial documents that have come out of these struggles, written in 1964: Amílcar Cabral, 'Brief Analysis of the Social Structure in Guinea', in *Revolution in Guinea: Selected Texts by Amílcar Cabral*, Stage One, 1969.

2. Cabral, 'Brief Analysis of the Social Structure in Guinea' (op. cit.).

3. Mabote's story is told more fully in Davidson, *In the Eye of the Storm: Angola's People* (op. cit.), pp. 179–80, with other examples of the same kind.

4. Cabral, 'Brief Analysis of the Social Structure in Guinea', op. cit.

5. The late Osvaldo Vieira, in a 1972 interview with the author.

6. Original in A. Cabral, *National Liberation and Culture*, Syracuse University, New York, 20 February 1970.

7. Fuller discussion in Davidson, *In the Eye of the Storm: Angola's People* (op. cit.), chapter 11. For Mondlane's development, see especially Mondlane, op. cit.

Chapter 6: The Line of March – and Diversions

1. e.g. J. Marcum, *The Angolan Revolution*, vol 1, M.I.T. Press, Cambridge, Mass., U.S.A., 1969; Davidson, *In the Eye of the Storm: Angola's People* (op. cit.).

2. A term originally invented by the Chinese Communists during their great guerrilla wars of the 1930s: the original, I am informed, is *Shan t'ou chu yi*. It describes those small groups of guerrillas who defected from the struggle by staying on this or that 'mountain top' in tacit or overt agreement with the Japanese or the Kuomintang, neither of whom needed the mountain top but the roads around it. During the Second World War in Yugoslavia, the *chetnik* bands of Draža Mihajlović were consistent 'mountain-topists'. Similar cases occurred in Northern Italy during early 1945. Such groups almost invariably become agents of the enemy, as notably with UNITA in Angola.

3. Much circumstantial evidence. See, for instance, *Afrique-Asie*, 61, Paris, 8 July 1974 for exchanges of letters in 1972 attributed to Jonas Savimbi, the UNITA leader, and the Portuguese army command in Angola. The content of these letters suggests that they would have been hard to fabricate. Nor does it seem that fabrication need be supposed. By June 1974 the Portuguese command was freely saying that it had contact with Savimbi, whose presence in Luanda was awaited as soon as 'certain clarifications' were available (see *Diario de*

Noticias, Lisbon, 28 June 1974). By July the extremist wing of the Luanda settlers were, for their part, openly in support of UNITA. In 1975, UNITA became the avowed ally of the S. African army.

In previous years, UNITA's propaganda in western Europe had specialized in 'revolutionary purity', and generally echoed a 'Maoist' line that received, for a while, a certain propaganda support in Peking foreign-language journals. What this 'purity' was really worth was suggested in a *Daily Telegraph* report from Luanda, published on 22 August 1974, that the UNITA leader, Jonas Savimbi, was being 'hailed as a future president by many of the Territory's Whites': by precisely those Whites, in fact, who were hoping for some kind of neo-colonial or settlers' régime. The UNITA collusion with the South African army's invasion of southern Angola in 1975 was logical enough

4. For the history of the FNLA and its parent movement, UPA, see Marcum, op. cit.; and Davidson, *In the Eye of the Storm*.

5. For evidence of Mobutu's early promotion by the CIA, see Jules Chomé, *L'Ascension du Sergent Mobutu*, Maspero, Paris, 1974. See also V. Marchetti and J. D. Marks, *The C.I.A.*, Jonathan Cape, 1974, pp. 31 and 118, where it is explained that Mobutu's career owed much to the CIA's support. Other public sources of information about the CIA made the same point in US press disclosures during 1975. The same disclosures reported that in 1961 the CIA began paying Holden an annual $10,000.

Chapter 7: Guerrilla Warfare

1. Quoted in Davidson, *The Liberation of Guiné* (op. cit.), p. 112, Cabral's emphasis.

2. Amílcar Cabral, quoted in *Afrique-Asie*, 66, Paris, 1974, p. xxv.

3. Quoted by G. Chaliand, *Armed Struggle in Africa*, Monthly Review Press, New York, 1969, pp. 78–9.

4. Amílcar Cabral, quoted in Davidson, *The Liberation of Guiné* (op. cit.), p. 52.

5. As to successful advances, the place of discussion can be seen in the relation between the 1964 congress of the PAIGC and the PAIGC's move to new organizational structures and mobile warfare. Responsible commanders and political workers were called from every sector of the struggle and made their way, often with great difficulty, to a rendezvous in the southern forest. Their gathering together, days of meeting, and return to their posts 'set back our armed struggle by six months, for the Portuguese profited by reoccupying many areas. But we had to do it, we had to see who we all were, we had to see where

we were going, we had to do all this together.' (A. Cabral and A. Pereira in an interview with the author, December 1972).

The same positive relation can be seen between the 1968 congress of FRELIMO (some delegates to the Niassa rendezvous had to be weeks on the way there, and more weeks on the way back) with subsequent discussion campaigns, and the firm unfolding of FRELIMO's successes in the early 1970s.

Or a contrary example may be seen in the relation between reduced internal discussion within the MPLA, after 1969, and the dissensions that appeared in 1973. Here, hostile geography played a crucial part.

6. Cabral, *National Liberation and Culture* (op. cit.).

Chapter 8: Practising What You Preach

1. As they did in Portuguese Africa, having found by harsh experience that urban struggle would not answer. The parallel here is with China of the late 1920s and early 1930s, or of Yugoslavia in the 1940s, although there is nothing to suggest (or, come to that, to deny) that these Africans were aware of following either.

2. Any detailed analysis of successful 'guerrilla warfare' would lay the strongest emphasis on the need to fight for the lives of villagers threatened by enemy offensives. Only those movements which have faced this need with self-sacrificing courage, while somehow conserving their own capacity to survive, have been able to succeed. The most impressive record known to me of what such a need can impose, whether in terms of courage or of suffering, is that of my old friend Todor Vujasinović: *Ozrenski Partizanski Odred*, Vojnoistorijski Institut, Belgrade, 1962, a book which much deserves translation.

3. There were exceptions to this in cases where the attitude of local Portuguese traders made their continued presence useful to the liberation movements which, for their part, campaigned against any racist objection to Portuguese or other Whites.

4. A. Cabral, *Identity and Dignity in the Context of the National Liberation Struggle*, UNESCO, 1972. Its critique of 'Négritude' and other such 'black returns to the source', whether on one side of the Atlantic or the other, is another aspect of this paper that will remain of permanent interest.

5. A. Cabral, *Resistençia Cultural*, seminar paper at PAIGC Conference of Cadres, 19–24 November 1969.

6. ibid.

7. Quoted in Davidson, *In the Eye of the Storm: Angola's People* (op. cit.), p. 279.

8. See interview and discussion in J. Slovo, 'Southern Africa:

Problems of Armed Struggle', *The Socialist Register, 1973*, Merlin Press, 1974, p. 319.

9. Samora Machel, *Mozambique: Sowing the Seeds of Revolution*, CFMAG, 12 Little Newport Street, London, 1974, p. 39.

10. A point well argued by John Saul, 'Neo-Colonialism vs Liberation Struggle', seminar paper of 1973; see also John Saul, 'FRELIMO and the Mozambique Revolution', in G. Arrighi and J. Saul, *Essays on the Political Economy of Africa*, Monthly Review Press, New York, 1973.

11. Luis Cabral, President of Guinea-Bissau and Deputy Secretary-General of the PAIGC, in August 1974 (interview with the author).

12. Havana, 1966: reprinted in Cabral, *Revolution in Guinea: Selected Texts by Amílcar Cabral* (op. cit.), p. 89.

Chapter 9: The End of the Beginning

1. In November 1970. A sufficient number of raiders were captured in Conakry to reveal the general machinery and authorship of the operation. All this was confirmed in 1974.

2. *Daily Telegraph*, 15 November 1970.

3. Emphasis in original. Spinola's views are quoted from Al. J. Venter, *Report on Portugal's War in Guiné-Bissau*, Munger Africana Library Notes, California Institute of Technology, Pasadena, April 1973, pp. 189–91. Venter's interview with Spinola was in April 1971.

4. A scenario in whose elaboration it will no doubt emerge, when the necessary records become available, that Portugal's allies had a leading hand.

5. 'Speech to the Nation' broadcast on 29 July, declaring the right of every people to its independence and announcing that a transfer of power to the peoples of Guinea-Bissau, Angola and Mozambique would begin forthwith.

6. America's interest in (Angola's) wealth needs no emphasis. So great was it that in February 1970, when Angola was still firmly under Portugal's thumb, the United States Govenment began a subtle shift in its policies towards southern Africa. Henry Kissinger prepared for President Nixon a typically 'realistic' set of secret policy options designed to foster American interests ... Kissinger's chief assumption was that white rule would continue for the foreseeable future. It was a classic miscalculation ... The April *coup* severely undermined the Portuguese section of this strategy. Kissinger's report had stated that 'the biggest U.S. interest in the area is Angola' ...

Sunday Times, 20 October 1974. All this was again confirmed during 1975 by greatly enlarged US aid to the enemies of the MPLA.

7. The Mbunda are a ciMbunda-speaking people to be distinguished from the Mbundu (plural: Ovimbundu) of the central districts.

Chapter 10: A New Situation

1. Marcelino dos Santos, vice-president of FRELIMO, in 1973: 'If our organization maintains a true revolutionary leadership, the special circumstances of the process of our liberation open up real possibilities for an advance from liberation to revolution.' Quoted in Slovo, op. cit., p. 336.

2. In Guinea-Bissau, for instance, the medical services of the PAIGC discovered (and even they were surprised by the discovery) that the total number of civilian doctors in the capital of Bissau, and all other towns held by the Portuguese until then, was exactly four; and one of these was too ill to work.

3. A large bibliography. For recent discussion and references see Basil Davidson, *Can Africa Survive?*, Heinemann, 1974. And in relation to Somalia, Basil Davidson, 'In Somalia Now', *Race and Class*, July 1975.

4. Perspectives sketched by Guinea-Bissau's Commissioner for Economics and Finance, Vasco Cabral, in September 1974. He pointed out that the colonial economy of Guinea-Bissau had rested on the maximization of ground-nut exports:

> This led to a disastrous consequence: the destruction of local growing of foodstuffs, without this being in any way compensated by a coherent industrialization...
>
> We have to start from this concrete situation that we inherit and, for the time being, found our whole economy on agriculture, so as to raise agriculture to a level that can serve as a basis for the future development of industry. That is our conviction. And that explains the measures we have already taken in our liberated areas.
>
> First of all, in order to break out of the colonial ground-nut system – a system which exhausted the soil by continually expanding ground-nut cultivation, reducing fallow, and ignoring rotation of crops – we have relaunched the cultivation of foodstuffs and tried to diversify it... (For) not only did the Portuguese fail to develop cultivation apart from ground-nuts: it's also the case that certain crops disappeared – cotton, for example... They even had to import rice, the staple food of our people...

In *Afrique-Asie*, Paris, 23 September 1974.

5. 'My own view is that there are no real conflicts between the peoples of Africa. There are only conflicts between their élites. When the people take power into their own hands, as they will do with the march of events in this continent, there will remain no great obstacles to

effective African solidarity.' A. Cabral in 1967, quoted in Davidson, *The Liberation of Guiné* (op. cit.), p. 139.

6. Like his fellow leaders in Guinea-Bissau and Mozambique, Agostinho Neto had long foreseen that the politics of armed struggle necessarily contained the seeds of a later ideological contention. 'Today,' he said in 1970,

> we are going through the stage of a movement for national liberation, a movement in which all tendencies and persons willing to take part in the struggle against Portuguese colonialism are accepted. We are bound together by the common will to fight against Portuguese colonialism . . . (but) while there is one organisational structure there is not one ideological position.

See Davidson, *In the Eye of the Storm: Angola's People*, (op. cit.), p. 332.

7. *Vitória Certa*, Luanda, no. 31: 20 December 1975, pp. 7 and 14.

8. One section of this 'left-wing trend', with views very reminiscent of the so-called 'Active Rebellion Group' which had appeared briefly and it must be said ingloriously on the scene in 1973, even went so far as to accuse the MPLA leadership of conducting a 'populist-fascist' policy, and called in October 1975, with the enemy almost at the gates of Luanda, for 'the organization of a Communist Party'. This was to operate, it said, within a 'broad anti-imperialist front . . . to be created as soon as possible': after, presumably, South African troops had destroyed MPLA. See the first two issues of the stencilled organ of 'The Communist Organization of Angola': *Jornal Comunista*, October 1975. The 'Active Rebellion Group', one may recall, had mustered fewer than twenty persons. This kind of thing, and other fantasies of CIA-like manufacture, also added to the ideological fireworks of those dramatic months.

Part Two:

South Africa – No Middle Road

Joe Slovo

Table 1

(a) Population of South Africa at 30 June 1974

Africans	*Coloureds*	*Asians*	*Whites*	*Total*
17,745,000	2,306,000	709,000	4,160,000	24,920,000
(71·2%)	(9·3%)	(2·8%)	(16·7%)	

Source: Bulletin of Statistics, December 1974, Department of Statistics, Pretoria. Estimates based in 1970 Census.

(b) Rate of population growth between 1960 and 1970

Africans	*Coloureds*	*Asians*	*Whites*
36·3%	32·3%	28·7%	2·4%

Source: Preliminary figures released by the Department of Statistics, Pretoria, for the period 8 September 1960 to 6 May 1970.

(c) Distribution of Africans between 'White South Africa' and the 'Homelands'

'White areas'	*'Homelands'*
8,060,773	6,994,179

Source: Bulletin of Statistics, December 1974, Department of Statistics, Pretoria. Figures based on 1970 population.

(d) Economically active persons total figures and as a percentage of whole population

Africans	*Coloureds*	*Asians*	*Whites*
6,389,000	807,000	208,000	1,673,000
(70·4%)	(8·9%)	(2·3%)	(18·4%)

Source: Minister of Statistics based on estimates for June 1974, Hansard 6, Col. 400, 9 September 1974.

(e) Distribution of Africans in 'White' areas

Urban	*Rural*
4,614,649	3,446,124

Source: Bulletin of Statistics, December 1974, Department of Statistics, Pretoria. Estimates based on 1970 Census.

(f) Growth of wage-gap in Rand per annum – excluding agriculture, domestic service & railways*

Year	*White*	*African*	*Gap*
1969	2,874	439	2,435
1970	3,213	472	2,741
1971	3,555	519	3,036
1972	3,824	578	3,246

Source: Bulletin of Statistics, March 1974, Department of Statistics, Pretoria.

* If these categories were included the gap would be considerably bigger.

I The Answer to Minority Rule

In a world increasingly hostile to race-based oligarchy, South Africa works unceasingly to widen its circle of accomplices. Its public relations machine orchestrates a perpetual wail on the theme 'why pick on us?'. It continually seeks admiration for its (often inaccurate) statistics on the incomes of its black inhabitants compared with the incomes of Africans living in areas of minimal resources and development.* It seizes upon every race riot, every famine, every exposure of intensive wage exploitation elsewhere in the hope that its own conduct will be judged by the lowest common denominator of human misery.

As a self-proclaimed 'bastion against Communism' South Africa claims an honoured place in the so-called 'free world' and finds it incomprehensible that in some respects (e.g. arms) even its friends and true allies can give it succour only by behaving like thieves in the night. It seeks acclaim for its terror-sanctioned stability by contrasting itself with the social disequilibrium in some areas of the Third World where newly-freed men are groping to lay a foundation for their future, while still contending with a historical heritage of colonial plunder and with continuing imperial interference.

But then the truth about apartheid has long been thoroughly

*In any case recent statistics show that the income of Africans in South Africa (by far the richest country on the continent) is only the 13th highest in Africa. The average per capita income of Africans in South Africa is R135. In Zambia, for example, it is R231. For the 7 million Africans in the homelands South Africa is near the bottom of the scale with an average per capita income of R72, of which half is earned in migrant workers' wages (Professor Jan Sadie, Dept. of Economics, University of Stellenbosch, quoted in *Rand Daily Mail*, 5 February 1975). South Africa's white population (just under 20% of the total) receives 76·5% of the country's gross domestic product (*Rand Daily Mail*, 9 August 1974).

and widely documented. Figures are easily available to show that there is no country on earth in which the ethnic origin alone of the overwhelming majority of the inhabitants condemns them to enjoy so trivial a proportion of its national riches. *This* surely is the test; not the unending stream of comparative statistics which pours forth from Pretoria.

And the ethical or moral qualities of apartheid are no more open to debate than the merits or demerits of Nazi race practices. For those who live apartheid's reality, not in debate but in their daily experience, the need to destroy it in all its manifestations is a self-evident truth. That is the starting point and the only remaining question is – how?

On this question the radical opposition movement within South Africa speaks with one voice: it is only through extra-legal mass action including armed struggle that the white monolith can be shifted and a just society won. The African National Congress's 'Strategy and Tactics' states:

> South Africa was conquered by force and is today ruled by force. At moments when white autocracy feels itself threatened, it does not hesitate to use the gun. When the gun is not in use, legal and administrative terror, fear, social and economic pressures, complacency and confusion generated by propaganda and 'education' are the devices brought into play in an attempt to harness the people's opposition. Behind these devices hovers force. Whether in reserve or in actual employment, force is ever-present and this has been so ever since the white man came to Africa.[1]

The illusion of the liberal gradualists, that apartheid will die a natural (albeit slow) death by the operation of the economic processes, has been demonstrably shattered by the events of the last three decades. This most dramatic period of economic advance, during which more and more Africans have been sucked into the modern industrial sector, has in fact been accompanied by a widening of the gulf between the races, by greater and not less repression, and by a growing gap between white and black incomes.

Before the Second World War, when South Africa was still on the threshold of its economic leap forward, the civic rights enjoyed by the black majority were paltry enough. They could by no stretch of the imagination be regarded as a suitable mechanism for achieving real change by constitutional methods. But since then, the little that had lingered on from the brave days of Cape liberalism has been systematically eroded. The Westminster-sanctioned compromise in 1909 between the all-white colonial governments in South Africa went the way of all compromises in which the victim is an unrepresented and powerless object of bargaining. The few Africans who had retained their place as electors on the Cape Common Roll were later segregated on a separate voters' roll, with three whites to represent them in the central legislature: only to have even this concession abolished – through a constitutional fraud – by the present régime.

The right to combine in political association across the colour line or on a platform of majority rule is no more. The outlawing of organizations such as the African National Congress, South African Communist Party, and Pan-Africanist Congress has been followed by a mass of draconian judicial and administrative measures to make effectual legal opposition impossible, and to harass and intimidate the voteless majority. What remained to blacks of the right to strike; marginal rights to freehold property in 87% of the national land area; the right to maintain a domicile in the urban complexes; the right to intimacy across the colour line; the right to study at the 'open' universities: these have all been diminished to the point of meaninglessness or simply swept away since 1948.

Indeed, if events in the post-war period prove anything, it is that the more dependent the white establishment becomes on black sweat and black skill, the more jealous it becomes of its monopoly over economic and political privileges, and the more finely it sharpens those instruments which ensure its hegemony.

To take issue with this generalization on the ground that it ignores the new 'liberalism' which post-Verwoerdian apartheid has been recently projecting, is to dispute not so much the fact as the yardstick for measuring its significance. If the essence of apartheid were only the segregated park bench, the all-white playing fields, the Verwoerdian language of 'baaskap', the permanent bar against black mobility into higher skilled occupations, and the refusal to delegate bureaucratic function, then we are indeed witnessing signs (however minimal) of a retreat. Official organs of the ruling party now join the 'unpatriotic' English press in making disparaging noises about 'petty apartheid'. Government Ministers belonging to the so-called enlightened (*Verligte*) faction talk about making the lot of the African urban dweller 'as happy as possible' and dismiss the idea that the homelands are 'dumping grounds for people we don't want in South Africa'.[2] Moreover, when Mr R. F. Botha, South Africa's chief delegate to the Security Council, told the United Nations in October 1974 that 'My Government does not condone discrimination purely on the grounds of race or colour, and we shall do everything in our power to move away from discrimination based on colour',[3] he seemed to have come a very long way from Strijdom's arrogant threat to the same body in 1950 that the Whites 'shall fight to the last drop of our blood to maintain white supremacy in South Africa'.[4]

But those who see in all this a significant indicator of a move from the top for the redistribution of power in favour of a society based on equality, confuse the politician's rhetoric with the reality which it hides. They ignore the fundamental premise from which all elements (whether *Verligte* or *Verkrampte*) in the régime proceed. What separates a Strijdom and a Botha is not a retreat from white supremacy but rather a differing approach to securing that supremacy in two distinct periods: a period when the risks of internal upheaval and external pressures were not yet immediately menacing; and the present period, when the prospect of a black revolutionary breakthrough is no longer a distant nightmare but a discernible cloud on the horizon, and the mood among the blacks inside the country and along the Republic's increasingly exposed borders is one of growing national assertiveness.

The significance of the reforms which have already been conceded and those which may still come, and their relevance to the struggle equation, will be referred to again. At this point it is enough to say that the pragmatism of the Vorster variety is little more than a tactical re-disposition calculated to streamline apartheid's machinery and to fortify the main citadel of white control in a situation which, according to de Villiers Graaff, leader of the opposition United Party, has 'dramatically reduced both the time and the space which stands between us and the relentless approach of insurgency towards South Africa itself'.[5]

To understand the true meaning of the reforms which have already been made and those which are still promised, it is essential that we recognize the point beyond which South Africa will not and cannot go.

First, white South Africa (if it is to survive as such) will not and cannot allow a challenge to the claim which it lays to ownership and control of the wealth in 87% of South Africa's land area. Its new-found vigour in promoting so-called black 'self-government' in the remaining 13% is designed to legitimize this monstrous historical swindle. Neither is the political kingdom negotiable except for the trappings of office in South Africa's backyards which are being graced by the name of 'homelands' or 'Bantustans'. For those – the majority of the black people – who are forced in their lifetime to minister to the labour needs of the urban complexes and rich farmlands where most of them were born, there is no question of the vote or any other constitutional access to real power. What has always united and continues to unite all white South Africans (except, in the words of General Smuts, 'those who are quite mad')[6] is the absolute and perpetual bar to political power-sharing in what is claimed to be 'white South Africa'.

'Call it paramountcy, baaskap or what you will,' said Strijdom,

> it is still domination. I am being as blunt as I can. I am making no excuses. Either the white man dominates or the black man takes over... The only way the European can maintain supremacy is by domination... And the only way they can maintain domination is by withholding the vote from the non-European. If it were not for that we would not be here in Parliament today.[7]

Such refreshing candour is no longer the fashion. The word 'paramountcy' is now seldom heard, and 'baaskap' is reserved for election time in the rural areas. But 'what you will' is very much alive, except that it attempts to hide its parentage so as to gain social acceptance.

White South Africa's exclusive control over South Africa's

riches is even less on offer.* Ninety-nine per cent of these are to be found in that part of South Africa which apartheid 'scholars' claim to be the white man's 'natural heritage'. *This racial monopoly over all the essential means of production is the real source of white political dictatorship.* And, in turn, exclusive control of the state apparatus sanctifies and maintains the vast racial imbalance by which South Africa's wealth is appropriated.

'In our country,' say the ANC,

> more than in any other part of the oppressed world, it is inconceivable for liberation to have meaning without a return of the wealth of the land to the people as a whole. It is therefore a fundamental feature of our strategy that victory must embrace more than formal political democracy. To allow the existing economic forces to retain their interests intact is to feed the root of racial supremacy and does not represent even a shadow of liberation.[8]

All that the recent signs of so-called enlightenment can be said with confidence to reflect is the system's ability to accommodate itself to internal and world pressures in those areas not crucial to its fundamental patterns of domination. At most we might dare to suggest that the observable back-pedalling at secondary levels of the system, accompanied by division and infighting in the ranks of the oligarchy on the pace of the 'reforms', is some evidence of a ferment within apartheid which renders it more vulnerable to revolutionary assault. As stated by Dr Yusuf Dadoo:

> From the point of view of the people, even the small successes such as the recent meagre wage rises create rising expectations and have given them new experience of the potential of united action on a much bigger scale. The forced retreat by the government on the question of certain levels of skilled work for blacks provides a spur for greater achievement in this field and highlights still further in the minds of the African workers the iniquitous wage gap between them and the whites who previously carried out the same work. The new deceptive labour law places more firmly on the agenda the urgent need to struggle for real trade union rights and the right to strike. Although it was never the régime's intention, the speeding up of the Bantustan programme

*'White South Africa' is in fact overwhelmingly black. It is white only in relation to access to wealth and power.

has put on the agenda as never before the whole question of real political power and national liberation.[9]

Those, then, who maintain that a substantial shift in political power could eventually come through changes by and within the system can only base their prophecy on the faith that the South African ruling class will set a precedent in history and abandon the real source of its power without a fight.

No system can survive without a legitimizing ideology which mobilizes its own battalions and blunts the aspirations of its opponents or accommodates these by deflecting them into channels which bypass the main issues. There are, of course, moments when, feeling itself vulnerable, the ruling class is compelled to venture into new territory, and so unintentionally triggers off fresh energies in its antagonists. But at the end of the day it will muster all its instruments of force to destroy these energies or divert them into non-vital areas.

So, whatever else may happen, the South African ruling class will not give up the main heights it commands without an intense struggle. It is precisely to prevent the threatened assault on these heights that adjustments are being made on fronts of secondary importance and more substance is being given to the Bantustan schemes.* And it is for the same reason that more action can be expected to remove or alleviate those levels of racial humiliation which are not indispensably functional to the system. The régime hopes in this way to gain black collaboration or acquiescence

*Ironically the apartheid publicists claim that the homelands scheme is an earnest of their sincerity in moving towards 'decolonization' and ending race discrimination. But like Humpty Dumpty in *Alice*, they are past masters at making a word mean 'just what I choose it to mean – neither more nor less'. Limited Indian representation in parliament (provided for in a 1946 statute but never implemented) was abolished by the *Indian Representation Act* of 1948. The pass laws were extended to women and to some previously exempted men in the Cape Province by the *Abolition of Passes Act* in 1952 (under this Act the annual rate of pass law arrests reached new heights). The meagre indirect representation of Africans (by three whites) in the central parliament was ended by the *Promotion of Bantu Self-Government Act* of 1959. In the same year the right of blacks to attend white universities was ended by the *Extension of University Education Act*. And joint political organization across the colour line was interfered with by the *Prohibition of Political Interference Act*, 1968.

inside and general support outside South Africa for its more fundamental purposes. It is a measure of the changed chemistry of the situation (inside South Africa, on its immediate borders and in the world generally) that apartheid realizes how necessary such collaboration is, if doom is to be postponed.

Even some good friends of the black liberation movements are sometimes tempted to allow a celebration of apartheid's reforms to weaken their moral and practical hostility towards it, and to foster the illusion that there may be a route to true democracy in South Africa short of the complete destruction of the white state and the economic base on which it rests. But the new society in South Africa will only come through a successful revolutionary assault by the deprived, in which increasing armed confrontation is unavoidable. To counsel otherwise is in fact to counsel submission.

A war in South Africa will doubtless bring about enormous human suffering. It may also, in its initial stages, see a line-up in which the main antagonists fall broadly into racial camps, and this would add a further tragic dimension to the conflict. Indeed if a reasonable prospect existed of a powerful enough group amongst the Whites joining in the foreseeable future with those who stand for majority rule, the case for revolt would be less compelling. As it is, the ANC claims that,

> The laager-minded white group as a whole moves more and more in the direction of a common defence of what is considered a common fate . . . this confrontation on the lines of colour – at least in the early stages of the conflict – is not of our choosing; it is of the enemy's making. It will not be easy to eliminate some of the more tragic consequences.[10]

There are those who argue that the consequences of such a conflict – tragic not only for both peoples but because it might well encourage outside forces to take sides on racial lines – are sufficient reasons in themselves to outweigh the passion for immediate radical change. But they are inventing for the black people of South Africa a code of social morality which no people in such conditions have ever accepted. To the black ear such reasoning has an especially hypocritical ring when it comes from editorial writers in Europe whose countries, in this century alone, have given the lives of scores of millions of their youth to ward off or destroy what they conceived to be tyranny. They would certainly endorse the spirit of Gladstone's remarks about Britain when he said: 'If the people of this country had obeyed the precept to eschew violence and maintain order, the liberties of this country would never have been obtained.'[11]

Nevertheless, a commitment to violence cannot be grounded on a speculation that the alternative would take a little longer. The path to which South Africa's national liberation movement is committed is not one which it has selected from a group of viable alternatives. There *is* no other path to the winning of majority rule over the whole of South Africa, for the simple reason that all other routes are permanently barred.

Yet one may concede all this and still continue to question the liberation movement's commitment to the strategy of revolutionary force. This may be done from one of two positions. Either (like some of the Bantustan leaders) one may dismiss the feasibility of victorious violent resistance in the context of such a vast imbalance of power and resources between the antagonists (an argument which will be considered later); or one may maintain that enlightened pressures from within the white group (although minimal at present) will escalate, and in the foreseeable future create conditions for a less painful road to democratic advance. In support of this hope, one cannot point to the adjustments which have already taken place; for this would be to overlook their peripheral and defensive nature and to ignore the factors which triggered them off.

When the white opposition leader voices the well-worn cliché of counter-insurgency that 'the only way to win the war against insurgency is to create conditions in which it could not take root',[12] he pays tribute to the impact which even the threat of force is making on the thinking of the white establishment. This kind of thinking (echoed by Nationalist politicians, army men and others), the ever-so-slight breeze of change suggested in the Progressive Party gains in the 1974 election, and in the marginal reforms which are being floated, underscore not growing white enlightenment, but the imperative relevance of the language of force. Dilute this language, and Vorster's so-called 'voice of reason' will become correspondingly less audible. Translate it into a sustained confrontation, and conditions may well emerge in which white intransigence on the main issues is forced to weaken, and talk of dialogue may no longer be a prescription for surrender.

Until then the seeds of revolt will continue to find nourishment, and no amount of surgery to remove 'unnecessary irritating laws' will prevent their germination. It is those laws and institutions that are considered 'necessary' to maintain white domination which count, and not the peripheral reforms which are both a response to the threat of force and, hopefully for Vorster, a defence against it. To create conditions in which insurgency cannot take root in the South African context means nothing less than to set the stage for an immediate advance towards majority rule. And this can only be brought about from a position of revolutionary strength and not supplication.

The inclusion of armed activity in the political struggle has not always been part of the strategy of South Africa's liberation movements, even though the dislodging of white supremacy in South Africa was never possible without it. Its adoption in the early sixties represented a departure from previous tactics (the significance of the change will be dealt with in Chapter 4). But let it be emphasized at the outset that in discussing revolutionary violence, the South African movement is not playing at war games. Insurgency in the context of a popular liberation struggle is not merely a confrontation between two bodies of armed combatants; if this were the case, no guerrilla force could, in the long term, match the professional armed might of the modern state. Its ability to commence military operations, to sustain itself and eventually to create an all-round climate of collapse in which a direct political solution becomes possible, is not the function of military tactics alone; it is dependent upon a comprehensive political strategy in which the core factor is the mobilization of a popular revolutionary base. Unless the struggle is supported by this base, serves it and is guided by it, it has as dismal a future as an isolated group of bandits would have. Looked at in this light, popular insurgency is a continuation of the political struggle by means which include armed actions.

Although the introduction of force influences every other level of political endeavour, it is nevertheless political and not military leadership that must remain supreme. For this to be so, there must be a unified political movement with a common understanding of the main perspectives and the tasks which flow from them at every given stage of the conflict: in other words, a movement which embraces a theory of revolution which is not just an academic exercise in social analysis but provides correct guidelines for action.

The starting point of our analysis and our assessments of the future perspectives must, therefore, be the theory of the South African revolution. This must be firmly rooted in the economic, political and historical peculiarities of the South African situation. But at the same time, if it is to dig beneath appearances and beyond the over-simplified race equation, such a theory must also draw on the treasure house of those fundamental propositions of Marxism which have a universal relevance, and on the experience of revolutionary forces which have fought other battles – both successful and unsuccessful – for radical change. The accumulated wisdom of revolutionary theory and experience is relevant to every part of the world; the accusation that Marxism is 'foreign ideology' is an attempt by a ruling class to put parochial blinkers on a subject people.

In attempting to discuss and elaborate the ideological framework of the South African revolution, I am certainly not venturing into virgin territory. South Africa is the home of two political organizations, the African National Congress and the South African Communist Party, which pioneered working-class and national movements on the African continent. Both have behind them a long history of struggle (much of it in conditions of illegality) in the course of which they have accumulated a wealth of revolutionary theory and practice. The one, the ANC, is the main constituent of the liberation front in its quest for immediate majority rule. Founded in 1912, it is a national mass movement representing the African people in whom it has helped to develop a common consciousness and a feeling of oneness – in the face of earlier tribal sectarianisms which made foreign piecemeal conquest so much easier. The other, founded in 1921, represents the aspirations of the working class and aims for the eventual establishment of a socialist South Africa.

Thus the two most important determinants in the South African socio-economic structure – class and race – have given birth to two complementary streams of revolutionary consciousness and revolutionary organization, each influencing the other and often standing in alliance on those aims they share in common. It is appropriate to begin our more detailed examination of the theory of the South African revolution with the complex interplay of race and class and its consequences for the perspectives of future struggle.

2 The Theory of the South African Revolution

South Africa's white and black groups are not homogeneous and within each there are varying kinds of class differentiation. Only a small minority of Whites owns and controls the country's basic means of production. Although the law and state-backed practice ensure that all Whites enjoy the processes of dominance, this does not mean that they all share equally in its fruits. Yet the programmatic and agitational documents of South Africa's revolutionary movement abound in such generalized expressions as 'white power', 'white domination' and 'white supremacy'.

These expressions reflect the immediately perceived reality that in such important spheres as political and civil rights, job access, or ownership and control of the means of production, it is colour and colour alone which, in law, lays down barriers against all Blacks. To be born white means by definition to be born privileged, and to be born black correspondingly deprived. To those actually engaged in revolutionary practice, it is obvious that the immediate struggle is for black liberation.

Yet for all the overt signs of race as the mechanism of domination, the legal and institutional domination of the white minority over the black majority has its origins in, and is perpetuated by, economic exploitation. This exploitation, in the contemporary period, serves the interests primarily of South Africa's all-white bourgeoisie, which is in turn linked to international capital. Since race discrimination is the mechanism of this exploitation and functional to it, since it is the *modus operandi* of South African capitalism, the struggle to destroy 'white supremacy' is ultimately bound up with the very destruction of capitalism itself. It is this interdependence of national and social liberation which gives the South African revolutionary struggle a distinctive form and shapes the role of the various classes within the dominant and subordinated majority.

The fundamental problem of theory posed by the South African revolution thus revolves around this question of the relationship between national and class struggle. The way this relationship is analysed and understood directly influences the tactical and strategic perspectives of those engaged in the conflict.

CLASS AND RACE

The continuous thread of South African history is the division of its peoples into dominant and subordinate groups defined primarily by criteria of colour. From the moment that the foreign settlers descended until the present day (class divisions and conflict within the dominant and subordinate groups notwithstanding), the economic, political and social status of individual members of each group has been profoundly influenced by ethnic origin. Explicit provisions in the law and state-backed social practice have ensured that whilst not every white man is a full member of the ruling class proper, no black man, whatever his economic status, can participate on equal terms with his white equivalent at any level of the social structure.

In each contemporary class category – whether it be capitalist, worker or peasant – the black man is fenced off from his white counterpart by a multitude of state-imposed boundaries. In contrast to most other capitalist societies, the process of class formation has always been inextricably linked with national domination, and extra-economic devices have been used to control and influence class mobility.

But South Africa is clearly a capitalist society. Its socio-economic structure rests ultimately on class relations of capitalist exploitation in which its race policies are rooted. The question presents itself whether the prime emphasis by every serious revolutionary force on the *national* content of the conflict is theoretically valid. Is there an irreconcilable contradiction between black consciousness and class consciousness? And what is the true relationship between them? To answer this we need to take a look at the concept of exploitation and class and the form it has assumed in the South African context.

In its strict economic sense, the term exploitation has a distinctive meaning. Under capitalism it describes the process whereby the owners of the means of production extract surplus value from that section of society which possesses no productive property except their capacity to labour. The bonds between workers and the factors which operate to set them apart as a distinct class from all other classes in the struggle for social change are rooted mainly in their common experience of exploitation in this primary meaning.

Differential wage scales between sections of the working class and even the use of guild mechanisms to protect the upper echelons have relevance to the degree and rate of exploitation but not to its essence, even at the level of what has been called the 'labour aristocracy'. Indeed, it is often the better-situated stratum of the working class which responds to the ideas of socialism more rapidly and easily, even though it is also in this stratum that there emerges a compromising element eager to protect its differential benefits.[1] Ultimately the most significant pointer to common class membership is the place a group occupies in the production relations of a given system of social production, and not the quantum of its earnings.

It follows that the white wage worker in South Africa is also an object of exploitation and could be said to occupy a place similar to that of the Black in the country's economic structure. But even if we accept further that in a class-defined society it is the struggle between historically antagonistic social classes which is the main motor force of social transformation, can we posit for South Africa a classic political confrontation between the working class (black and white) in alliance with the peasantry (black and white) against the capitalist class (black and white)?

To South Africa's revolutionary movement, including that part of it which is inspired by Marxism, such a perspective in the contemporary scene is a nonsensical one. It is nonsensical because it flows from a mechanical application of the valid 'ideal' model of class struggles to a situation in which the familiar categories of 'class' and 'exploitation' have not only a general but also a particular connotation, not in form or appearance alone but also in substance.

WHITE AND BLACK WORKERS

This becomes immediately apparent if we examine the dual nature of the exploitation to which the black worker is subjected. As a *worker* the fruits of his labour are appropriated by the owners of the means of production (which, of course, does not include all the Whites); but in addition, as a *black* worker he has particular disabilities to contend with – disabilities designed by the ruling class to facilitate a more intense rate of exploitation.

His role at the point of production is fixed by law as a category distinct from the rest of the working class. There is an absolute extra-economic bar against his acquiring productive property in the existing preserves of the white group. His relation to the white worker is not just that of the unskilled worker to the labour aristocrat. The white workers constitute an exclusive privileged group, membership of which is *completely* barred to the mass of the black working class by legal and social devices, and which is politically integrated into the ruling class so as to play an active role in maximizing the exploitation of the black worker. In such a context it would be pedantic to maintain that the black and white workers are political class brothers. The very fact that it does not seem incongruous to talk of the 'white working class' and the 'black working class' is a recognition that at an important level, both in theory and in practice, the two groups occupy a distinct and colour-defined position in relation to the means of production. Their respective roles in the social organization of labour differ,* as does the share of the social wealth of which they dispose and the mode of acquiring it.†

*Over half the white workers (700,000 out of 1·27 million in 1970) occupy non-productive roles mainly in the tertiary sectors (civil service, finance, professions, wholesale and retail trade, etc.), and where they are more directly engaged in the production of commodites, it is increasingly in the role of overseers.

†The well known definition by Lenin of the word class is: 'Classes are large groups of people differing from each other by the place they occupy in a historically determined system of social production, by their relation (in

In other words, the white worker (whose militant class postures earlier this century will be discussed in Chapter 3) is not just a part of an aristocracy of labour which has been corrupted ideologically by some concession from the ruling class: he is, in a sense which has no precedent in any other capitalist country, a part (albeit subordinate) of that ruling class in its broader meaning. Indeed, his economic, political and social interests are objectively served by its survival rather than its destruction. In this sense, white consciousness amongst the white workers is not a false consciousness; it reflects their material interests as a group. Conversely, black awareness amongst the black workers is not inconsistent with class consciousness but is an integral part of it. For these reasons the class struggle, particularly since the early twenties, has undoubtedly also involved antagonistic postures between black and white workers. Perhaps a less high-flown but more profound indicator of this is the familiar language of the factory and shop floor. Here the role of the white wage-earner as part of the exploitative machine is given recognition in the almost mandatory use by the black workers of the word 'baas' or 'master' to address him.

The white worker frequently constitutes a more recalcitrant opponent of African industrial advancement than the employer, particularly in the area of job elevation and differential awards for labour. Militant industrial action by white workers, as in the 1922 white miners' strike, often included an attempt to block African workers' advancement. In practice, principles which are seminal to every trade union movement in the world, such as 'the rate for the job' and 'one united trade union centre', have in the South African context been designed by the white workers to entrench rather than to undermine group inequality and to maximize rather than to minimize exploitation of the black worker.

The organized white trade union movement relies heavily on

---

most cases fixed and formulated by law) to the means of production, by their role in the social organization of labour, and, consequently, by the divisions of the share of social wealth of which they dispose and the mode of acquiring it.' ('A Great Beginning', *Collected Works*, Vol. 29, Lawrence & Wishart, p. 421.)

its considerable political influence with the white establishment to back and even initiate devices such as job reservation and to ensure its privileged trade union status. Even when lip-service is paid to the need for legally recognized African trade unions, it is usually qualified by conditions which would, in practice, make them appendages of the white workers' organizations. When economic pressures force a change in the racial policies relating to skilled and semi-skilled jobs, the shift is strictly a parallel one, and the racial gap in wage differentials is maintained or widened on the initiative of the white workers.* Between 1960 and 1970 the gap between white and black per capita income had grown from 13:1 to 14:1.[2]

The special place occupied by the black worker in South Africa's class framework is underlined by the fact that every economic action he takes immediately raises the question of his rights and aspirations not just as a worker but as a worker belonging to an oppressed group. In pressing for simple demands with a purely economic content, he is invariably forced to join issue not only with the boss and the state but more often than not with the organized white workers as well.

Thus, in the case of the black worker, the starting point of political consciousness – the economic struggle – invariably involves a national as well as a class disposition. It is instructive to note that some of the most significant industrial actions by the black workers – the 'bucket strike' of 1917, the mine strike of 1920, the great miners' strike of 1946, and many others – were closely linked with, and in some cases led by, political organizations whose leaders were thereafter prosecuted under laws relating to sedition, subversion and treason.

*In the mines, for example, the latest wage agreement with the 7,000 white artisans gives them an immediate rise of R100 per month in exchange for allowing Africans to do certain artisan tasks under their supervision. This rise alone is five times the average monthly earnings of the black miner even after the recent increases.

THE RURAL POPULATION

(a) On the white farms

If the exploitation of the black worker is so intimately bound up with his national status, this factor impinges even more clearly in the case of the black population in the rural areas. For all practical purposes, there are no white peasants or rural labourers. Those on the land are there as capitalist farmers or overseers on their behalf. They have exclusive rights to farm 87% of South Africa's land area; and no Black, whatever his economic status, has the legal right to cultivate this soil except in the employ and for the benefit of the white owner. The diminishing numbers of black squatters on white farms have no proprietary or tenure rights to the land they cultivate. Essentially they are rural labourers obliged to render service to the landowner but whose labour time is paid for partly in kind by the allocation of family small-holdings. All together, there are 3·3 million Africans (including families) on the white-owned farms as squatters or contract wage labourers.[3]

Thus, in the white areas, the process of 'liberating' the black peasant from productive property by conquest and its aftermath is absolutely complete. Here, at any rate, the words 'white man' and 'boss' are absolutely interchangeable.

(b) In the Reserves

In the balance of the land area (13%), statistics relating to black peasant farmers are difficult to acquire. There are now over 7,000,000 Blacks crowded into these areas. Between 1960 and 1970 alone, 1·6 million were 'repatriated' from 'white South Africa' to the reserves; of whom 1·2 million were squatters or labour tenants on white farms.[4] These have now joined millions of other rural people who have neither land nor any other form of employment. In the Transkei, for example, a recent survey in the Umtata district showed that ninety-five per cent of families have much less than the 3·4 hectares of land each: the area regarded as minimally necessary to sustain family life. In the Ciskei a survey in the late sixties showed that one-third of all families had no arable land at all. In fact, most inhabitants of the Reserves constitute a colonizer's dream: a massive army of landless unemployed, geographically separate from the colonists but ever-available as migrant labourers for use by white industrialists or capitalist farmers. This Reserve system is clearly designed to meet the exploitative needs of the capitalist system and in particular its unending quest to ensure the production and reproduction of cheap labour power.

No reliable figures are available of the extent to which the legally limited land area available to Blacks in the Reserves has become concentrated in the hands of a minority of black peasant families. But there can be no doubt that the overwhelming majority who eke out part of their living from working the land, are not commodity producers for the market and fall into the lowest rung of rural economic categories. In other words, insofar as there may be a handful of middle or rich black peasants, they have, *for the moment*, minimal significance as direct economic exploiters, and the class picture in the case of those who have any access to land at all is completely dominated by a poor black peasantry. Their poverty and land-hunger is, even more clearly than in the case of a black worker, connected with their national status. Even conceptually they have no actual or potential white class brothers.

The pursuit of the aspirations of the land-starved peasants and landless unemployed in the Reserves must, in a most immediate sense, bring them into direct political collision with the ruling class as a whole and its state apparatus. Here, there is no intermediate stage of a poor peasants' struggle against landlords and kulaks (as was the case, say, in China or Russia), with localized economic confrontations paving the way towards a wider political consciousness. In South Africa the day-to-day struggle of the black peasants and aspirant peasants as a class is inseparable from their struggle as a subject people. Even localized struggles invariably assume a political form connected with their status as members of a subject group.

THE BLACK MIDDLE STRATA

The African middle strata in the white areas and the paltry few amongst them who have themselves become petty capitalist exploiters are similarly hemmed in by national disabilities which frustrate their aspirations and which, consequently, place them in a hostile position towards their white counterparts. In general the unreliable and vacillating nature of any political commitment by the petit bourgeoisie in capitalist society is legendary: since this class occupies the intermediate area between the mass of the working people and its exploiters. Its members often enter and leave the ranks of the latter of they play the role of appendages of the ruling class, mainly in the tertiary sectors. In the case of the black middle strata, however, class mobility cannot proceed beyond a certain point; and, again, this point is defined in race rather than in economic terms. Objectively speaking, therefore, the immediate fate of the black middle sections is linked much more with that of the black workers and peasants than with their equivalents across the colour line.*

In the Bantustans, exceptionally, however, there is emerging a significant group of petty capitalists and, in some areas, farming entrepreneurs. Between 1959–60 and 1972–3 the Bantu Investment Corporation (B.I.C.) granted 1,413 loans worth R9,817,755 to African businessmen: eighty-five per cent for commercial enterprises, twelve-and-a-half per cent for service industries and two-and-a-half per cent for other industries. Also by the end of March 1973, the B.I.C. erected 392 business buildings for leasing to African businessmen.[5] In a recent paper presented to a conference on development at the University of

*I have so far used the word 'Black' to refer mainly to the African people. The 2 million Coloured people and the ¾ million Indians are subjected to similar disabilities as groups even though the degree of discrimination and exploitation is in their case not as far-reaching and intense. It is only amongst the Indian group (the overwhelming majority of whom are workers) that there has emerged a sizeable group of commercial bourgeoisie which is, nevertheless, barred from using its economic resources to break into the top layer of the capitalist structures. In general, the Coloured and Indian people form a natural ally of the African masses even though the ruling class often attempts to use their slightly more favourable position to divert them from full involvement in the struggle for all-round radical change.

the Witwatersrand, the Minister of Agriculture of the Bophuthaswana stated:

It is notable that in recent times a new breed of farming entrepreneur has emerged amongst the Tswana people. It is not uncommon to find farmers running herds of several hundred cattle. Stud breeders have also been forthcoming, and also in the field of crop husbandry, men, owning tractor units and producing up to 6,000 bags of grain per annum are operating on portions of land leased from other farmers or on vacant government land.[6]

If the pattern in other neo-colonial régimes in Africa repeats itself, the new administrative class which is being established to help run the Bantustans can also be expected to use their positions to advance themselves in the economic sphere.

Although they have not yet taken off as a significantly large direct exploiter of their people, the role of these petty capitalists and the bureaucratic élite, as appendages of dependent neo-colonial development, will undoubtedly grow. As a dependent fraction of the white state's dominating classes they will feed on its patronage and, as a group, tend to serve its exploitative designs.*

THE MAIN LINE-UP AND SECONDARY CONTRADICTIONS

Class differences and antagonisms within the oppressed groups have a significant bearing on our later remarks on the issue of which class stands in the forefront of the struggle for social change, and of respective roles in relation to the imperative linking of the national with the social revolution. For the moment I have concentrated on what the national liberation movement in South Africa believes to be the valid projection of an objective basis for revolutionary actions by all social groups amongst the Blacks. These, *by and large*, face an alliance – also rooted in objective economic factors – of all social groups amongst the politically dominant white community.

This projection is based on existing realities and tendencies. But historically there have always been differences within the ruling class centred on competing claims for labour resources

* See also pages 142–4 below.

and on the reallocation of the surplus generated by the super-exploitation of the Blacks.

It is true of the South African ruling class, as of any other, that 'the separate individuals form a class only insofar as they have to carry on a common battle against another class; otherwise they are on hostile terms with each other as competitors'.[7] So, in the early stages of conquest, a complex interplay of competitiveness between rival imperialist powers for the establishment of control over South Africa's natural and labour resources, and conflict at the top within the owning imperialist power, left its impact on the forms devised for domination over the indigenous people. The emergence of a landed settler group and the growth of an indigenous commercial class, led to conflicts with the colonial office on questions such as local labour policy and the pace of forced land grabbing by the wandering Boer communities anxious to free themselves of imperial direction.

The discovery of diamonds and gold gave a fresh impetus to the completion of the colonization process over the whole of what is today South Africa; and (the black wars of resistance aside) this whole period was also punctuated with conflict originating in the contradictions between external imperialist interests and the newly established internal settler states. Looked at from the viewpoint of the close on one million Africans in the Transvaal, the Anglo-Boer War (1899–1902) was an anti-imperialist struggle only in an extremely technical and qualified sense. To their ears the characterization of Kruger's campaign as a progressive anti-colonial war must have sounded very odd indeed, for they were living in a semi-feudal state whose rigidly enforced constitution, after acknowledging its authority from the Almighty (who is also, by the way, the acknowledged inspirer of the current South Africa Act), proclaimed that there shall be no equality between Black and White in church and State.

The later period which eventually culminated in a political handover to white local interests is also not free of internecine conflict within the ruling class, based largely on competing claims over the utilization of black labour resources and the re-allocation of the surplus. Farming interests versus mining labour needs; mining labour needs versus the labour needs of the emerging secondary industry; the struggle by white workers to entrench their monopoly of skills and privileged status; the attempts by 'Afrikaner capital' to win a place at the top dominated for so long by the English: all these factors, together with the changes that were taking place in the socio-economic structure as a whole, have an important bearing on the shifts in emphasis which have taken place at the level of state policy over the years and the ideological infighting between different sectors of the ruling class.

The movement from the policy of segregation to that of apartheid is partly connected with these interactions. It is also the response of the system as a whole to the reduced capacity of the reserve economies as subsidizing wage factors, and to the growing threat (especially after the Second World War) from a black proletariat, whose permanent establishment in the industrial centres the previous policies of segregation had failed to prevent. The political and economic consequences of this failure affected the different segments of the ruling class in different ways. Industrial capitalists benefited economically from the growth of a settled urban proletariat, whereas farming capital saw a threat to its supply of cheap migratory labour. Mining capital had a schizophrenic approach stemming from the duality of its interests. On the one hand, the mining industry itself profited greatly from the system of migratory labour, for whose pattern it was chiefly responsible. On the other hand, its steady advance into industrial and finance capital gave it a stake also in the establishment of a more permanent work force in the industrial centres. Perhaps this is a partial explanation of the fact that during the late forties and thereafter, quite a few of the mining magnates who were involved in white politics tended to favour the greater stabilization of the labour force in the towns. To cope with mining labour needs, the industry sought external supplies, which by the fifties constituted seventy-five per cent of its labour force.

With the passage of time, the closer interlocking between mining industrial finance and even farming capital as a result of monopoly trends, has lessened some of the contradictions between the previously separate elements of capital, and this perhaps explains the decline of sharp political opposition to the régime from within the white camp.* The white working class, too, determined as always to perpetuate its monopoly of skills and privileged status, turned more and more politically to those who promised to protect it and to 'keep the Kaffir in his place'. Significantly, the ideological roots of modern apartheid are to be found as far back as the middle twenties in the platform of the all-white South African Labour Party,[8] which disappeared after 1948 when the white workers found their aspirations so well served by the new Nationalist régime.

Nevertheless, those divisions which persist in the ruling establishment – and some of them now also stem from differences on how to respond to the growing threat from the liberation movements and its external allies – have obvious tactical relevance because they weaken the cohesion of the ruling class and make it possible for the liberation movement to isolate the most racist elements amongst them. So far, however, the dominant tendency has been for the white political and economic oligarchy and its allies to close ranks when faced with a real threat from the majority deprived of rights.

But future developments could alter the relatively monolithic character of the present line-up by the ruling class and its allies. A combination of factors – economic crisis, successful pressure from the liberation movements, etc. – may force a break with existing patterns at the top in an attempt to ensure the survival of capitalism. It could, for example, lead to jettisoning some of the institutionalized privileges of the white workers.

Already the labour shortage, reaching crisis proportions in many industrial sectors, has been the main impulse to the present upward mobility of black workers from positions of labourers into semi-skilled and skilled categories. Until now, this has been carried out with the agreement of the white trade unions, which

*A great deal more research and analytical work needs to be done to determine more precisely the correlation of the roles of the different segments of capital and the way these reflect themselves at the level of ruling-class policy and ideology.

have insisted on the simultaneous elevation of displaced Whites into supervisory and administrative positions. But if, in the long run, the system proves incapable of accommodating the white working class as a whole in this way, those sections which are no longer assured of their racial economic privileges might well become more receptive to class rather than race solidarity. In anticipation of such a possibility, the ANC believes that even now no opportunity should be missed to win over these white workers 'who are ready to break with the policy of racial domination'.[9]

In the light of existing tendencies, however, it is in general unrealistic to expect that any significant group in the dominant white alliance will throw in its lot with the forces struggling for revolutionary change. It does not, however, follow, either theoretically or practically, that there is no place in South Africa's liberation movement for non-Africans either as individuals or as groups. Certainly the 2 million Coloured community and the $\frac{3}{4}$ million Indians are vital and indispensable contingents in a struggle which undoubtedly includes their own liberation as well. In the case of the white community, there is obviously little possibility *at this stage* of winning over a sizeable portion to the side of the liberation movement. But even here it would be doing violence to the basic premise of the liberation movement's policy, that it is fighting to create a non-racial society, if it were not to welcome those few amongst the Whites who show a readiness to break with race-infected rule and unconditionally make common cause with the struggle for full liberation.

The weakness of the slogan of POQO (We Alone), which dominated the thinking of the breakaway Pan-Africanist Congress group in 1958, is thus exposed. An emotional and apolitical cry, it is objectively liable to alienate vital potential allies in the struggle and to make it easier for the enemy to win them over as opponents of the liberation thrust. It ignores the very kernel of the art of political leadership, which demands in the first place the widest possible yoking of actual and potential allies, and the exploitation of division and weakness within the enemy camp; without, of course, compromising the main direction of the struggle. An emphasis on the liberation of the African people does not therefore imply a line-up of the Africans against the rest. In addition, the tactics of the liberation struggle demand that advantage must be taken

of differences and divisions which our successes will inevitably spark off to isolate the most vociferous, the most uncompromising and the most reactionary elements amongst the whites. Our policy must continually stress in the future (as it has in the past) that there is room in South Africa for all who live in it but only on the basis of absolute democracy.[10]

But it remains true that for the moment the mainspring of the conflict is black liberation, with the African majority as the main force. It involves amongst other things a stimulation and deepening of their national confidence, national pride and national assertiveness. A response to national oppression is undoubtedly the chief mobilizing factor. It has over-riding validity at the level of the immediate political struggle and (as we shall show later) has strategic relevance in the struggle for social emancipation as well.

THE THEORY OF INTERNAL COLONIALISM

A revolutionary theory has relevance only as an instrument of social change. To perform this role it must give pride of place to uncovering the real correlation of class and national forces and the mobilizing factors which will set in motion groups who, by their nature, will be historically compelled to destroy South Africa's exploitative system. The overall characteristics of this system have been described by South Africa's revolutionary movement as Internal Colonialism. It is based on the historical analogy of the classic imperialist–colonialist situation in which the ruling class of the dominant nation 'owns' and controls the colonial territory, and uses its instruments of force to maintain its economic, political and military supremacy against any would-be external competitors. All are agreed that in such a situation the elimination of direct foreign control is item one on the agenda of the struggle.

But analogies are not carbon copies; they are resemblances between situations otherwise different. For this case, it is immediately apparent that although South Africa is by no means free of external imperialist involvement, economic control and political supremacy are in general now exercised by an indigenous ruling class with a unitary state which purports to represent the general will of all the inhabitants. Broadly speaking, its peoples are geographically and in every other way part of a single socio-economic formation, divided along class lines; although they occupy distinct racial positions in relation to the manner in which the wealth is appropriated and in the political structure. That formation is now capitalist in essence, even though some specific marks remain from its historical genesis which involved not only the almost total destruction of the pre-capitalist mode of production which the settler found amongst the indigenous people, but also the re-structuring of this mode to serve the dominant capitalist production relations.

If then the overwhelmingly dominant mode of production within this unitary state is capitalist, is it analytically correct or useful to talk of 'two South Africas' defined, *at a certain level*, in national rather than class terms? Both the SACP's Programme and the ANC's 'Strategy and Tactics' do precisely this.

The SACP Programme says, under the chapter heading 'Colonialism of a Special Type':

> On one level, that of 'white South Africa', there are all the features of an advanced capitalist state in its final stage of imperialism. There are highly developed industrial monopolies and the merging of industrial and finance capital. The land is farmed along capitalist lines, employing wage labour, and producing cash crops for the local export market. The South African monopoly capitalists, who are closely linked with British, United States and other foreign imperialist interests, export capital abroad especially in Africa. Greedy for expansion, South African imperialism reaches out to incorporate other territories – South West Africa and the Protectorates.
>
> But on another level, that of 'non-white South Africa', there are all the features of a colony. The indigenous population is subjected to extreme national oppression, poverty and exploitation, lack of all democratic rights and political domination by a group which does everything it can to emphasise and perpetuate its alien 'European' character.[11]

And the ANC's 'Strategy and Tactics' says:

> South Africa's social and economic structure and the relationships which it generates are perhaps unique. It is not a colony, yet it has, in regard to the overwhelming majority of its people, most of the features of the classical colonial structures. Conquest and domination by an alien people, a system of discrimination and exploitation based on race, techniques of indirect rule; these and more are the traditional trappings of the classical colonial framework. Whilst at one level, it is an 'independent' national state, at another level it is a country subjugated by a minority race. What makes the structure unique and adds to its complexity is that the exploiting nation is not, as in the typical imperialist relationship, situated in a geographically distinct mother country, but is settled within its border. What is more, the roots of the dominant nation have been imbedded in our country for more than three centuries of presence. It is thus an alien body only in the historical sense.

This characterization provides the theoretical foundation for the conclusion that the main content of the *immediate* struggle for change is the national liberation of the African people and, with it, the destruction of all forms of racial discrimination.

Neither in its classical connotations nor in its very specialized use (Colonialism of a Special Type) in the South African context, does the word 'colonialism' necessarily imply that there exist two homogeneous and undifferentiated nations standing in a simple oppressed–oppressor relationship. In both situations the relations of exploitation and domination have their ultimate roots in class exploitation. Even in a more typical anti-imperialist struggle, as in pre-1948 India, the emphasis on British oppression of the Indian people did not preclude a recognition of the class divisions in British society nor the different commitments and roles of the various classes in Indian society in the anti-imperialist movement.

In South Africa the thesis of internal colonialism sees class relations in an historically specific context in which internal group domination has lent shape to, and influenced the content of, the exploitative processes. The thesis, however, stresses the existence of internal class divisions in both the dominant and subject groups, with these class divisions influencing political and ideological positions in the struggle for social change. To identify 'white South Africa' with an imperialist state and 'non-white South Africa' with the 'colony' is undoubtedly a useful shorthand, *at one level*, to depict the reality of the historically specific race factor in both the genesis and the existing nature of class rule.

In this respect there is no great divide between the period when South Africa was a colony in the classical mould, ruled from London with the help of the white settler, and the time when the white settler won autonomy and then political independence. In the latter period a dominant oligarchy restricted to white settlers assumed more and more of the functions of the British ruling class towards the black majority whose subject and colonial status as a group dominated the whole subsequent process of class formation, class mobility and class exploitation. Of course, the whole character of the socio-economic structure has altered fundamentally. But exploitation of the Blacks as a group and the racist ideology which this has spawned are not functions of latter-day monopoly capitalism only. This has been a pattern of exploitative relations from the early days of slavery at the Cape, in the period of primitive capital accumulation and during the phase of commercial and pre-monopoly capitalism.* It would be pedantic to argue that the colonial status of the black majority disappeared in 1910 or with the granting of Dominion Status by the Statutes of Westminster in 1934, even though there was a shift towards internal political sovereignty. The ruling and exploitative establishment has always been drawn from the dominant white group (either local or foreign), and the Blacks as a group have always had a subject or colonial status. This reality in its altered form remains the pattern today.

*This is not to say that the content of economic exploitation has remained unchanged since the days of slavery. I am dealing here with one of the common threads to emphasize the historical continuity of national domination in the different stages of socio-economic developments.

FROM INTERNAL COLONIALISM TO NEO-COLONIALISM

Indeed this continuing pattern has provided the impetus for the new administrative procedures we see being established in the nine separate 'homelands' carved out of the Reserves. The main function of the Reserve system was to ensure the reproduction of black labour power within the traditional subsistence economy which the ruling class, from time to time, re-structured to serve its changing needs. This ensured a continuous supply of cheap migratory labour which could be easily dealt with in the political sphere; and, at the same time, provided the rationale for below-minimum wage levels. What remained of the subsistence economy based on tribal and family units of production purported to serve as indirect wages generated outside the capitalist framework; and to provide some kind of 'social security' when age, sickness or surfeit of labour needs made the presence of the African workers in the white industrial areas economically 'redundant'.

In unguarded moments the real function of the Reserve system has been made crudely obvious: as, for example, in the Chamber of Mines evidence placed before the Lansdowne Commission on Mine Wages in 1943:

> It (the Reserves policy) aims at the preservation of the economic and social structure of the native people in the native areas where that structure can be sheltered and developed. The policy is a coherent whole and is the antithesis of a policy of assimilation and the encouragement of a black proletariat in the towns divorced from its tribal heritage. The ability of the mines to maintain their native labour force by means of tribal natives from the Reserves *at rates of pay which are adequate for this migratory class of native but inadequate for the detribalized native is a fundamental factor in the economy of the gold mining industry.* (my emphasis)[12]

The maintenance of separate geographic areas for the subordinate majority has always constituted an important part of the specific internal colonialist relationship which characterized the socio-economic structure in both its pre-monopoly and monopoly phases. But with the completion of the conquest, the Reserves system, pioneered by Shepstone in the 1850s to ensure cheap labour supplies to the settler farmers, became an integral part of the unitary state structure established in 1910. Currently there appears to be a real move to institutionalize the Reserve system into a group of tribal states which, so it is claimed, will soon enjoy full political sovereignty within their areas.

What general purpose is the re-structured Reserve system designed to meet and how will it alter the relationships of internal colonialism? In brief, *it is an attempt partially to externalize the colonial relationship in the shape of ethnic states*, eventually having all the attributes of *formal* political independence.

In other words, the ruling class is, under pressure, searching for a neo-colonial solution especially adapted to South African conditions. It is unable to follow precisely in the footsteps of the main imperialist powers who, when faced with anti-colonial pressures, were able to concede a measure of national-political sovereignty to their colonies whilst contriving to keep intact their economic dominion.

Unlike the classical imperialist rulers, it cannot 'withdraw' to its real power base in some distant metropolis, after a negotiated handover to a submissive bureaucratic élite. It is unable to hold out anything to the colonial subject except neo-colonial office and a few small-scale business opportunities in the scattered rural backwaters. Hence, its own brand of neo-colonialism can operate only on the basis of a *politically* fragmented South Africa. This, if successfully pursued, will reintroduce a more typical content to the colonial relationship and provide a new institutional 'justification' for the absolute bar to black political advancement in 'white' South Africa. It would obviously facilitate the piecemeal manipulation and exploitation of the ethnic groups which make up the African people as a totality. Already the Bantustan administrations are competing for foreign and local imperialist investment on the basis of the only commodity that they all have in abundance – 'cheap, problem-free labour'.* And,

*Examples of the contents of the investment appeals were referred to in the *Financial Mail*, 11 October 1974, pp. 146–8.

' "*Stop pussyfooting around. If you want a nice, fat, highly-profitable overseas operation, invest in SA. But make sure you build your factory in a Black area.*" '

So runs the appeal to foreign investors by Chief Wessels Mota, chief execu-

hopefully for South Africa's ruling class, it is this kind of labour which will continue to be the main export commodity to service an economy which despite the rhetoric of the apartheid idealists has become more than ever dependent on black workers.

These new steps to transform the Reserve system reflect a policy which is, therefore, in the direct line of succession from the present internal form of colonialism, showing the strains of its lack of sufficient geographic definition. It is an attempt to legitimize the foreign conquest in a new way and to use black 'governments' and administrations to carry out the more important functions of the old 'Native Commissioners'.

This is not to say that we should discount the contradictions which are implicit in this new attempt to hide the real mechanism of race domination. We have already witnessed a measure of sharp verbal infighting between some of the less sycophantic Bantustan leaders and the government on questions like land consolidation and allocation of economic resources. But the implied premise from which these confrontations proceed is an acceptance of the white myth that the indigenous majority has claim only to an ethnic solution on the basis of so-called 'natural homelands' into which the conquest squeezed the fighting tribes, and not to a national one. Some Bantustan leaders (e.g. Chief Gatsha Buthelezi of KwaZulu) qualify the acceptance of this myth by an insistence that it is, for the moment, a justifiable temporary compromise warranted by black powerlessness. Nevertheless, even such qualified acceptance is objectively calculated to disarm nationwide revolutionary endeavour on the real issue of immediate majority rule and to replace national

---

tive councillor of Basotho Qua Qua, in a recent advertisement by the Bantu Investment Corporation in *The Economist*.

'KwaZulu's Gatsha Buthelezi offers "problem-free labour resources", while Lebowa's Cedric Phatudi declares: "The Black proletariat in the Homelands is ready, willing, and able to do a decent day's work for a fair salary."

'Just how "fair" are these salaries? A survey by Wits University's Wages Commission earlier this year found, for example, that Kool Look Wigs (Pty), the largest single employer in the Homelands and the first to move there (as distinct from a border area), was paying unskilled workers a basic wage of R2,50 to R3,25 a week.'

consciousness with regional and ethnic consciousness which, for obvious reasons, can be more easily manipulated. It serves also to undermine the most significant achievement of the ANC in advancing the 'one nation' concept as opposed to tribal separatism.

NATIONAL LIBERATION AND THE DESTRUCTION OF CAPITALISM

True national liberation is impossible without social liberation; and a nationalist ideology which ignores the class basis of racism is false. No doubt the necessary emphasis on the national content of the struggle could, as a by-product, encourage a disregard of its ultimately class basis and with it the emergence of pure bourgeois nationalism, backward racialism and chauvinism. Some recent academic criticisms of the internal colonialist thesis and the national liberation strategy which it suggests have questioned the validity of the thesis on the grounds that it would undervalue (and, some say, already has undervalued) the class factors in the conflict. Insofar as this danger exists it must, of course, be continuously countered by the spread of true revolutionary ideology, and by ensuring that a working class imbued with class and political consciousness plays its proper role in the coalition of forces which constitutes the liberation front. Indeed, both the theory and practice of South Africa's revolutionary movements have emphasized the special role of the working class in the national struggle and the social goals of the liberation struggle.

On the immediate role of the working class in the struggle for national and social liberation, the SACP Programme says, in a paragraph which is printed in emphasis, that only under working class leadership can the 'full aim of the revolution be achieved'. On the nature of South Africa's national struggle, the ANC's 'Strategy and Tactics' says:

The national character of the struggle must therefore dominate our approach. But it is a national struggle which is taking place in a different era and in a different context from those which characterized the early struggles against colonialism. It is happening in a new kind of world – a world which is no longer monopolized by the imperialist world system; a world in which the existence of the powerful socialist system and a significant sector of newly liberated areas has altered the balance of forces; a world in which the horizons liberated from foreign oppression extend beyond mere formal political control and encompass the elements which make such control meaningful – economic emancipation. It is also happening in a new kind of South Africa; in which there is a large and well-developed working class whose class consciousness and independent expressions of the working people – their political organs and trade unions – are very much part of the liberation front. Thus our nationalism must not be confused with chauvinism or narrow nationalism of a previous epoch. *It must not be confused with the classical drive by an élitist group among the oppressed people to gain ascendancy so that they can replace the oppressor in the exploitation of the mass* . . . (my emphasis).

This perspective of a speedy progression from formal liberation to genuine and lasting emancipation is made more real by the existence in our country of a large and growing working class whose class consciousness complements national consciousness. Its political organizations and the trade unions have played a fundamental role in shaping and advancing our revolutionary cause.

This special place of the working class within the national movement and the part played by independent working class organizations in a liberation alliance accords an immediate role to class-based action and is an obvious obstacle to any tendency for the national struggle to fall under bourgeois hegemony.

There is objective ground for the belief that 'under South African conditions the national democratic revolution has great prospects of proceeding at once to socialist solutions'.[13] This follows from the undoubted reality that no significant national demand can be successfully won without the destruction of the existing capitalist structure. It is precisely because in South Africa capitalist production relations are the foundation of national repression that the national struggle itself has an objective coincidence with the elimination of all forms of exploitation. The elimination of national inequality, if it is to be more than a mere gesture, involves a *complete* change of the way in which the country's wealth is appropriated. This must surely be the major premise of every social group or class in the subordinate majority, even if its ideology is limited solely to an urge for national vindication. This premise bears on the correction of historical injustice stemming from conquest; it is concerned with the fundamental source of existing grievance, and it has vital relevance to the question of future power relationships. If every racist statute were to be repealed tomorrow, leaving the economic status quo undisturbed, 'white domination' in its most essential aspects would remain.

National liberation, in its true sense, must therefore imply the expropriation of the owners of the means of production (monopolized by a bourgeoisie drawn from the white group) and the complete destruction of the state which serves them. There can be no half-way house unless the national struggle is stopped in its tracks and is satisfied with the co-option of a small black élite into the presently forbidden areas of economic and political power. For the overwhelming mass, such a result would perpetuate the historic consequences of national conquest. It therefore stands opposed not only to the class aims of the working people but also to the aims of the genuine nationalist to be found in the ranks of other social groups. This explains the relative ease of the progression from national to class political consciousness by so many black South African activists who begin their political life as 'pure' nationalists.

South Africa's ruling class is, of course, able to find individual collaborators amongst the black people through the lure of status, more lucrative jobs, etc. But is there a social group within the national movement which will be served by a purely nationalist solution (of the type seen in some parts of Africa), which would keep the existing economic and state structure essentially intact? The destruction of this structure is, at the moment, the factor which gives a common content to the aspirations of all the social groups amongst the black people except, perhaps, those who have a vested interest in Bantustan separatism. It is in this sense that a broadly based assault on white supremacy involves the expropriation of the main contingents of South Africa's oligarchy and its state apparatus; in other words, the destruction of the capitalist system as we know it.

A FUTURE BLACK EXPLOITING CLASS?

Beyond the political chemistry of the existing situation, it is not out of place to speculate about the tendencies within the system which, although not yet dominant, may grow in importance. The contrast between the large and experienced black working class (which, together with the rural landless, forms the overwhelming base for the national struggle) and the relatively undeveloped state of the black bourgeoisie, is an obvious obstacle to the importation of bourgeois ideology into the national movement.

But since group colour domination is, in general, not an indispensable condition for capitalist exploitation, is there a possibility that a capitalist society could still evolve within the present South African framework which jettisons the race factor altogether?

One of the preconditions for such a development would have to be the fostered growth of a black bourgeoisie and its co-option into the ruling class. But I have already argued that the South African ruling class will be compelled by its very nature to resist any incursion into its existing sources of wealth and the state power which underwrites it. *The racial exclusiveness of its economic and political power is a primary and not a secondary feature of the structure as a whole.* Even if it were willing to take some members of the black middle strata into its fold, this could only be in an auxiliary and dependent capacity, without even the consolation (as elsewhere in Africa) of political office. They would be playing a role in the economic sphere similar to that of black policemen in the state apparatus – as collaborators in a continued system of race repression. Such a group can have no place in the national movement of the sort occupied by the small independent national bourgeoisie of the colonies, precisely because its interests would visibly stand in contradiction to those of the people as a whole, even in the context of purely national aims.

At the moment, insofar as we can speak of an African bourgeoisie at all, it is pathetically small and has arrived too late on the historical scene to play a classic class role either as a leading element in the national struggle or as the main beneficiary of mass revolutionary sacrifice. Indeed, for a black bourgeoisie to gain ascendancy, the whole 'normal' process would have to be reversed, in the sense that *its real class formation would have to follow and not precede political power*. Since the aspirations of all the main classes amongst the oppressed majority can, at the moment, only be served by the destruction of the economic and political power of the existing ruling class, the question which remains is whether the role of the all-white bourgeoisie could conceivably be assumed by a black equivalent *in the future* which would act to stop the revolution in its tracks and subvert the social aims of real national emancipation.

This possibility cannot, of course, be discounted altogether. Within the white group itself, we have seen during the last twenty-five years in particular how the wielding of political power has facilitated the breakthrough of 'Afrikaner capital' into finance and mining; areas previously the preserve of so-called 'English capital'. In some other parts of the continent, too, political office has been used as an instrument by those at the top to enrich themselves through state-backed projects and by providing the necessary local participation in neo-colonialist enterprises.

It is only in the projected neo-colonies (Bantustans) that there are any signs at all of an emerging administrative and, as yet small, commercial class which aspires to greater rights of participation at the top of the exploitative machine than is permitted in 'white' South Africa. Together with the traditional elements, this group is being offered a vested interest in the fragmentation of South Africa, to stifle the national movement as we know it and replace it with ethnic and parochial nationalism.

The eventual creation of these satellite client states, on whose behalf 'development' capital is being canvassed in 'white' South Africa and in the West with the lure of cheap 'problem-free' black labour, is clearly designed by the régime to help perpetuate a newly camouflaged version of race exploitation with black collaboration. However, unlike its counterpart in some parts of Africa, a Bantustan-based commercial and bureaucratic élite is at a disadvantage in any attempts to mobilize the allegiance of the African people as a whole on the basis of a 'solution' which, even at the superficial level (a political take-over), fails to meet their *national* aspirations with regard to South Africa as a whole. Those, therefore, who use their status as aspirant administrators or businessmen to entrench the Bantustans, fall outside the mainstream of the national struggle.

THE NATURE OF THE NEW STATE

So far we have attempted to describe those factors in the existing class make-up of the African people and its main allies which provide an objective basis for a national struggle, to strike at the existing framework of capitalist exploitation throughout the whole of South Africa. But we need to look further and consider the type of society which will replace it. This is not merely speculation about the future; it bears immediately and directly on the main class content and direction of the struggle, not only for social but also for national emancipation. What then is the revolutionary movement's projection in this respect?

Broad guidelines are provided by the *Freedom Charter* (formulated by the most representative assembly ever held in South Africa, the 1955 Congress of the People, and thereafter endorsed by both the African National Congress and the South African Communist Party), and that section of the SACP's Programme (adopted in 1962) which deals with the national democratic state as the immediate form of the post-revolutionary state in South Africa.

The *Freedom Charter*[14] (an extremely short document – less than 1,500 words) is devoted largely to a description of the type of 'democratic' state sought. It sets out under separate headings the changes which will be necessary in order to eradicate racial discrimination at every level. It calls for the restoration of all South Africa's wealth to the people, which involves the transfer of 'the mineral wealth beneath the soil, the banks and monopoly industry . . . to the ownership of the people'. It cites the need to control the rest of industry and trade 'to assist the well-being of the people' and proclaims that all people 'shall have equal rights to trade where they choose, to manufacture and to enter all trades, crafts and professions'. It refers to the ending of 'restrictions on land ownership on a racial basis', and a redivision of the land 'amongst those who work it'.

The SACP Programme, although it states that the *Freedom Charter* is not a programme for socialism but rather 'a common programme for a free, democratic South Africa agreed on by socialists and non-socialists', pledges the Party's 'unqualified support' for its implementation. It sees the achievement of the aims of the *Freedom Charter* as laying 'the indispensable basis for the advance of our country along non-capitalist lines to a socialist and communist future'. And, it calls for '*a national democratic revolution which will overthrow the colonialist state of white supremacy and establish an independent state of national democracy in South Africa*'.

Some critics of the formulations have concluded that what is implicit in them is an unwarranted duality between the struggle for national and social emancipation, with the latter appearing on the agenda only after the destruction of the race structures by the 'national democratic state'. I have already referred to the interdependence of the struggle against the race structures and the capitalist system which is served by them. There can be little doubt that the implementation of the *Freedom Charter* will in itself be a giant step towards social as well as national emancipation. But clearly a number of phases is envisaged.

It is important to emphasize that the reference to the tasks of 'immediate' and 'future' phases does not necessarily involve a commitment to the step by step creation of two distinct socio-economic formations: first a non-racist bourgeois democracy and then a socialist order. Lenin's theoretical commitment to a bourgeois democratic phase in pre-February Russia was bound up with the slogan of a 'revolutionary democratic dictatorship of workers and peasants' and not that of the bourgeoisie. In fact, the leading role which the workers and peasants played in the 'first phase' (not, by the way, on the slogan of class against class) resulted in a relatively quick development from February to October. The struggle for bourgeois democratic rights at the dawn of capitalism, when it represented mainly the class aims of the emerging bourgeoisie, is to be distinguished from the period when the working class emerges as an independent political force, with the capacity to become the most decisive element in the struggle for democratic changes.

This distinction becomes even more relevant to a situation of the South African type in which the emergence of a significantly large bourgeoisie amongst the subordinate group has been frustrated by the dominant ruling class, and in which the main drive for social change must come from the large black proletariat in alliance with rural labourers and the millions of landless and land-hungry people in the countryside. This is not to say that the main mobilizing slogan at this stage is class against class; nor does it imply that the forces of immediate struggle for a revolutionary breakthrough will necessarily be in a position to proclaim a socialist South Africa at the moment of victory against the racist state.

The problem of creating a socialist order, even where the working class is the dominant force in the newly created state power, is connected with yet another factor. Unlike emerging classes in all previous progressions from one class order to another, the working class does not achieve a measure of control and ownership of productive property within the old society itself. When it gains political ascendancy as a result of a revolutionary breakthrough, it has no ready-made socialist economic structures which grow within the womb of the old society, in the way that capitalist property and capitalist relations of production evolved over a long period of time within feudalism. The advanced levels of division of labour and of the social organization of production under capitalism, provide a foundation for socialization but do not, in themselves, constitute socialist property. Laying the basis for the construction of a *socialist economic order* is only possible after the achievement of political power. In this sense every contemporary revolution in which the working class has a dominant role, has gone through a series of interim phases before it was able to establish a socialist economic order. Thus there is a distinction between the creation of the new state form and the building of a new socialist economic formation. The former is made possible by a revolutionary seizure of power; the latter, though the exercise of that political power by a class whose interests are unconditionally served by a socialist order.

The *Freedom Charter* and the SACP Programme do not, as we have seen, project socialism as the immediate consequence of expropriating the main contingents of the ruling class. A non-monopoly private sector, controlled so as 'to assist the well-being of the people', will still be tolerated. Rural policy involves confiscation, redistribution and redivision of the land amongst the people; *implying an extension of private ownership*. This is qualified by the words 'those who work it'; and in a 1968 commentary on the *Freedom Charter* the thought is added that the land is to be 'divided amongst the small farmers, peasants and landless of all races *who do not exploit the labour of others*'.[15]*

It should be emphasized that this projection of a liberated South Africa not yet socialist, is not just a device to provide a basis in the struggle for an alliance of the different social forces amongst the oppressed. It is rather a recognition of the reality that the construction of socialism is a process which is not consummated but begun by a successful revolutionary seizure of power. And during the course of this process a vital role, under restrictive controls, may still be required of a private and (let us not balk at the issue) exploitative sector. This type of interim phase has been experienced by every socialist country, including Russia and China.

All-purpose words or phrases to characterize this kind of pre-socialist interim economic formation have built-in limitations. Concepts such as 'people's democracies', 'national democratic state' can become a source of theoretical ambiguity if used abstractly to describe a whole range of situations whose only

*Whilst it is premature to speculate about future agrarian policy in detail, a literal and mechanical implementation of this land policy would, I believe, unnecessarily proliferate petit-bourgeois and bourgeois aspirations in the rural areas and may create serious economic problems for the country as a whole. A basis certainly already exists for the transformation of the large, rich and mechanized capitalist forms (worked by the millions of black rural proletarians) into communally-run farms. Economic considerations aside, this would also serve to create a relatively advanced rural revolutionary base for the new state.

common feature is that successful assault on an existing social order has not yet matured into a socialist order.

The fundamental question is: which class or alliance of classes exercises state power in the immediate post-liberation period? Kwame Nkrumah's injunction to struggling national liberation movements was 'Seek ye first the Political Kingdom'. But where, as in some of the ex-colonies, the inchoate state of class formation led to a loose alliance at the top, of mainly petit bourgeois elements, the capacity of the new Political Kingdoms to make planned advances towards socialism has been beset by difficulties and sudden reverses. If, on the other hand, the liberation struggle should bring to power a revolutionary democratic alliance dominated by the proletariat and the peasantry (*which is on the agenda in South Africa*), the post-revolutionary phase can surely become the first stage *in a continuous process* along the road to socialism: a road which ultimately can only be charted by the proletariat and its natural allies.

In both basic statements of programme previously cited, a speedy progression from formal liberation to lasting emancipation is advanced as the main perspective of the post-liberation state; a state dominated by the working class and peasantry which will, from its inception, begin to lay the basis for taking the country along the road to socialism. Without this there can be no real solution to the national or social problems for the majority of the South African people.

But this outcome is inevitable only in the abstract or conceptual sense. Its translation into reality must be dependent on a number of vital subjective factors. The most important of these are the ideological perception of the movements which constitute the liberation alliance; the extent to which the most revolutionary class – the proletariat – is politicized and participates as a leading force in the coming struggles and in the state forms which are constructed in place of the old; the degree to which petit bourgeois ideology and narrow nationalism is successfully combated within the national movement; and the extent to which the rural millions can be mobilized on the side of true liberation.

Masses do not of their own accord generate an ideology which provides true guidelines on the main direction of the struggle, or which makes them conscious of the necessity to create non-exploitative relations of production. Even in regard to the proletariat 'there can be no talk of an independent ideology formulated by the working masses themselves in the process of the movement . . . There is a lot of talk about spontaneity but a spontaneous development of the working-class movement leads to its subordination to bourgeois ideology'.[16] And if it is true that workers left to themselves in direct conflict with their class enemy tend to be subordinated to bourgeois ideology, how much more true is this of a struggle whose main immediate content is national in character? The continuing role of an independent class-based movement as part of the revolutionary front is thus historically vital, despite the absence of any basic policy divergence between the ANC and the SACP on the main strategy and thrust of liberation aims.

Revolutionary leadership by a movement experienced in struggle is therefore the precondition for real victory. In South Africa the resistance to the conquest and its aftermath has been long and continuous. The organizational forms which have emerged to express and lead this resistance have their roots in specific historical factors and in the changes that have taken place in the socio-economic structure. We now turn to a brief examination of those main phases in the struggle which have a bearing on the development of the strategy and tactics of the South African revolution.

3 The Resistance

Broadly speaking, the struggle against national domination in South Africa can be sub-divided into three phases: the wars of resistance; the pre-1960 responses to conquest; and the current phase, in which the armed perspective is once again part of the drive for liberation.

THE WARS OF RESISTANCE

First contacts between the indigenous people and foreigners were not always hostile. Trade in ivory, cattle and labour in exchange for European commodities took place. The use of land by white farmers, sometimes 'contractually' arranged with the Chiefs in the name of their people, was permitted in the spirit of indigenous custom which excluded Western concepts of individual ownership of property.

But even these relations of commercial intercourse were always one-sided and fragile. The 'new civilization' tolerated the politics of coexistence as long as it made possible unequal exchange, willing surrender by the tribes of the best pasture lands, and supplies of near-slave labour. Punitive military expeditions always hovered in the background as a reserve weapon for the continuation of colonial politics by war.

In the century between 1779 and 1879, history tells of ten major wars of indigenous resistance to foreign control. But between these bloody armed clashes (and even before the first 'official' war in 1779), settler expansionism into the interior was accompanied by numerous guerrilla skirmishes.

By 1770, the systematic extermination of the San hunter (in so-called 'bushman' country abutting the Cape settlement in the north-east) was already well advanced.

On the Eastern Cape frontier, warfare between settler raiding parties and the Xhosa tribes raged intermittently. The Xhosas, with a more advanced social system based on cattle breeding and agriculture, and more effective military organization and traditions, made a less easy prey than the San for the marauding settler bands. The *King William's Town Gazette* of 14 August 1856 said of the Xhosas: 'We have observed, in connection with the native character, that lean and starving men are always tractable and civil, but the well-fed and sleek, impudent and easily led to mischief.'[1]

This 'impudence and mischief' put a heavy price on the conquest. The saga of Xhosa resistance over a long period of time was heroic in its proportions. But the ultimate crushing of the resistance was perhaps historically inevitable. Not only did the colonists possess overwhelming military resources (grapeshot against the spear); but in the age-old tradition of 'divide and rule', they were able to play on tribal divisions.

The Xhosa version of the conflict is not yet fully recorded. However, the Xhosa grasp of the issues involved is impressively described in a British soldier's account of an address by a Xhosa counsellor to the English commander, Colonel Willshire, after the Xhosa defeat in the fifth War of Resistance (1818–19). The counsellor was part of a group which had come to offer itself in exchange for the defeated Xhosa leader, Makana, imprisoned on Robben Island for life.

'The war, British Chiefs, is an unjust one. You are striving to extirpate a people whom you forced to take up arms.' Initial contact between the settlers and Xhosas was friendly and warm 'until the herds of the Xhosas increased so as to make the hearts of the Boers sore. What those covetous men could not get from our fathers for old buttons, they took by force. Our fathers were men; they loved their cattle, their wives; their wives and children live upon milk; they fought for their property. They began to hate the colonists who coveted their all and aimed at their destruction . . . If we had succeeded, our right was good, for you began the war. We failed and you are here.'[2]

On this occasion, some 3,000 square miles of Xhosa land and 30,000 head of cattle constituted the cost of the failure. Makana was to drown off Blaauwberg beach in an unsuccessful attempt to escape from the prison island which today, once again, keeps African resistance leaders under lock and key.

In other parts of the sub-continent, the story was the same. North of the Orange River, the independent Griqua states fell to the Boer conquest of the 1860s. Sotho resistance under Moshweshwe I – a general in the Shaka mould and a statesman of great talent – was also fierce. Before his death in 1870 the Basotho had retained a measure of independence under British 'protection' which eventually prevented the incorporation of their remaining lands into the Union of South Africa. The new Boer Republics in the North found the process of subduing the existing African traditional societies costly. The Pedi under Sekhukhune in the East and the Setswana in the West fiercely resisted the land grabbing and labour hunting. And it was not until 1898 that the South African Republic succeeded in defeating the Venda.

The great Zulu kingdom in the end also succumbed to overwhelming force, but not without a struggle which became legendary. Under Dingiswayo it had begun the welding of the tribal factions into nationhood. This was already well advanced by the mid-nineteenth century.*

In Zululand, as in the Eastern Cape, the colonists originally hoped to achieve their territorial ambitions through the lure of trinkets. Simon van der Stel sent a galliot to Port Natal (now Durban) with instructions to purchase 'that bay with some surrounding land from the King and Chief of those parts for some merchandise consisting of copper arm and neck rings and other articles'.[3] Later, when war rather than commerce became the instrument of settler expansionism, the cohesion of the Zulus and their advanced military techniques (pioneered by Shaka) made them a formidable foe.

It was not the so-called 'war-like' Zulu chiefs who chose

*It was undoubtedly accompanied by inter-tribal war and attendant cruelties. Racist historians who attempt to denigrate the process by harping on the atrocities not only exaggerate the element of violence but also, more often than not, conveniently omit comparison with the savage destruction of both life and property which surrounded nation-building in Europe and elsewhere.

armed confrontation. The events leading to the tenth war of resistance in 1879 without a doubt demonstrate settler intentions to provoke a conflict in order to destroy the Zulu kingdom, and the army which was its defence. The prize would not only be cattle and land, but the prospect expressed by Governor Shepstone that Zulu warriors would 'be changed to labourers working for wages'.[4] But before the change was enforced, these warriors gave more than a good account of themselves. At the battle of Isandhlawana in 1879, Europe's foremost army, with modern breech-loading guns, sustained a military defeat at the hands of Zulu soldiers with stabbing spears. Before the battle, when the British intention to destroy Zulu power had become crystal clear to him, Cetshwayo told a messenger who brought an ultimatum from the British: 'Go back and tell the English that I shall now act on my own account and if they wish me to argue I shall become a wanderer but I shall not go without having acted.'[5]

In the end, having acted, Cetshwayo became a 'wanderer'. After a successful British assault on his stronghold at Ulundi, he was tracked down in the Ngomi forest and banished from his kingdom.

The scene was thus set for the fulfilment of Shepstone's dream. Zululand was split into thirteen parts under separate chiefs salaried by the government. New tax laws were promulgated, designed to force the Zulu warrior to offer himself as a labourer to settler farmers: a device soon to be followed by administrations in other parts of Southern Africa. This provoked the final episode of old-style resistance when, in 1906 in Natal, Bambata led an unsuccessful armed uprising against these taxes. To destroy the myth of Bambata's invulnerability, his head was cut off by his 'Christian' conquerors and publicly paraded.

The destruction of Bambata and his guerrillas in the Nkandle forest represents a watershed in indigenous resistance to colonial rule. Resistance of that type could no longer be sustained by traditional African tribal societies. The independent tribe with its military organization – the base of the resistance – had been destroyed throughout the whole of Southern Africa. There had been no concerted African resistance; the enemy had exploited the divisions between and within the different tribes, some of whom were temporarily inveigled onto the side of the colonists only to be destroyed in their turn when they had served their purpose; there had been an absolute disparity in weaponry. Each of these factors played a part in the ultimate defeat.

The period of imperialist primitive accumulation – so familiar in colonies throughout the world – had run its course. The usual progression from trade, through to conquest, followed by economic and political control, was complete.

AFTER THE CONQUEST

A new era of political struggle opened. It began uncertainly because the core of former resistance in the countryside had been destroyed, and the new forces were not yet fully developed.

The early stages of both national and working-class struggle bore the marks of this transition. They saw the emergence of nationally orientated organizations amongst the Indian and Coloured peoples, and in 1912 the creation of the African National Congress. With the lessons of the conquest behind it, the African National Congress set itself the task of promoting a national African consciousness and of eliminating the historical hangover of tribalism and regionalism. This was also the time when developing capitalist relations of production stimulated the growth of political and trade union organizations, which began to assert workers' interests in the economic and political spheres.

The history of the early responses of various national groups and class forces to the conquest has been set out in works by Roux (*Time Longer Than Rope*), Lerumo (*Fifty Fighting Years*) and, above all, by H. J. and R. E. Simons in their richly documented *Class and Colour in South Africa 1850–1950*. It is impossible here to do more than concentrate on a number of important themes which highlight the way in which both national and class forces grappled, sometimes uncertainly, with the new tasks posed by changed and continuously changing conditions.

It will be seen that, in the course of time, the attitudes of the main political organizations were radically transformed on a number of fundamental questions.

The African National Congress of today, for example, led by men like Tambo and Mandela, with an unqualified demand for people's power to be achieved by revolutionary force, is a far cry from the African National Congress of the twenties, which was still shy to challenge the roots of white supremacy, and still looked to the imperialists at Whitehall to ameliorate the conditions of Africans.

The Communist Party, too, has come a long way since its formative years and the days of the 1922 general strike. Despite efforts by Communists to steer this white miners' strike away from racialism, the Communist Party nonetheless ranged itself with those forces which supported the retention of the job colour bar on the mines. But this same organization was shortly afterwards to play an important role in pioneering the concept of immediate majority rule, and in elaborating an integrated appreciation of the relationship of class to national struggle.

The same process of radicalization occurred in the organizations of the Indian minority. The early beginnings of resistance by the Indian community had been led by Mahatma Gandhi, who founded the Natal and Transvaal organizations that later merged to form the South African Indian Congress. Gandhi pioneered the technique of passive resistance which was to be used so effectively in the following half-century by the whole national movement as a means of mobilization and resistance. But, like the early leaders of the African national movement, Gandhi still had illusions about the nature of the British Empire, and was unable to see an imperative need for all-black unity. In 1906, for example, he considered it tactically wise to side with the British in the brutal crushing of the Bambata rebellion. When the Dadoo–Naicker group won the leadership battle in the late forties, the South African Indian Congress and its constituents turned from former moderate and sectional policies to joint action with the African National Congress.

Early organizations of the Coloured people, such as the African People's Organization, also suffered similar limitations.

The partial Coloured franchise of those times, now totally abolished, 'proved to be more demoralizing than total disenfranchisement. Coloured politicians tended to become appendages of white parties, which denied them membership and rewarded them with scraps of political loot'.[6] But, by the fifties, the newly-created Coloured People's Congress was becoming an integral part of the liberation alliance.

A brief examination of a few of the main phases in the history of two of these organizations – the South African Communist Party and the African National Congress – will help to relate some of their earlier ideological limitations to the realities of the period in which they occurred. It will also shed light on the mutual interaction between the national and the class movements from which evolved those strategic perspectives common to the whole liberation movement today.

THE SOUTH AFRICAN COMMUNIST PARTY

The Communist Party held its founding conference on 30 July 1921. Like many of its counterparts, especially in Western Europe, it was constituted by those who had broken with social democracy on the question of its support for the First World War. Initially, in 1915, a small group of left-wingers, led by people like Bill Andrews, broke with the all-white South African Labour Party and formed the International Socialist League. This group, together with smaller left-wing groups, took the initiative in establishing the Party and affiliating it to the Comintern. The Party operated as a legal body until 1950, when it was declared illegal under the Suppression of Communism Act. After a lapse of three years, it reconstituted itself in clandestine conditions. The most concise and all-round definition of its theory of the South African revolution is contained in its programme, *The Road to South African Freedom*, which was adopted in 1962 at its sixth underground conference held in Johannesburg.

Between the first conference in 1921 and the programme conference in 1962, a fundamental re-shaping had taken place in the Communist approach to many of the basic problems of the

South African revolution. Some of these changes were responses to a changing situation; but in the case of others, the changing situation served only to put in question some of the Party's earlier assumptions about the fundamental character of the political conflict, about the main forces for change, and about the precise character and role of the Party itself.

The composition of the delegates attending and of the leading bodies elected at these two conferences tells its own story. At the 1921 conference every delegate was white, and so was every member of the executive. At the 1962 conference the great majority of the delegates were black, and a predominantly black Central Committee was elected.

But the contrast between the main programmatic documents is equally stark. The earlier conference posited, as an immediate task, an advance to a classless society, with the industrial workers – then predominantly white – providing the 'storm troops' of the approaching revolution. The 1962 programme, however, set out a perspective of a national democratic revolution whose main content would be the liberation of the African people. Radical change must have seemed closer to the delegates in 1921, in the post-October Revolution euphoria, than it seemed in 1962. And indeed, shortly after the founding conference, the white miners on the Rand initiated a strike which developed close to insurrection, in which armed commandos took to the streets and pitched battles between them and the state's armed forces took place.

But with the benefit of hindsight there can surely be no situation more bizarre. The red flag is hoisted over the Johannesburg city hall. A huge demonstration of miners takes to the streets on 7 February 1922, led by a brass band blaring the Red Flag, and followed by a slogan which proclaimed 'Workers of the World Fight and Unite for a White South Africa'. The Rand Revolt, as it became known, was sparked off by an attempt by the Chamber of Mines to ease – for its own purposes and in a limited sphere – the job colour bar on the mines. The employment of black mineworkers to do skilled or semi-skilled work was not yet prohibited by law. The 1917 *status quo* agreement between the mine owners and the white workers had fixed the ratio of white to black labour. Whilst attempting to steer the strike away from its anti-black tendencies, Communists found themselves arguing that the true interests of the workers (white or black) were to defend the white monopoly of skilled work and thus to defend the rates of white workers' pay which the bosses were attacking by their ploy. They declared that the leaders of what they called the 'bourgeois National Congress', by advocating the immediate removal of the colour bar, were 'playing the game of the capitalists'.[7]

The Communists were undoubtedly right in questioning the motives behind the mine-owners' attempt to dilute the colour bar. But in the absence of an alternative demand for the immediate ending of the race quotas, their actions and attitudes objectively reinforced and 'justified' the retention of the colour bar.

What explains this association of the Communists at that time with a movement whose proclaimed aim was to entrench white racial privilege at the point of production? Given their thesis of class struggle in which the national element played little or no part, and given the overwhelmingly white composition of the Communist movement at that time, it is easy to understand why they thought of the white working class as *the* revolutionary force. After all, the white workers had been engaged for more than a decade in bitter class struggles against the bosses and had fought many heroic battles, occasionally with guns in hand. In contrast, the African proletariat proper was still in its formative stages. If, as they understood it, the working class was the vanguard in the struggle for socialism, who but the most articulate and most highly organized sector of the working class could be seen to fill this role? The racial prejudice of the white workers was evident; but, it was believed, the industrial system would gradually wean them away from racialism, and a truly international class consciousness would emerge in the course of struggle.

It was, of course, exceedingly difficult for these early Communists – many of them utterly selfless in the cause of socialism – to uncover the true character of the process that was taking place. The white workers had not yet won the place at the ruler's table which they have today, and their undoubted militancy was a mixture of motives and aims, that included a class hostility to capitalism. From their struggles were born the radical political movements with broadly socialist orientation which, as we have seen, led ultimately to the formation of the Communist Party of South Africa. On the other hand, the black worker had neither effective industrial organization nor a militant national consciousness or national movement which could hold out an immediate prospect of revolutionary struggle.

South African Communists were not alone in believing that on a world scale the early twenties would see a major revolutionary breakthrough. With hindsight it is easier to see that their perspective of a working-class power, based as it could only be on the white working class, was a mistaken one. Their internationalism expressed itself in the concept of a white proletariat taking power and then proceeding to free South Africa's oppressed nations. Rigid adherence to this concept led to political stances which, however well-intentioned, were objectively at best utopian, and at worst a pandering to white reaction.

The victory of the alliance between the white South African Labour Party and the Nationalist Party at the polls in 1924 was the real culmination of the strivings of the privilege-seeking white workers. The basic aims of the 1922 strike were given statutory recognition. The new government made vast concessions, and the process of making the white workers appendages of the ruling group in every sphere of life – economic, political and social – began in earnest. Laws were passed effectively making skilled work a right of white workers alone. A so-called 'civilized labour policy' was implemented to maintain Africans as unskilled cheap labour and to prevent the emergence of an organized African working class. Africans (i.e. all who were obliged to carry passes) were excluded from the definition of 'employee' in the new industrial legislation. This deprived them of the legal right to strike (in any industrial dispute) or to form their own registered trade unions.

The faith in the revolutionary potential of the white working class soon began to fade within the Communist movement. Those who had never really envisaged a socialism to embrace the black people withdrew from politics, or found a home in the racialist Labour Party, or in a few cases in the fascist-oriented Nationalist Party. But men like Andrews – not without personal difficulty on some issues – continued to play a leading role in the Party, whose emphasis was swinging towards African liberation. By 1928, of the 1,750 members of the Communist Party, 1,600 were African.

For the first time the concept of Black Rule was advanced. James La Guma, a Coloured leader of the Communist Party. attended the 1927 Brussels conference of the League Against Imperialism which asserted the doctrine of 'Africa for the Africans'. From there he went to Moscow. In the course of this visit the basis was laid for the Comintern to formulate its line on South Africa, the adoption of which, in terms of Comintern rules, was obligatory on the South African Party. This line proclaimed that the main task of the revolution was to struggle for what it called an 'independent native republic (with minority rights) as a stage towards the overthrow of capitalism in South Africa'.

As with the modern-day slogan of black power, the 'Native Republic' slogan was calculated to dissolve traditional African subservience to whites. The attainment of equality was dependent not upon white goodwill but African power: as far as it went a very sound thesis, which not only brought about a revolution in the thinking of Communists but also helped transform the very character of the national movement itself. But the pendulum had swung to an opposite position and the correct balance of a revolutionary strategy was still lacking.

The Party now saw the struggle as a colonial one with Africans of all classes fighting for self-determination and aiming at the establishment of a bourgeois democratic republic. This was the era of the so-called 'Black Republic'. Work amongst workers of other sections declined and almost exclusive attention was paid to mobilizing Africans in the struggle for freedom and independence.

This approach obviously had difficulties of its own. Was South Africa a colony in the accepted sense? From whom was independence to be wrested? From the South African ruling class? From the imperialists in Britain who were economically dominant in South Africa? Against whom was the main blow to be directed?[8]

Thus, although the slogan of a Black Republic was, by and large, a move in the right direction, there were deficiencies in the exposition which, not for the first time in the experience of revolutionary movements, mechanically divided the phases of social change into rigid chronological categories. In the early period the perspective had been one purely of class struggle, led by the organized whites and leading to a workers' and peasants' republic which would then set about solving the national problems. In the later period the emphasis was in an exactly opposite direction; on the achievement of full equality and democratic rights as a distinct phase, after which the search for socialist solutions of South Africa's other ills could begin.

In the 1962 programme the synthesis of these two positions is completed. This synthesis is based on the concept that it is just as impossible to conceive of workers' power in South Africa separated from national liberation, as it is to conceive of true national liberation separated from the destruction of capitalism.

This more fully worked out ideological integration of these two elements in South Africa's strategy of struggle owes a great deal to black Communists like Moses Kotane (the Secretary General of the Communist Party since 1939 and a top-level leader of the ANC since the early forties) and Dr Yusuf Dadoo (Chairman of the Communist Party and one of the most prominent leaders of the Indian community). In the hands of revolutionary activists of their calibre, the practical Party campaigns to mobilize people on issues close to their experience injected an indigenous revolutionary vitality into what had, for some time in the 1930s, remained a somewhat sterile exercise in theory.

THE AFRICAN NATIONAL CONGRESS

But if the early Communist Party suffered from the twin legacy of its genesis in the white labour movement and its unreal belief in the immediate prospect of a working-class breakthrough in South Africa, the new national organization remained for some time the prisoner of other limitations. The defeats of armed resistance in the countryside had been piecemeal, made easier by the enemy's manipulation of one tribe against another. The bulk of the African people remained tied to these demoralized tribal groupings; in the urban centres new black forces for change were still in their infancy. It was to be some time before the economic and political processes matured sufficiently to create a common all-African experience of oppression and exploitation which would cut across tribal boundaries.

Understandably the initiatives to develop a single national consciousness out of all the diverse groups and cultures came from the small group of black intellectuals, for whom a wider world had begun to open beyond the narrow confines of tribal allegiances. Writing in IMVO on 24 October 1911, a young Natal lawyer, P. Ka. I. Seme, advocated the formation of a national organization dedicated to creating unity amongst Africans.

'The demon of racialism,' wrote Seme,

> the aberrations of the Xhosa-Fingo feud, the animosity that exists between the Zulus and the Tongas, between the Basotho and every other native, must be buried and forgotten. We are one people. These divisions and jealousies are the cause of all our woes and of all our backwardness and ignorance today.

Those who, on 8 January 1912, responded to this call, took a revolutionary step forward when they created the South African Natives' Congress. Revolutionary? The composition of the delegates and certain of the political platforms adopted may suggest otherwise. Traditional rulers and chiefs and the few black intelligentsia dominated the proceedings and the elected leadership. Inspired by the Westminster constitutional model, an 'upper house' of chiefs was created to share the leadership. Amongst the policies adopted were those 'to encourage a spirit of loyalty to the British Crown and all lawful authority' and 'to bring about better understanding between the white and black inhabitants'.

For many decades after its formation, cap-in-hand nationalism formed a part of Congress's ideological stance, even when it was engaging in radical actions. Congress fought the 1913 Land Act (the first all-Union statute to legitimize the Reserve system) by sending a deputation to London. In election speeches for one of the African seats in the Cape Provincial Council, one of the Congress Vice-Presidents, the Rev. Walter Rubusana, was still acknowledging on behalf of his people the superiority of the white race. Rallies in 1919 ended in the singing of *Rule Britannia* and *God Save the King*. In 1923 the Congress restricted itself to demanding 'equal rights for all civilized men', the notorious Rhodes formula for assuring white rule while assuaging the liberal conscience. In 1928, when the Communists were already talking of an 'Independent Native Republic' as a stage towards socialism, the Congress upper house of chiefs passed a motion disapproving of the growing 'fraternization' between the ANC and the Communist Party, swayed by the argument of the proposer that 'the Tsar was a great man in his country, of royal blood like us chiefs, and where is he now?'

As with the first years of the South African Communist Party, it is facile to judge this phase in the life of the African National Congress by standards of abstract revolutionary formulae, and to allow the examples of moderation and conciliation quoted above to overshadow the organization's overall revolutionary significance.

Bringing the important chiefs together under one national umbrella was a great stride forward, even though their traditions as resistance leaders were being rapidly overtaken by their integration as minor cogs in the white man's administrative apparatus. It meant that new ideas of non-tribal politics could begin to seep through to the African people, most of whom were still living in a tribal environment. The absence of a militant strategy for the destruction of the white state reflected the reality of black powerlessness; it encouraged a lingering and desperate illusion that divisions between British and Boer imperialism – had they not just fought a war? – could somehow be exploited to win Whitehall support for advancing black aspirations.

But even in those early stages ANC politics were not totally confined to conciliation, deputation and petition. Five ANC leaders were amongst the eight accused (the other three were members of the ISL) charged with incitement to violence in a trial arising out of the strike by Johannesburg black sanitary workers (the 'bucket strike') in 1918. The ANC was involved in the strike by 40,000 black miners in February 1920, and its rally in support of this strike was broken up by armed force. In March of the same year it organized a passive resistance campaign against the Pass Laws, which led to more than 700 arrests. And in the 1922 white miners' General Strike, Congress sensed more clearly than the Communists the essentially retrogressive implications of the white miners' 'class'-inspired opposition to a dilution of the works Colour Bar.

But it was not until the forties that the ANC outgrew its moderate leaders and began to free itself from the limitations of its formative period. The first leap forward was marked by the 1943 adoption of its 'African Claims' and 'Bill of Rights'. The ANC President-General, Dr A. B. Xuma, declared that Africans had an 'undisputed claim to full citizenship'. But the radical strategy for pressing this claim only emerged four years later, when the ANC adopted its Programme of Action, which asserted an absolute right to black self-determination. A Council of Action was appointed to implement the programme by methods which were to include boycott, strikes, civil disobedience and non-co-operation.

This radicalization resulted from the interaction between changes in the socio-economic structures and a range of subjective factors. The first major spurt towards black urbanization took place in the post-First World War period, when the ANC was not yet ready to break out of its 1912 élitist mould. As a consequence it was effectively eclipsed by the newly-formed Industrial and Commercial Workers' Union of Africa (ICU), a trade union movement for African workers which proclaimed direct political aims, including national liberation and the establishment of a socialist South Africa.

The Second World War and the consequent industrial boom accelerated the process of black urbanization. The focus of the struggle for social change, more clearly than ever before, moved to the cities, where the relatively detribalized black proletariat became the vital force in liberation politics. White intransigence was also reaching a climax with the election of a Nationalist

Party government in 1948 dedicated to the complete destruction of black opposition and to the reversal of any trend towards African national cohesion.

The militant nationalists in the youth section of Congress (ANCYL) responded to the new conditions. In 1948 a number of the moderates were displaced and men like Tambo, Sisulu and Mandela elected to the executive. Together with Communists in the ANC leadership like Kotane, Marks and Mofutsanyana they won support for more dynamic policies, and more radical political action to back them up. This set the scene for the rousing mass struggles of the fifties, and these struggles, in turn, set the scene for the complete 1961 break with the period in which resistance politics stopped short of violent revolution.

THE MASS STRUGGLES OF THE FIFTIES

Starting from nation-wide strikes on 26 June 1950, to protest at the May-Day police killings of demonstrators against the Suppression of Communism Act,* the fifties were punctuated by an unprecedented series of mass struggles in the urban and rural areas.

In 1952 a Defiance Campaign against selected racial laws was launched; in the course of it 8,000 volunteers in every part of the country were jailed for deliberately flouting apartheid measures. Following upon this campaign, a nation-wide movement was launched to convene a 'Congress of the People'. After sixteen months of public campaigning, over 3,000 delegates met in Kliptown, Johannesburg, and, surrounded by armed police, this, the most representative assembly ever held in South Africa, adopted the *Freedom Charter*.

When the COP campaign was announced by Chief Albert Lutuli, the President-General of the ANC, on 8 May 1954, he also called for a separate campaign of resistance to all apartheid measures. Amongst the acts of resistance subsequently advo-

*This Act outlawed the SACP, introduced the offence of 'Statutory Communism' (which covered all radical opposition to racism), and gave the executive arbitrary powers to deal administratively with individuals and groups in the whole liberation opposition.

cated was the campaign against the removal of Africans from Sophiatown in 1955 (the only area in Johannesburg in which Africans still enjoyed freehold rights); and the boycott of all Government-controlled schools as a protest against the implementation of the 1953 Bantu Education Act.

On 6 December 1956, 156 leaders (Africans, Indians, Coloureds and Whites) were arrested in nation-wide swoops and charged with high treason arising out of their involvement in the Congress of the People and other campaigns. The trial was to end in favour of the accused over four years later. 1956 also saw a major women's anti-pass campaign which involved the burning of passes and led to thousands of arrests. In more than one urban centre militant bus boycotts were organized in protest against rising fares, and whole townships (like Alexandra in Johannesburg) marched in daily demonstrations through white suburbs to reach their places of work. For the first time in South African history, national general strikes were called for political purposes. Time and again the big industrial complexes of the Witwatersrand, the Eastern Cape, Natal and elsewhere were seriously disrupted as hundreds of thousands of black workers went on strike in support of political demands.

In the countryside, too, a new militancy was in evidence. In Sekhukhuniland partly-armed peasants doggedly resisted government attempts to integrate the chieftanship more closely into the Government's apparatus. In Zululand, similar resistance developed. In Zeerust, pass burning by women was followed by a period of violent clashes between people and police. In Pondoland, peasant resistance reached the most impressive heights: the sizeable popular movement set up its own unofficial administrative units, including People's Courts. The movement took its name 'Intaba' (the mountain) from the spot where thousands of peasants assembled illegally to decide their own actions. Many of these peasant eruptions were spontaneous, but all were stimulated by the new climate of organized mass resistance. The Pondo Revolt, for example, had its origins in purely local grievances, but it soon embraced the platform of the African National Congress – the attainment of full political rights for the oppressed majority.[9]

THE PRELUDE TO VIOLENCE

Measured by the yardstick of immediate achievement, each of these campaigns against specific measures failed. The laws selected as the targets of the Defiance Campaign remained on the statute book. Sophiatown was bulldozed into the ground and replaced by a white suburb which (with typical white insensitivity) was given the name of Triomf (triumph). The attempt by Congress to provide alternative education for African children through cultural clubs eventually collapsed (unofficial schools were outlawed), and the Bantu Education Act was fully implemented. Anti-pass actions did not, in the end, prevent the more intense application of the pass laws. Peasant resistance was to be crushed by emergency legislation and military action. And the strikes did not loosen the hold of white supremacy.

But 'failure' measured in such narrow terms has been the universal experience of every revolutionary movement. Until the moment of successful revolutionary take-over, each individual act of resistance usually fails, and is often crushed; and the radical demands of political action remain unsatisfied. In this sense 'failure' is the constant companion of all political endeavour by a dominated group which is not yet capable of winning power. The rare moment in history which makes possible the final victorious revolutionary assault is a compound of many elements. Amongst the most important of these is a people and a movement with an accumulated heritage of resistance which, through all the immediate 'failures', perpetuates and reinforces the tradition of struggle. It is often only through the experience of these so-called 'failures' that the masses begin to understand the need for conquering state power and thus for revolution. And when the moment of revolution arrives, only a political organization which has been with the people through all their earlier experiences can hope to command their allegiance.

The immediate tactical aims articulated by the Congress movement in the fifties did not yet raise directly the concept of violent revolution, although the demands increasingly centred on the issue of majority rule implicit in the slogan of 'one man one vote'.

Each one of these campaigns was met with varying degrees of violent repression from government forces. Yet the organizers attempted throughout to steer mass activity along non-violent lines, while not shirking the need for constant, direct confrontation.

The decision to prepare deliberately for armed struggle was not taken until the early sixties. Why was the decision taken only then and not in the fifties or forties or thirties? There had never been a moment in history since 1652 when the white ruling class would have given up power without a battle outside the polite arena of the white man's parliament. The answer is that the conditions which make violence a revolutionary imperative had still to mature.

> The revolutionary sounding phrase does not always reflect a revolutionary policy, and revolutionary sounding policies not always the springboard for revolutionary advance. Indeed what appears to be 'militant' and 'revolutionary' can often be counter-revolutionary. It is surely a question whether, in the given concrete situation, the course or policy advocated will aid or impede the prospect of the conquest of power . . . Untimely, ill-planned or premature manifestations of violence impede and do not advance the prospect for revolutionary change and are clearly counter-revolutionary. It is obvious, therefore, that policy and organizational structures must grow out of the real situation if they are not to become meaningless clichés.[10]

The answer to the central question of whether violence should have been on the agenda from the early fifties cannot be plucked out of a collection of textbook models. A serious movement poses the idea of revolution seriously only when the objective conditions make it possible to prepare for it. Until then it can articulate the idea of *a* revolution *ad nauseam* (as many obscure revolutionary groups do to small effect but their own gratification) without advancing *the* revolution one jot.

Conditions for armed struggle are not brought into existence by subjective and ideological activity alone; they grow out of the real situation both locally and internationally. Already by the early fifties, the increasing use of state violence to frustrate every level of organized black protest, stimulated thought and action in the direction of people's counter-violence. The defiance campaign ended in bloody riots in almost every major city. The government's 'shoot first' order to the police led to regular killings of demonstrators and strikers who, more than once, retaliated with rudimentary weapons. In the rural areas (particularly in Pondoland) the struggles against the imposition of Bantu Authorities were accompanied by a great deal of violence. The evidence at the Treason Trial showed that more and more ANC activists were, in their speeches, reflecting the people's groping towards a strategy of retaliation in kind. But the longer-term problem for the revolutionary movement was how to express this changing mood in terms of armed rather than spontaneous violent activities, a people's war rather than mere retaliation or self-defence. For a number of reasons such a strategy could not be effectively projected during the fifties. An attempt to do so would have given the régime a pretext (which it clearly sought at the time) for a massive attempt at intimidation. Also, the possibilities of legal and semi-legal mass mobilization by a Congress movement still enjoying a precarious legality had not yet been completely blocked. Both at important levels of the liberation alliance and amongst sections of the people a belief lingered in the potential of mass pressure short of organized force.

In the rest of the continent, black self-rule had not yet become a reality, nor were there in existence friendly external base areas (within reasonable reach) such as proved to be of undoubted importance in the launching and sustaining of armed struggle in countries like Guinea-Bissau and Mozambique. Without even the prospect of such base areas until the late fifties and early sixties, preparations for modern-type guerrilla struggle seemed unrealistic; and even more so in a situation where, almost uniquely, the black people were absolutely barred from access to weaponry even in the army, or to any modern combatant experience or know-how. The crushing of the tribal armed resistance by means of unequal material odds was still fresh in the collective memory of the African people, and the example of successful armed challenges to colonialism in Africa (as in Algeria) by new techniques of people's war had still not made its impact.

But it was not only the sweep of African decolonization which provided the spur for a more radical strategy. When the movement began to alter the emphasis of its approach, it was reflecting the more militant political climate which it had itself helped bring about inside South Africa by the radical leadership it had provided in the preceding period. The decision of the Planning Council in 1952 to call for a *defiance* campaign, and not a *passive* resistance campaign, was calculated. It was a conscious attempt to begin promoting defiance of the white state, and was certainly 'not designed to end the system of white supremacy by the sacrifices of its victims'.[11]

Although immediately directed against selected laws, the longer term purpose was clearly expressed in the letter written by the President and Secretary General of the African National Congress to the government when the campaign was announced:

> We firmly believe that the freedom of the African people, the elimination of the exploitation of man by man and the restitution of democracy, liberty and harmony in South Africa, are such vital and fundamental matters that the Government and the public must know that we are fully resolved to achieve them in our lifetime.

Deliberate defiance by selected volunteers was to be the first phase of the campaign. A later phase was to be 'mass action, which as far as possible should broaden out on a countrywide scale . . .'.[12]

The Congress of the People, the pass-burning campaigns, the demand for majority rule backed by the general political strike: all these were designed to inject a spirit of organized defiance and to show the need of state power for realizing the new vision of South Africa as set out in the *Freedom Charter*. Certainly the ruling class understood the strategy in these terms when it eventually moved to destroy the leadership with the charges of high treason: and, when that miscarried, through the outlawing of the African National Congress.

The conduct of campaigns in a way which would narrow the enemy's opportunities for violent retaliation against a people not yet equipped to fight back was also calculated. A call for physical assault on white power at that stage would have perhaps been answered by the advance guard. But it would have isolated the advance guard from the people and enabled the authorities to pick them off separately. Under these circumstances the call would be stifled before the masses even began to respond.

The emphasis placed by the leaders of the movement on non-violence no doubt fed those reformist tendencies rooted in the earlier period and may well have given rise to some illusions of possible constitutional advance. Against this danger the movement may not have guarded sufficiently. But the overall strategy can as little be condemned on this score, as can the strategy of violence because of the risks it may run of encouraging adventurism and heedlessness of the political factors. The strategic turning point came in the early sixties, because that was approximately the time when the ruling class made clear its intention of smashing the black opposition totally: that was the time when it finally sealed off all avenues for effective opposition without the element of organized force.

THE CONGRESS ALLIANCE

The decade of the fifties was also the high point of active collaboration between the mass organizations of the different groups constituting the Congress Alliance. The Communist Party, already outlawed, could not, for obvious reasons, be formally associated with it. The Joint Planning Council which co-ordinated the Defiance Campaign was followed by a National Consultative Committee (NCC), which consisted of representatives of the African National Congress, South African Indian Congress, Coloured People's Congress, South African Congress of Trade Unions and the Congress of Democrats (a white group created on the initiative of the African National Congress during the Defiance Campaign). The NCC was not a super-executive. As the name implies, it was consultative in character; formed to co-ordinate the efforts of the organizations which were part of it.

Critics of this Congress Alliance, such as the Pan-Africanist Congress, echoed government allegations that it was infiltrated by communist elements and saw participation by the minority groups as a dilution of the 'African image'. But on neither count can the charge be sustained.

The leading Communists who participated at the top level of the Congress Alliance – men like Kotane, Dadoo, J. B. Marks and Mofutsenyana – did so in their capacity as long-standing leaders of the national organizations. They did not hide their political affiliations but won their leading status by long and active participation in the organizations in which they had been elected to high positions.

The South African Communist Party saw its role in relation to the national movement as follows:

> South African experience has fully proved that a strong Communist Party is vital to the strength and the vigour of the movement as a whole. The Central Committee is vigorously opposed to any conception of counterposing the Party or 'the Communists' to the rest of the movement. We have never considered that the way to play a 'vanguard' role is by 'proclaiming' it or by contesting for positions. In the fight against white supremacy we have no aims separate from those of our non-Communist comrades and colleagues in the liberation and working-class movements. Leadership consists in each and every one of our members, in whatever field he may be working, and at whatever level, setting an example of firmness and devotion in the common patriotic struggle against the common enemy. We maintain that our ideology of Marxism–Leninism enables our members to be better Congressites, better trade unionists, better fighters for the freedom of our country. We maintain that the movement as a whole can only gain by our Party playing its full role as a partner in the liberation alliance.[13]

The charge of minority domination of the Alliance is equally groundless. There are moments

> . . . after 1960 in which co-operation between some organizations which were legal (e.g. SAIC, CPC, COD) and those that were illegal (e.g. ANC) sometimes led to the superficial impression that the legal organizations – because they could speak and operate more publicly and thus more noticeably – may have had more than their deserved place in the leadership of the Alliance.[14]

But in general the ANC was undoubtedly the leading organization in the Alliance, and was recognized as such by the other organizations in it.

Rhetoric apart, the PAC was to show in practice that it was not so much opposed to participation by minority groups in the national liberation struggle as to the left ideological positions held by many of the leaders of the SAIC, CPC and COD. Its real objection to the broad alliance was made clear by Leballo (the present PAC leader in exile) in 1958:

The African people do not want to be allied with the Congress of Democrats. They know these people to be leftists and when they want to fight for our rights these people weaken us. This is so because they use campaigns for their own ends and *also because the government will not listen to our requests and demands because of their outlook** (my emphasis).[15]

In contrast to those who feared that minority participation was diluting the 'African image' of the struggle, others like the Non-European Unity Movement raised theoretical objection to what it called 'voluntary segregation' of the black community into separate national organizations.

Apart from the Communist Party and SACTU (with class rather than national roots), membership of each of the constituent organizations of the Congress Alliance was effectively restricted to individuals belonging to the different communities. The idea of creating a single mass organization to struggle against white rule accords with the general truth that all black groups suffer from race exploitation. Indeed, the ideologically advanced could have no principled objection to the inclusion even of committed white supporters into one movement. But a single liberation organization cannot be established by 'advanced decisions' from the top, and organizations like the Non-European Unity Movement which attempted to move in that direction never made an impact in the country on any significant scale.

Historically, as we have seen, each group gave birth to its own

*Soon after its formation the PAC was to count amongst its leaders and external representatives men like Patrick Duncan – a right-wing member of the SA Liberal Party, who edited *Contact* which devoted its columns to memorials to 'the victims of Mau Mau terrorism' (27 December 1958), to supporting 'peaceful arrangement of affairs with the ex-colonial powers' (13 December 1958), and to supporting US military action against the Chinese People's Republic (18 October 1958).

national movement. The explanation for this must be sought in the fact that Coloureds and Indians had not only been physically and culturally separated from each other and from the Africans, but that the oppression of each group always differed in important respects. There were therefore tendencies towards both unity and diversity – unity in response to the fundamental fact of South African life, white supremacy; diversity because of the differential techniques of domination and exploitation of each group.

Until recently a section of the Coloured and Indian people in the Western Cape had been included in the Common Voters' Roll, and there have always been fewer obstacles in the way of the Coloured people engaging in skilled industrial occupations. The most onerous racial laws – e.g. the Pass Laws which restrict freedom of movement – have never applied to Coloureds or Indians. Despite legal obstacles, a small Indian merchant class emerged and has been a significant factor in the life of that community. But, apart from a petty trader element, no analagous group existed amongst Africans or Coloureds. For both the Indian and Coloured communities, with only minimal peasant elements, the land question (except in a very limited sense for trading and residential purposes) had little direct significance.

The different levels of national consciousness, the historical legacy of separate national movements, and even some inter-black prejudices (always encouraged by the government),* could not be made to disappear simply by ignoring them or by ideological appeals only. It was only the active collaboration between the various national organizations in the campaigns of the fifties which made possible a high level of concerted black action and thus moved the masses towards the achievement of real unity. But later events were to pose new problems in this area.

In 1960 the African National Congress was outlawed, and the period of repression which followed led to the virtual destruction at all levels of the liberation movement's organization. The SAIC and the CPC ceased to exist, either within or outside

* In January 1949 clashes between Africans and Indians in Durban led to an estimated 142 deaths and 1,087 wounded.

the country, in the sense of having a defined and functioning leadership with the allegiance of an organized rank and file. The COD disappeared completely. In fact, of the groups which once constituted the Congress Alliance, only the African National Congress and the South African Communist Party continued to operate, each with a recognized leadership and organized rank-and-file organization, even though for some years outside the country only. But the Congress Alliance in the form in which it was known in the fifties ceased to exist. The new period of internal reconstruction which followed therefore posed anew the problem of appropriate organizational forms for a united struggle in new circumstances.

FUTURE LIBERATION UNITY

Broad guidelines of the ANC's approach to unity are set out in its 'Strategy and Tactics'.

Whatever instruments are created to give expression to the unity of the liberation drive, they must accommodate two fundamental propositions: *firstly*, they must not be ambiguous on the question of the primary role of the most oppressed African mass, and, *secondly*, those belonging to the other oppressed groups and those few white revolutionaries who show themselves ready to make common cause with their aspirations, must be fully integrated on the basis of individual equality.

Approached in the right spirit these two propositions do not stand in conflict but reinforce one another. Equality of participation in our national front does not mean a mechanical parity between the various national groups. Not only would this in practice amount to inequality (again at the expense of the majority), but it would lend flavour to the slander which our enemies are ever-ready to spread of a multi-racial alliance dominated by minority groups. This has never been so and will never be so.

Therefore not only the substance but the form of our structural creations must in a way which people can see, give expression to the main emphasis of the present stage of our struggle. This approach is not a pandering to chauvinism, to racialism or to other such backward attitudes. We are revolutionaries, not narrow nationalists. Committed revolutionaries are our brothers to whatever group they belong. There can be no second-class participation in our movement. It is for the enemy we reserve our assertiveness and our justified sense of grievance.

In the councils of the OAU and especially its Liberation Committee, unity in South Africa's liberation struggle is seen by some in terms of a formal alliance between the external missions of the ANC and PAC. But FRELIMO's approach to this question was underlined by its Vice-President, Marcelino Dos Santos in an interview:

> When we speak about unity we mean, in the first place, unity of the people; not just groups who claim to represent the people. Every situation generates numerous individuals and groups who have the ambition to exploit a struggle for their own ends . . . Unity between organizations only has meaning if they have a real base amongst the people, otherwise it is purely formal and does not serve the interest of a people. Such a kind of unity may even serve to divide the people rather than unite them.[16]

The attempts in other parts of the sub-continent to impose a formal unity from the top between contending national movements has, too often, proved abortive and become a drag on real revolutionary effort.

The ANC has emphasized that today, as in the fifties, the building of a democratic front against minority domination in South Africa is a priority but can only be achieved as 'a unity in action, in the field, a genuine unity forged on the anvil of the struggle inside the country'.*

How then is such unity to be forged inside the country?

The form of the liberation alliance is not fixed. It shifts and develops to suit not only changing objective conditions, but also ideological changes amongst the masses who are constantly re-educated by political activity. In the present situation it obviously has to take into account a number of new factors. The armed wing of the liberation movement – Umkhonto We Sizwe – is overwhelmingly African in its leadership and composition but admits membership from the other groups. Some of these have already given their lives in the struggle and many others are serving long sentences in South Africa's jails. The needs of a totally underground organization, like today's in South Africa,

* Memorandum submitted by the ANC delegation to a meeting of the OAU Liberation Committee held in 1974.

cannot be met by the forms which grew up when all or most were open and legal. It is obviously both impractical and inefficient to encourage a number of parallel underground organizations of Africans, Coloureds, Indians and the few white revolutionaries, each with its own leadership. Yet a place needs to be found for those revolutionaries from the minority groups who are unconditionally devoted to the liberation struggle and who are ready to participate in underground work.

In the sphere of legal political activity, there have also been new developments which bear on the future of liberation unity. The last few years have witnessed the emergence of such bodies as the Black People's Convention and the South African Students' Organization, which are predominantly African but also have some Coloured and Indian members. They have not yet defined their relation to the older liberation organizations and, generally speaking, have canvassed for support on the basis of a vaguely defined platform of 'black consciousness'. The term does not in itself express a coherent programme, still less an ideology. It is in the first place a response to the arrogance of the white supremacists; and, insofar as it encourages black assertiveness, its spread is undoubtedly a contribution to the 'psychological' liberation of the black people. Both organizations have attracted a mixture of individuals ranging from militants seeking new ways to express their radicalism, to those who had been associated with the predominantly white moderate Liberal Party.

There has been a recent attempt – hampered by government administrative measures – to revive the Indian Congress which, like the CPC is still legal, although administrative repression of its leaders and activists continues. The CPC itself seems to be completely dormant inside the country. Radical leadership of the Coloured community in the legal sphere has come from the newly-formed Coloured Labour Party which won a majority of seats in the elections to the Coloured Representative Council (yet another of the government's dummy institutions) but was deprived of control by the régime's subterfuge in handing over control to the defeated Federal Party. Most of the leaders of the Coloured Labour Party are committed to a complete rejection of this type of 'representation' and they increasingly emphasize their belief in the common fate of all the black groups.

In the trade union field a new organization – the Black Allied Workers' Union – was formed recently as an offshoot of the Black People's Convention. From its inception, government and police measures have prevented 'normal' organizational activity, and there appears to be a decline in the rate of its growth. SACTU itself is still a long way from recovering its internal organizational strength, and it is only in the recent period that there is some evidence of revived activity on a relatively small scale. The recent impressive strike wave, involving about 200,000 workers since the beginning of 1972, was, however, semi-spontaneous in character. Although activists of both trade union organizations played important roles in some of the strikes, there was no overall centralized direction.

In the countryside, the legal political stage has been dominated by Bantustan politics; and new ethnic political groups and parties, both official and opposition, are emerging with a wide panorama of attitudes on the future of the Homelands and other issues.

It follows from this rough sketch of the new developments which are taking place, both in the area of underground activity and of legal and semi-legal opposition, that the old type of Congress Alliance (which in its original form is in any case dead) can no longer satisfy the overall needs of liberation unity. These needs must obviously be met by a flexible approach which accommodates these new interrelated realities and cannot be expressed in a single rigidly-defined structure. But, structures aside, it seems clear that effective liberation unity means a unity, under the overall leadership of the African National Congress, of *all* the black people, the involvement of the small group of white revolutionaries, and, above all, a recognition of the special role of South Africa's working class.

4 Perspectives of Armed Struggle

On 16 December 1961 organized units of Umkhonto We Sizwe ('The Spear of The Nation' – MK)' formed on the initiative of the ANC and SACP, carried out bomb attacks against Government installations in every major South African city. These attacks were the first in the modern period to give public notice that radical change would be sought by a strategy which included organized violence. There were to be over 150 acts of sabotage during the following eighteen months. In a proclamation widely distributed on the day of the first acts of sabotage, MK declared: 'The people's patience is not endless. The time comes in the life of any nation when there remain only two choices – submit or fight. That time has now come in South Africa.'

Had that time come? Was the moment of action well chosen; and, if so, was the method used appropriate? Did the leadership have a strategy other than an immediate expression of militant anger? Was the movement in a state of readiness sufficient to safeguard its units and personnel against massive enemy reprisals, which should undoubtedly have been anticipated?

In attempting to answer questions of this type, those whose vocation is only to dispense praise or censure have an obvious advantage over those who acted: the advantage of knowing the result. In Clausewitz's perceptive aphorism:

> The state of circumstances from which an event proceeded can never be placed before the eye of the critic exactly as it lay before the eye of the person acting, [. . . because, above all . . .], it is almost impossible that the knowledge of (the result) should not have an effect on the judgement passed on events which preceded it.[1]

Examining only the result of MK sabotage in its narrow immediate sense, critics who have turned their pens to this period have had a gala day. The form of violence chosen was, by its nature, restricted. Sabotage of property, even on a more sophisticated scale than MK was capable of mounting, is at best a weapon auxiliary to revolutionary armed struggle. It could neither bring about the downfall of the government, nor draw into action those not already in the fairly small conspiratorial groups of activists.

The organized beginnings of sabotage, and the semi-spontaneous terrorist outbursts of the PAC-inspired Poqo in 1962, acted however as a spur to government counter-action, culminating in blows which led to the virtual destruction of all effective levels of leadership and organization within the country. The police raid on the Rivonia headquarters of South Africa's underground and its follow-up resulted in the arrest and imprisonment of almost the whole of the liberation movement's internal leadership and activist rank-and-file. The state security structure, refashioned to counter threatened insurgency, succeeded in silencing all significant liberation opposition. In the period that followed, those leaders who had previously been selected for external missions together with the MK cadres sent abroad for military training, continued to make renewed efforts to get the struggle off the ground.

HAD THE TIME COME?

In thc carly sixtics, all scctions of South Africa's liberation movement believed that a move towards armed struggle was a revolutionary imperative. By then the strategy of mass struggle along non-violent lines had exhausted its potential for mobilizing the people. The régime had turned to the use of undisguised terror against all militant opposition to race rule; the liberation organizations had been outlawed. These facts had put paid to any lingering illusions that radical change could be won by action which did not include armed activity.

The formal turning point from the old to the new strategy was the régime's massive mobilization of armed force to frustrate the liberation movement's last attempt in May 1961 to pursue old-style tactics, in the call for a general strike to protest against the declaration of a Republic without consulting the black majority. It became clear that old methods would no longer strike a chord amongst the people. Like the workers in Russia in the wake of the 1905 revolution, the peaceful strike and the demonstration.

> ceased to satisfy the workers; they asked: what is to be done next...? The proletariat sensed sooner than the leaders the change in the objective conditions of struggle ... as is always the case practice marched ahead of theory.[2]

Events outside South Africa also played an important part in developing a more offensive mood amongst the people, and stimulated a search for a new strategy to destroy minority rule 'in our lifetime'. The international isolation of South Africa was reaching a high point. In Africa itself direct imperialist control of the continent was being undermined; one country after another was obtaining independence; the prospects of self-rule were firing the imagination of people throughout Africa, the South included. Friendly borders were creeping closer to the beleaguered South and, with these, the prospect of vital practical aid from the newly emergent states. For the first time in modern Africa, successful armed struggles were being waged, first in Algeria, then in Guinea-Bissau and Angola, and later in Mozambique; in these areas armed national liberation forces could be seen to be challenging enemies with overwhelmingly superior military and material resources.

Untimely inaction can often be as politically damaging as untimely action. There can be no doubt that in late 1961, failure by the ANC and its allies to make a public break with the tactics of the previous decade would have been seen by their supporters as 'inaction' – and as an abdication of their leadership role. But if a sharp break with previous tactics was called for, could the perspective of armed struggle reasonably be placed on the agenda? And were the initial techniques for doing so adequate or correct? Before we can answer these questions, we must first consider the general place of armed tactics in the struggle for revolutionary change.

INSURRECTION AND ARMED STRUGGLE

It is necessary to separate two distinct problems. The *first* relates to what may broadly be called 'a revolutionary situation', in which revolution involving armed uprising is properly on the agenda. The *second* relates to the use of organized violence as part of a planned build-up towards a protracted people's war. A confusion of these two concepts has sometimes prevented a revolutionary movement from seeing the revolutionary possibilities of its own situation. Recent history has provided a number of examples of revolutionary parties which rejected military activity because they did not discriminate between the separate questions, and paid dearly in consequence. In Algeria, for instance, the beginning of armed activity took the Algerian Communist Party by surprise; it regarded the launching of the national liberation war in November 1954 as premature, since 'the conditions for an armed uprising as formulated by Lenin did not exist'.[3]

Lenin's formulation is presumably that in *'Left-Wing' Communism – An Infantile Disorder*:

> It is not enough for revolution that the exploited and oppressed masses should understand the impossibility of living the old way and demand changes; it is essential for revolution that the exploiters should not be able to live and rule in the old way . . . revolution is impossible without a nation-wide crisis (affecting both the exploited and the exploiters.)[4]

Lenin was here discussing the problems of a general insurrection or uprising at that time in the advanced or relatively advanced capitalist countries. He was not stating a law. He was always at pains to emphasize that the general theory and practice of communism must be adapted to specific conditions. The solution to problems of the colonial areas, 'You will not find in any communist book . . . you will have to tackle that problem and solve it through your independent experience.'[5]

In his formulation in *'Left-Wing' Communism*, Lenin did not deal with the question of whether a vanguard organization could help create favourable conditions for the conquest of power by its own activities. He was dealing with the objective conditions themselves. But this has not always been appreciated.

Of course favourable conditions for armed struggle ripen historically. But the historical process should not be regarded as a mystical force outside of man, which in a crude deterministic way sets him tasks to which he mechanically responds. Simply to sit back and await the evolution of the objective conditions for a 'revolutionary situation' can amount to a dereliction of leadership. What people in organized activities do or abstain from doing, hastens or retards the historical process, and helps or hinders the maturing of favourable conditions for successful armed struggle.

On the continent of Africa there have been – or are – people's armed struggles in Algeria, Guinea-Bissau, Angola, Mozambique, Zimbabwe, and Namibia. In none of these territories can it be claimed that hostilities started in a classical situation either of revolutionary crisis or when a general insurrection could be immediately anticipated. Yet a combination of internal non-armed strategy used to exhaustion, and favourable external conditions made it possible for armed activity to promote a revolutionary advance.

Although no single incident provides the sole point of departure from non-armed to armed conflict, in each country one can recognise an event or a sequence of events which dramatically signalled the need for fundamentally new approaches. In Guinea-Bissau the signal event was the bloody repression of the August 1959 strike at the Pidgiguiti docks of Bissau, in which fifty workers were killed and many injured. In Mozambique it was the 1960 Mueda massacre of 600 at a peaceful meeting. In Angola it was the killing of thirty and the wounding of 200 at a meeting in Catete to protest at the arrest of the MPLA leader Agostinho Neto, combined with brutal repression of the Maria uprising led by a militant Christian sect. In Zimbabwe serious preparations for armed struggle were prompted by the settlers' successful Unilateral Declaration of Independence, which shattered any remaining illusion that Britain might act against the interest of its 'kith and kin' to enforce majority rule. In Namibia, the turn to armed resistance occurred immediately after the abortive 1966 judgment of the International Court of Justice, when the process of international and legal pressure had been tested to its limits and found wanting.

These examples must not be taken to support the dangerous illusion that in any country in which there is severe repression, the mere injection of armed groups will of itself, and subject only to the professional skill of the armed groups, slowly spread revolution like an oil patch. They do, however, make clear that, *given certain minimum pre-conditions*, the actual commencement and continuation of violent action can hasten the development of insurrectionary conditions.* What are these pre-conditions, particularly in a colonial-type situation?

First, disillusionment (based on hard experience), amongst the majority of the people, with the prospect of achieving liberation by traditional and non-violent processes. *Second*, the readiness of the people to respond to the call for armed confrontation, at the beginning in the form of sympathy and later with practical support. *Third*, the existence of a leadership capable not only of gaining the peoples organized allegiance for armed struggle, but of carrying out the immensely difficult tasks of planning, preparing and directing the conduct of the whole struggle.

There are, of course, other factors: such as the international context in which the struggle takes place, and the physical possibilities (terrain, friendly borders, availability of trained personnel and arms, etc.) Whether a propitious situation exists in any given country cannot be determined solely by reference to generalized theoretical models. In each case it is for the indigenous political activists who are intimately involved in the special complexities of their situation, to assess what is possible.

*It is a matter of historical record that in many colonial countries, the commencement of organized armed activities did not take the form of an armed uprising in the classical sense; nor did it wait upon the time when it could properly be claimed that there existed a 'nation-wide crisis affecting both the exploiters and the exploited'. It would be difficult, if not altogether impossible, to find in China in the early 1920s, Algeria in 1954, or Cuba in 1958 a traditional type of revolutionary upsurge to provide a classical basis for armed activities. In these countries protracted armed activity undoubtedly played *the* major role in bringing about the conditions for nation-wide revolutionary upsurge and eventual victory.

Of course, no political struggle (and this is what people's armed struggle essentially is) can be taken up only on condition that its success can be guaranteed. In the South African case, some serious mistakes were made, which proved all too costly. But if assessing these mistakes is not just an exercise in criticism, but an aid to future conduct, it should avoid seeing the struggle as a purely subjective process in which all reverses are due to avoidable errors. The real world in which struggle takes place is not a laboratory model.* We must never forget that events which are now well behind us were at one stage ahead, and that those who acted did not have then – as they have now – the benefit of experience.

THE SIXTIES – A FORWARD LOOK

In South Africa during the early sixties, there could not be a strategy for the immediate unleashing of an armed struggle; there was a gap between the people's disenchantment with exclusively non-violent methods, and their readiness and capacity to storm the citadels of the enemy. That gap could not be bridged merely by brave calls to action. Sabotage by selected units was therefore considered to be the proper departure point of the new liberation strategy. It was not presented as an ultimate weapon in people's war; nor as a form of physical pressure which, on its own, could gather force so as to create a climate of crisis and collapse in the enemy camp. It was designed rather to meet the specific ideological and practical needs of the new direction of struggle in the conditions of that time.

It was vital that the political leadership demonstrate that it was placing before the people new perspectives which would mark a sharp and open break with the politics of non-violent resistance that had dominated the preceding half century or more. Inside the movement the ideological momentum of the previous period was still evident. Strong voices continued to echo the hope that the old techniques could still succeed with-

*'World history would indeed be very easy to make if the struggle were taken up only on condition of infallibly favourable chances.' – Karl Marx in a letter to L. Kugelman, 17 April 1871.

out resort to armed confrontation. Although calls for old-style actions were attracting a diminishing response from the people, the alternative strategy had still to gain currency. The people had experienced escalating state violence in every peaceful campaign of the fifties, and on more than one occasion had reacted with spontaneous counter-violence. But riot and head-on clash by enraged crowds with state forces was little more than a transient reflex. It did not – and could not – provide the basis for an effective armed challenge. A new approach was necessary:

> The strategy adopted, and the structure devised to implement it, envisaged a long term, multi-staged campaign of disciplined violence in which a hard core of trained militants, supported by mass-based political activity and crucial external aid, confront state power with the ultimate goal of seizing it.[6]

To lay the foundations for this strategy, the ANC and its allies publicly launched the first phase: 'controlled violence' in the form of the sabotage campaign. Politically the campaign was designed to serve a number of purposes. It would be a graphic pointer to the need for carefully planned action rather than spontaneous or terroristic acts of retaliation. And it would demonstrate that responsibility for the slide towards bloody civil war lay squarely with the régime. A proclamation accompanying the first sabotage acts declared:

> We of Umkhonto We Sizwe have always sought to achieve liberation without bloodshed and civil clash. We hope, even at this late hour, that our first actions will awaken everyone to a realization of the disastrous situation to which the Nationalist policy is leading. We hope that we will bring the government and its supporters to their senses before it is too late, so that both the government and its policies can be changed before matters reach the desperate stage of civil war.[7]

However forlorn the hope, its expression – backed up by a form of violence which deliberately avoided the taking of life – was a politically useful bridge between the period of non-violent campaigning and the future people's armed struggle.

But another need had also to be met. If the armed tactic was to play a part in the political struggle, it was necessary to begin building a revolutionary armed force, under the overall leadership and direction of the political movement but with a distinctive apparatus and function. The sabotage campaign thus bebecame a proving ground for establishing which activists of the existing organizations could make the transitions to the new tactics; and, by means of these acts of armed propaganda, the atmosphere was created in which other young militants would be inspired to join.

That sabotage was to form only the opening phase in the unfolding of armed struggle is revealed by other steps which were taken at the same time. Before MK was formed, leading personnel had been sent out of the country to be trained in the art of guerrilla struggle. An intensive drive had been initiated for the recruitment of large numbers of other cadres; and an underground railway had been set up which carried hundreds of recruits abroad for guerrilla-type instruction. Early in 1962 – almost immediately after the beginnings of sabotage – Nelson Mandela had toured Africa and Europe to obtain support for the armed struggle and training facilities for guerrillas; efforts afterwards continued by the external missions of the ANC and its allies.

At the same time the National High Command of MK elaborated an ambitious plan to prepare for the next phase, the initiation of guerrilla warfare. The plan envisaged the establishment of MK regions in urban and rural areas, each with full time organizers. It included the mobilization of both home and foreign resources to enable trained personnel with their equipment to return to chosen strategic areas. These trained cadres, acting together with a local network which the High Command would build in the interim, would form the hard-core of guerrilla activity. Emphasis would be placed on the country areas in the initial stages. All these technical and organizational measures would be accompanied by an intensive campaign of mass mobilization by the political organizations which, for tactical reasons, did not yet publicly admit MK to be their creation. The precise timing of guerrilla action would depend on implementation of the preparatory steps, although the euphoric mood led to unreal expectations.

The draft document (Operation Mayibuye) which set out

the main elements of the plan emphasized that the struggle ahead was likely to be protracted, and that there would be tremendous difficulties in acting against a state which was powerfully armed and could rely on the support of the indigenous white population. But it declared, 'the time for small thinking is over because history leaves us no choice'. The successful beginnings of guerrilla warfare could well lead to a collapse of the state structure 'far sooner than we can at the moment envisage'. As it turned out, that speculation could not be tested. Although some aspects of the strategy contained in Operation Mayibuye were implemented – the most successful being the training abroad of large groups of MK cadres – it is now a matter of history that its main purpose was completely frustrated; and the enemy's reprisals rendered the whole movement abysmally weak in the years that followed.

It is vital to identify the main reasons why this happened, not merely for purposes of historical record, but because the experiences have obvious relevance to present day endeavours.

Given the imperative of armed struggle in South Africa, the broad conception behind the plan cannot be faulted. The plan had been prepared by the MK High Command and its details were still being discussed by the political leadership when it was captured at Rivonia. Whether then, now, or in the future, there can be no strategy for commitment to guerrilla-type struggle in South Africa without the main steps which the plan envisaged: the training of sufficient skilled military personnel which, in the absence of liberated areas, could only be effectively done outside the country; their return to selected regions; their equipment with a reserve of weapons to sustain operations in the initial period; and the preparation of organized political and military support for them amongst the people, especially in the areas selected for the first actions. Indeed, this was the pattern in Guinea-Bissau, Angola and Mozambique, and also of the beginnings of armed conflict in Zimbabwe and Namibia. But it is now clear that the objective obstacles to the implementation of such a plan in the 1963 South African situation were not properly appreciated.

THE EXTERNAL FACTORS

In the special conditions in which struggles on the African continent have had to be initiated and pursued, the external element was and continues to be a crucial factor. The support of the socialist world and of contiguous countries (as, for example, Guinea next door to Guinea-Bissau; Tanzania and Zambia adjoining Mozambique and Angola; the Caprivi Strip as an entry point to Namibia; and the liberated territories of Mozambique for freedom fighters striking into Rhodesia) has enabled the liberation movements to start the early phases of armed struggle sooner than would otherwise have been possible. In each of these territories, the initial phases of armed action could not have been organized from inside the countries themselves. Leaderships had to be constituted externally, and in this opening phase, supplies and trained personnel had to flow into the country from outside.

In the case of Guinea-Bissau, the decisive step was the installation of a leadership group in the newly independent Republic of Guinea in 1961, where the basic PAIGC core, both political and military, was formed.[8] For Angola it was only after Congo-Brazzaville granted haven to the MPLA leadership in 1963, following the overthrow of the puppet French régime of Abbé Youlou, that MPLA was able to begin in earnest the long task of reconstructing their forces in friendly territory.[9] Another decisive break-through was the opening of the Eastern Front made possible by Zambian support. In the case of Mozambique, the early beginnings of FRELIMO were at a congress in Tanzania in 1962 of three organizations, all exile-based. Tanzanian facilities, encouragement and unstinting support contributed immeasurably to FRELIMO's ability to begin guerrilla struggle and to sustain it for ten years.

In the South African case there were not then in existence any contiguous friendly states with the capacity to risk open confrontation with the strong racist régime. South Africa was surrounded by a *cordon sanitaire* of states which stood in alliance with white supremacy or, like Botswana, Lesotho and Swaziland, were still hostages to its economic and military power. For the liberation movement this made the vital link between internal and external resources extremely complex. As it turned out, this complexity was underestimated; and, at the same time, the prospects of assistance from independent Africa on the required scale were overestimated. Indeed, the OAU had to accommodate itself to a unity which incorporated disparate levels of commitment to the anti-imperialist struggle. As a consequence, the ANC often received less assistance and facilities than the amount needed to implement its projects. It thus found itself in the vicious circle where its inability to begin armed actions was used as a justification for only lukewarm support, which in turn, made the task even more difficult.

Also over-optimistic was the assessment of the likely effect of the campaign to isolate and weaken the South African régime. For example, in 1963, the SACP Central Committee claimed that:

> Looked at from the viewpoint of the historical process, the South African régime is steadily and swiftly being driven into a position of isolation in which the armaments, capital and other forms of material and moral support which sustain it from abroad will one after another be cut short.[10]

Though the level of its own support was thus overestimated, the tenacity of external imperialist economic and military support for the racialist régime was under-estimated.

THE INTERNAL FACTORS

Although of some importance, the external factor is only one aspect of the problem. It is obvious that both then and now the progress of the struggle depends essentially upon political organization within the country and its capacity to mobilize internal revolutionary energies.

But every attempt to raise a struggle to a higher level involves new complexities and creates new dangers for both the organization and its membership. In answer to those who looked only to the organizational disasters which followed the armed struggle in the 1905 revolution, Lenin said:

Every new form of struggle, accompanied as it is by new dangers and new sacrifices inevitably 'disorganizes' organizations which are unprepared for this new form of struggle. Our propagandist circles were disorganized by recourse to methods of agitation. Our Committees were subsequently disorganized by recourse to demonstrations. Every military action in any war to a certain extent disorganizes the ranks of the fighters. But this does not mean that one must not fight. It means that one must learn to fight. That is all.[11]

He went on to point out that what would have disorganized the movement even more than organized guerrilla warfare, would have been the absence of resistance altogether. The same could well be said of South Africa. But it is nevertheless of capital importance for the future of the South African struggle to pinpoint those errors and misjudgements which contributed to the régime's successful counter-offensive.

In retrospect the main weaknesses are now apparent. First, the movement's own security screen which had seemed adequate in the previous period (despite ten years of illegal activity, the SACP, for example, did not suffer a single casualty until 1962), proved inadequate after the régime had refashioned its own instruments to meet the new challenge. The immunity of the earlier period had bred a mood of carelessness and bravado which was, in the end, to prove costly. The majority of leaders and rank-and-filers taking part in illegal activity were well known to the authorities from the period of open public campaigning, and very few of them 'went underground' in the sense of changing their existing identities and operating under a protective security screen. Only a few, like Mandela and Sisulu, went into hiding. But even their safety was daily threatened by their regular contact with others who were equally vulnerable, but who continued to lead their normal lives.

By mid-1963 the Rivonia underground headquarters had become a point of security weakness to the whole movement. The organizational nerve centre of the struggle came to be centred around this one headquarters; and there the lines of demarcation between the political and the military organizations became impermissibly blurred. The site of headquarters became known to more and more cadres who were drawn into its underground work. Decisions were taken from time to time to remove the headquarters, and to disperse some of its activities; but, influenced by a long period of safe operation which bred an unjustified contempt for the enemy's security police techniques, the implementation of these decisions lacked the necessary urgency. In June 1963 a well-prepared police raid on Rivonia resulted in the arrest of all the top leaders and the capture of valuable archives. This was followed by the rounding up of numerous other members of the ANC and MK whose detention and torture under the infamous 90-day law led to further successes by the security forces. South Africa's judicial framework, with all its inequalities, had up to then provided a degree of protection for those who fell into police hands. The new laws and interrogation techniques (learnt from the French army in Algeria and from the Portugese political police) gave the security forces a charter to force information out of those detained. Many resisted bravely but the majority who were subjected to standing torture, sleep deprivation and similar methods proved unable to resist.

Since casualties are unavoidable, it is a basic rule of conspiratorial work that the destructive effect be contained within the smallest possible limits. Those who take part in such work should obviously know only what is absolutely necessary for the performance of their tasks. This rule too was infringed, and thus successful interrogation under torture of many of those detained set up a chain reaction which made it easier for the security forces to immobilize almost every level of the movement's apparatus.

In the political sphere, too, distortions crept in. The commencement of armed struggle tends to monopolize more and more of the energies and resources of a movement, especially one unpractised in the art of the new strategy. It therefore requires a deliberate effort to ensure that the mass political and organizational factors are not, directly or indirectly, belittled. In the South Africa case, the energies and resources devoted to the planning and execution of acts of sabotage and to the military apparatus (and all its auxiliary requirements) began to affect the pace of political work amongst the people. If anything, the new strategy called for an intensification of mass propaganda and organization. In the words of Giap:

> If insurrection is said to be an art, the main content of this art is to know how to give to the struggle forms appropriate to the political situation at each stage, how to maintain the correct relation between forms of political struggle and those of armed struggle in each period. At the beginning the political struggle is the main task, the armed struggle a secondary one.[12]

In South Africa in the early sixties the increasing concentration of the liberation movements on military preparation helped to generate an attitude both within the organization and amongst the people that the fate of the struggle depended upon the sophisticated actions of a professional conspiratorial élite. The importance of the mass base was theoretically appreciated; but in practice mass political work was minimal. This attitude was to persist for some years after 1963 with propaganda tending to say too little about what initiatives people should be taking, and to treat them only as support groups for guerrilla units which would soon appear amongst them.

THE PROBLEMS OF THE POST-RIVONIA PERIOD

A few brave efforts were made inside the country after 1963 to create a new internal structure, but in the decade that followed the task of propaganda, reconstruction and further preparations for armed activities were assumed by the exile leadership.

The fact that, during this period, there was no effective leadership centre within the country also generated its own special problems: not least in the lack of intimate contact by the exile leadership with internal conditions and with the state of consciousness of the people, which effective revolutionary leadership demands.

From 1966 onwards, internal ANC and SACP propaganda once again appeared regularly, and numerous efforts were made to return trained personnel with equipment.

Unsuccessful attempts were made to filter back small groups through Botswana and other territories. Beginning in August

1967, joint ANC/ZAPU guerrilla units entered Zimbabwe. In the case of the ANC contingents, it was made plain that they were *en route* home but their interception by Rhodesian and South African security forces led to armed engagements. Although the battles which were fought took place outside South African territory, this was MK's baptism of battle with South African military forces called in by Smith. By all accounts confirmed by enemy reports they acted with heroism and competence. But one of the prime reasons for the failure of this incursion by the joint ANC/ZAPU groups was that, within Zimbabwe, there was not the requisite level of internal organization, mass mobilization and mass support without which armed activity may easily be strangled. For the liberation movements, the Zimbabwe incursions once again underlined the need for careful political preparation of the population and for guerrilla groups to be integrated within the community rather than functioning as isolated *foci*.

But if it remained true that armed tactics were a vital part of any future realistic advance in the struggle, the dilemma of timing still persisted. Experience of South Africa and other highly organized police states has shown that, until the new type of action is started, it is doubtful whether political mobilization and organization can be developed beyond a certain point. Given the disillusionment of the people with the old forms of struggle, a demonstration of the liberation movement's capacity to meet and sustain the struggle in a new way is in itself a vital way of attracting organized allegiance and support. Therefore, postponing all armed activity until political mobilization and organizational reconstruction have reached a high enough level to sustain its more advanced forms would undermine the prospects of full political mobilization itself.

Military planning, as opposed to political planning, has some mechanical aspects which inevitably require certain static assumptions to be made about the future. Creating a core of trained professional armed cadres, putting them into the field with adequate logistical support, and with adequate contact to carry them through the initial period, requires long-term planning. It cannot be an overnight response to a sudden twist in the political situation. If operations go smoothly and according to plan, the beginnings of armed action will be the result of a deliberate decision. If not, they could be triggered off prematurely, as for instance by the need of the armed group to defend itself against enemy attacks as happened in the 1967–8 Zimbabwe campaign. The exact moment when actual armed action takes place, therefore, does not always coincide with the most favourable local or national situation.

In general there can be no all-embracing formula which correlates the level of all-round readiness with the precise timing of armed actions. But, despite the degree of uncertainty inherent in this type of action, a case could be made out to show that, both in the sabotage campaign and in some of the subsequent efforts at armed activities, insufficient internal political and organizational preparation had been made to justify the chosen timing. Historically, however, 'the correctness and feasibility of this general policy decision (for armed struggle) were not, and are not, dependent on the success or failure of any particular scheme or operation.[13]

We must remember also that not every success of an enemy stems from a failure or a mistake on the part of the revolutionary force. A struggle is a contest in which there are two sides. The antagonist is not a passive object which feeds only on those items foolishly thrown in its direction. It is in continuous active engagement with those who threaten it; and when it scores, it often does so from its own strength and not only from the other side's miscalculations. To engage in struggle is to invite enemy counteraction. To make certain that no blows are ever inflicted means not to engage in struggle. This is not advanced as an apologia for some of the failings cited (all of which have been publicly admitted by the liberation movements): but it emphasizes the need to see these failings in the context of real social struggle, and not just as drawing-board miscalculations.

Certainly, it is fallacious to characterize the years which followed 1961 as wasted and to attribute the setbacks solely to organizational distortions, deficiencies in planning, or ill-judged timing. The inevitable future victory will undoubtedly owe a great deal to the persistence of the liberation movement's turn to a policy of armed struggle. Had it failed to act at all, it would have disappeared as a viable agency for change. Without actions which continued to emphasize that force is vital in the struggle for people's power, it would have left the field clear for a more ready acceptance at home and abroad of a reformist rather than a revolutionary solution. The régime's pursuit of its Bantustan policies and its endeavours, on the basis of these policies and other minor reforms, to seek an accommodation with independent Africa, would face fewer obstacles, if the potential armed alternative had not been kept alive by the persistent attempts of the liberation movement. The current resurgence of black political militancy within the country, particularly amongst the workers and youth, is primarily a response to a whole set of changing objective factors, including (in the case of the workers) the growing gap between wages and prices. But the revolutionary tradition perpetuated by the liberation movement's actions, not only played a part in this resurgence but serves to inform it with more radical aims.

THE GUERRILLA PERSPECTIVE

It is clear that the South African liberation movement's endeavour to lay a basis for sustained armed struggle is perhaps the most difficult on the whole African continent. The enemy here is in stable command of a rich and varied economy, which can finance a massive military budget, of £594 million in 1975, even at the stage when it is not required to extend itself. It has a well-trained army and para-military police force. It can draw on considerable manpower resources from amongst the overwhelming majority of the four million privileged whites, who can be expected to fight with great ferocity and conviction to sustain their privileges. In addition it has rich and influential allies to help build its military and economic potential. It faces an unarmed people historically deprived of opportunities to learn the skills of modern warfare. And it has one of the most sophisticated repressive security machines in the world. If then the employment of force is a subjective imperative, what about these objective difficulties?

The recent history of guerrilla struggle has underlined the fact that the material strength of the enemy is by no means a decisive factor. Witness the resources at the disposal of the French in Algeria; at the height of the fighting, 600,000 troops were supplied and serviced by a leading industrial nation from an economic base quite outside the reach of military operations. Consider the unsurpassed superiority of pure material strength and almost limitless resources of the U.S.A. in Vietnam? Yet neither modern industrial backing, technical know-how nor fire-power swayed the balance in favour of the invaders. Grivas and his Cyprus group challenged the British Army with forty-seven rifles, twenty-seven automatic weapons and seven revolvers. ('It was with these arms and these alone that I kept the fight going for almost a year without any appreciable reinforcements.')[14]

Guerrilla warfare, almost by definition, posits a situation of vast imbalance in material and military resources between the opposing sides. It is designed to cope particularly with a situation in which the enemy is infinitely superior in every conventional factor of warfare. It is supremely the weapon of the materially weak against the materially strong. With a populace increasingly supporting and protecting it whilst opposing and exposing the enemy, a people's army is assured of survival and growth by skilful exercise of tactics. Surprise, mobility and tactical retreat make it difficult for the enemy to bring its superior fire-power into play in any decisive battles. No individual battle is fought under circumstances unfavourable to the guerrilla. Superior force can be harassed, weakened and, in the end, destroyed.

The absence of an orthodox front of fighting lines; the need of the enemy to attenuate his resources and lines of communication over vast distances; his need to protect the widely scattered installations on which his economy is dependent (because the guerrilla pops up now here, now there): these are amongst the factors which serve in the long run, to compensate the guerrillas for their disparity in initial strength. I stress the words 'in the long run' because it would be idle to dispute that for a long time the enemy has considerable military advantages from his high level of industrialization, his ready-to-hand reserves of manpower and his excellent roads, railways and air transport which facilitate swift manoeuvre and speedy concentration of personnel.

But over a period of time, many of these very factors could begin to operate in favour of the liberation force. The resources, including food production, depend overwhelmingly upon black labour which will not remain docile and co-operative if the struggle grows in intensity. The white manpower resources, adequate initially, must become dangerously stretched as guerrilla warfare develops. The mobilization of a large force for a protracted struggle would place a further burden on the workings of the economy. The South African Director-General of Strategic Studies, General J. H. Robbertze, stressed the vulnerability of the South African economy in a paper *On the strategic implications of recent developments in South Africa*, presented to an international conference in Paris in early 1975.[15] He apprehensively predicted the establishment of 'active guerrilla bases' in both Angola and Mozambique. Of South Africa's agricultural production, he declared that, 'in the event of civil war or generalized violence this intricate economic machinery will be disrupted or destroyed'. Many installations, vital power and water supplies might be disrupted with disastrous effects; mines could be flooded. All this, General Robbertze maintains, could lead directly to a virtual paralysis of industrial activity in the country.

In contrast to many other major guerrilla struggles (Cuba was one of the exceptions), the enemy's economic and manpower resources are all situated within South Africa, the theatre of war. There is no economic base area which can remain safe from sabotage, mass action and guerrilla strikes. In an underdeveloped country, the interruption of supplies to any given region may be no more than a local setback. But in a highly sensitive modern economic structure of the South African type, the successful interruption of transport to any major industrial complex would inflict immense damage on the whole economy and on the morale of the enemy. The South African forces would have the task of keeping intact about 30,000 miles of railway lines spread across an area of over 400,000 square miles.

One of the more popular misconceptions concerning guerrilla warfare is that a physical environment which conforms to a special pattern is indispensable: thick jungle, inaccessible mountain ranges, swamps, and so forth. The availability of such terrain is, to be sure, of enormous advantage to the guerrillas, especially in the early non-operational phase when training and other preparatory steps are undertaken, and no external bases are available for this purpose. However, when the operations commence, the guerrilla cannot survive, let alone flourish, unless he moves to areas where people live and work and where the enemy can be engaged in combat. If he is fortunate enough to have behind him a friendly border or areas of difficult access which can provide temporary refuge, it is of course advantageous; although it sometimes brings with it its own set of problems, connected mainly with supplies. But guerrilla warfare can, and has been, successfully waged in every conceivable type of terrain; in deserts, in swamps, in farm fields, in built-up areas, in plains, in the bush and in countries without friendly borders.

The sole question is one of adjusting survival tactics to the sort of terrain in which operations have to be conducted. In any case, in the vast expanse that is South Africa, a people's force will find a multitude of variations in topography; deserts, mountain forests, veld, and swamps. There might not be a single impregnable Sierra Maestra or impenetrable jungle, but the country abounds in terrain which in general is certainly no less favourable for guerrilla operations than some of the terrain in which the Algerians or the resistance movements in occupied Europe operated. Tito, when told that a certain area was 'as level as the palm of your hand and with very little forests', retorted: 'What a first-class example it is of the relative unimportance of geographical factors in the development of a rising.'

In particular, South Africa's great size will make it extremely difficult, if not impossible, for the ruling power to keep the whole of it under armed surveillance in strength and in depth. Hence, an early development of a relatively safe (though shifting) rear is not beyond the realm of possibility. The undetected existence of a SWAPO training camp inside Namibia for over a year and, more especially, the survival for years in the mountains and hills in the Transkei of the leaders of 'Intaba' during the military occupation of the area after the 1960 Pondo Revolt, support this possibility.

A LOOK AHEAD

But, theory aside, the stark reality is that after more than ten years of effort, there is as yet no evidence of any form of military engagement inside the country. Critics of the liberation movement's strategy during this period have attributed its lack of success to a combination of organizational mistakes and formidable objective obstacles. They point to the fact that since the immediate post-Sharpeville low, the régime has shown a relative economic and political stability, has strengthened its external ties, and has not faced a crisis of the proportions which normally precedes a revolutionary break-through. They question whether there are 'grounds for declaring that (the people) prefer death to oppression, the finality of annihilation to the indeterminacy of existence',[16] and ask whether there is a psychological readiness and a motivation amongst the Africans to use violence.[17]

Some academic analysts also conclude that the people's readiness to seek a solution by force seems minimal since, 'in spite of the structural violence embodied in South African society, individual violent reactions against this situation have been remarkably limited'.[18] Doubt is expressed whether there are present in South Africa the very specialized conditions in which armed revolutions have made headway elsewhere.[19] It is also suggested that the 'reformist option' persisted 'long past the point in time when a decision to shift from non-violent struggle might have stood a remote chance of possible success'.[20]

In one form or another, all the critics stress the difficulties of an unarmed people, deprived of opportunities to learn the skills of modern warfare, engaging a powerful and highly industrialized enemy; a factor aggravated by the absence of friendly border states. Most also allude to the negative effects of exile politics in a period in which internal national leadership had been destroyed.

To recognise the validity or partial validity of some of these assessments does not imply that the armed tactic has no place in South Africa's future liberation strategy. Indeed, the ANC and its allies continue to regard the introduction of force as one of the main foundations of such a strategy. They do so for a number of reasons. In the first place (as emphasized in chapter 1) the struggle for majority rule in South Africa today has no realistic backing without it. To abandon the armed tactic is to abandon the people to forces willing to settle for the scraps of power and not its substance. However long the struggle still takes and however many lessons there are still to be learnt, it is unthinkable for South African revolutionaries, in this era, to return to struggle for reforms only within the white framework; for this is the only alternative.

The obstacles facing the liberation movement in pursuit of its strategy may have disappointed earlier hopes and defied some of the more optimistic predictions. But the defeatist conclusions of many academic analysts are static in their conception and show an onlooker's separation from the demands and processes of active revolutionary struggle. Was there any demonstrable evidence in Mozambique in 1962, when FRELIMO charted the armed path, that the mass preferred 'death to oppression' or that they were psychologically ready to use violence? Were there any more individual reactions against violence in pre-1958 Guinea-Bissau than there are in South Africa? Were the French occupiers of Algeria or the Portuguese occupiers of Angola passing through an identifiable moment of economic or political collapse when the liberation forces in these territories launched their own armed activities? Did the Cubans have a friendly border? Did none of these movements make serious tactical mistakes and were they not also, for a time, dogged by the exile syndrome?

The combination of favourable and unfavourable conditions in which each of these struggles had to be launched was different in each territory. South Africa, too, is a special case. But what is common to them all is that a people which has exhausted the 'reformist option' responds to the revolutionary one when the feasibility of hitting the enemy has been demonstrated by deeds as well as words.

Experiences have been gained and lessons learnt by the ANC and its allies. Against the background of the changing external and internal situations, a more hopeful basis is emerging for the success of a strategy which includes the factor of organized force.

Inside the country there are once again signs of a significant upswing in political awareness and militancy. This will gain momentum as the system remains incapable of overcoming the ever-recurring financial and economic crises inherent in the capitalist mode of production, and more especially as the special contradictions which flow from its internal racialist-colonialist character intensify. The efforts to slow down and reverse the process of permanent black urbanization has not succeeded, and white dependance on black labour is growing inexorably.* This, together with the depressed state of black wages, has already triggered off economic struggles in the recent period which are giving the workers a renewed consciousness of their collective strength. The mining industry, so dependent on foreign labour, faces severe difficulties of labour supply and is being forced to reconsider its migratory labour policies. The creation of a more permanent black work force would, for obvious reason, strengthen the potential for class-based economic and political pressures.

In the Reserves a situation with enormous explosive potential is being created by the crowding into its limited area of more and more millions of impoverished, land-hungry and unemployed Africans.†

*According to Dr Cyril Wyndham of the Chamber of Mines Human Sciences Laboratory, by 1980 South Africa will have an economically active population of 10·4 million of which only 1·7 million will be white. *Financial Mail*, 2 August 1974, p. 408.

†The Government's Tomlinson Commission (1956) talked of the need to create 500,000 new jobs over a ten-year period in and around the Reserves if progress were to be made in the implementation of apartheid. According to the Government-supporting Afrikaanse Handels Instituut (*Rand Daily Mail*, 18 August 1973) only 8,000 new jobs had been created in all the Bantustans in the previous 10 years. In the 'border' regions the figure for the 11½ years from June 1960 to December 1972 is 78,451. Tomlinson also claimed that the Reserves, which now have a population of 7 million, could only reasonably support life for 2·3 million people even if his recommendations for development investment were carried out.

The working and student youth in particular are in search of a strategy which will begin to lay the basis of the struggle for power. At the universities and in the schools the mood is one of growing hostility to white rule. Organizations such as SASO have not only challenged government policy at the educational institutions but have involved themselves in wider political struggles.

Government attempts to gain Coloured and Indian acceptance of relatively powerless communal institutions as a substitute for direct political representation have made little headway. The Coloured Labour Party, in particular, has once again (in the March 1975 elections) won overwhelming support for its rejection of differential institutions. Indian workers in Natal showed an impressive degree of solidarity with the striking Africans, and many Indian youths have begun to play an active role in newly formed black organizations with militant anti-Apartheid postures. New attempts have been made to revive the Indian Congress movement.

But in all these areas of reawakening, it is already clear that police harassment and intimidation set a limit to the activity and growth of purely legal mass structures. Beyond the struggle for 'moderate' reforms within the framework of continuing white domination, there hovers the state's legal and administrative hatchet. Thus the renewed awareness can no longer express itself, as it could during the fifties, in sustained mass demonstrations. Nor can the struggle for power be mounted by mass legal pressures alone, although these constitute an essential ingredient in the unfolding of the struggle. Without the direct or indirect backing of offensive and defensive force and effective underground mass leadership, the limits are self-evident; but, with it, this ferment once again sets a more hopeful scene for radical political advances.

If the elusive psychological factor is to be given its place in the projection of future responses to armed activity, there can be no doubt that it has become more favourable for South Africa's liberation movement. The armed victories in the former Portuguese territories and the perceptible progress of armed actions in Zimbabwe and in the Caprivi Strip have had a great inspirational impact on South Africa's black people: because, unlike other such victories, they have happened and are happening next door. And, as already emphasized, these events have also driven home to South Africa's ruling class the growing likelihood of internal insurgency in the not-too-distant future.

But the people's expectations and the enemy's fears aside, there can be no doubt that the dramatic transformation which has taken place in southern Africa has eliminated one of the most serious obstacles in the path of people's insurgency. South Africa is no longer cushioned by states actively hostile to the South African liberation movement. This is not to belittle South Africa's internal strength, which is shored up by direct and behind-the-scenes support from the West. Nor can we dismiss the continued possibility of 'some independent African states taking a leading part in championing the cause of what amounts to collaboration with the counter-revolution'.[21] But despite these factors, both the internal and external balance of forces have become much more favourable to liberation endeavours. The changes that have taken place, especially on South Africa's borders, provide the more militant lobby in the OAU with renewed incentives to oppose the trend of compromise perceptible in the Lusaka Manifesto and in the recent dialogue manoeuvres.

But at the end of the day, the tendencies to support the liberation drive will only become lasting realities through the efforts of the liberation movement itself and its support groups throughout the world. Above all, the extent to which the world translates its verbal condemnation of the racist régime into significant action against it and more direct support for the liberation movement, will depend upon events inside the country.

The liberation movement recognizes that well-planned activities by its armed wing is not the only immediate perspective of struggle in South Africa. Mass political mobilization of people in the urban and rural areas is a vital ingredient and requires a combination of all methods: legal, semi-legal and clandestine. The muscle power of the black working class needs to find stronger organizational expression through the building of a powerful trade union movement. The Bantustan deception must be exposed and fought both inside and outside the so-called 'homelands'. The struggle can no longer be centred on pleas for civil rights or for reforms within the framework of white dominance; it is a struggle for people's power, in which mass ferment and the growing importance of the armed factor go hand in hand. The liberation movement points to this as the only path which can be trodden by the oppressed mass if it is not to submit permanently to white overlordship. An underground leadership presence within the country itself is the most vital element in the phase ahead, and there are signs that this is closer than at any time since the pre-Rivonia period.

All this does not mean that the revolution is around the corner. It rather signifies that conditions for its unfolding are perhaps more favourable today than at any time this century.

Oliver Tambo, the Acting President-General of the ANC, in a speech delivered in June 1973, said:

> In South Africa, the long stalemate since Rivonia is undeniably over. Everywhere in Southern Africa our struggles are gathering a new momentum and our peoples are striking out in several directions against the Apartheid and colonialist régimes. There is no peace for the enemy. They live in a state of apprehension, doubt and fear. They no longer strut about with arrogant confidence in the permanence of their power. Instead they are now frantically directing their energies into repairing the floodgates which menacingly threaten to burst open in revolution throughout the Southern African region.[22]

When Tambo spoke these words, the situation seemed on the surface less promising than he claimed. FRELIMO, MPLA, and PAIGC were still locked in struggle with Portuguese colonialism; Smith, with Vorster's backing, still clung arrogantly to his belief in the permanence of white rule in Zimbabwe; Namibia was still a routine item on the U.N. agenda; and Vorster seemed unthreatened in his racialist fortress. But the turbulence below, which Tambo so correctly sensed, was to surface dramatically. Within a year Portuguese colonialism was no more. Smith was talking a less assured language while Zimbabwean guerrillas cut deep into his territory. Vorster was frantically making his gestures on 'petty Apartheid' and Namibia. Although these and other gestures were of little substance, they nevertheless marked the measure of his apprehension of things to come.

This dramatic lunge forward in the sub-continent's history was the fruit of protracted endeavour and sacrifice by the liberation movements. The unexpectedly swift change was, however, triggered off by an event thousands of miles away: the overthrow of the Fascist dictatorship in Portugal. But the apparently 'accidental' trigger of Lisbon's April Coup was, like all such 'so-called accidents', merely 'the form behind which necessity lurks.'[23]

In South Africa too, struggle in the new conditions sets the scene for the fulfilment of its historical necessity – the early achievement of liberation and freedom from exploitation.

Notes

Chapter 1: The Answer to Minority Rule

1. 'Strategy and Tactics of the African National Congress': adopted by the Third Consultative Conference of the African National Congress in April 1969 at Morogoro, Tanzania. The Conference was attended by over seventy delegates and included about a dozen delegates selected by the ANC Executive by virtue of their connection with the allied organization – South African Indian Congress, South African Congress of Trade Unions, Coloured People's Congress, and the South African Communist Party. Published in *Sechaba*, 3 July 1969.

2. Punt Jansen, Deputy Minister of Bantu Administration, quoted in the *Rand Daily Mail*, 10 August 1973.

3. *The Times*, 8 October 1974.

4. Karel Roskam, *Inter-Racial Relationships in the Union of South Africa*, Leiden, p. 111.

5. House of Assembly speech, quoted in the *Rand Daily Mail*, 31 August 1974.

6. House of Assembly speech quoted in Roskam, op. cit., p. 94.

7. H. J. May, *The South African Constitution*, Allen and Unwin, 1955, p. 153.

8. 'Strategy and Tactics', (ANC), op. cit.

9. Report to a Plenary Session of the Central Committee of the South African Communist Party, *African Communist*, 1st Quarter 1974, p. 32.

10. 'Strategy and Tactics', (ANC), op. cit.

11. Quoted by Harold J. Laski, 6th Roy Calvert Memorial Lecture, 1940.

12. *Rand Daily Mail*, 31 August 1974.

Chapter 2: The Theory of the South African Revolution

1. V. I. Lenin, 'A Retrograde Trend in Russian Social Democracy', *Collected Works*, Vol. 4, Lawrence and Wishart, p. 280.

2. *Financial Mail*, 6 September 1974, p. 901 (quoting Mike McGrath in a paper presented to a Durban economics conference).

3. *Survey of Race Relations*, South African Institute of Race Relations (SAIRR), 1974, p. 52.

4. '*Fact Paper*', SAIRR, 14 February 1972.

5. *Survey of Race Relations*, SAIRR, 1974, pp. 210–11.

6. T. M. Molathlwa, *South African Institute of Internal Affairs*, December 1974, pp. 11–12.

7. Karl Marx, *The German Ideology*, Part One, Lawrence and Wishart, 1970, p. 82.

8. H. J. Simons, 'What is Apartheid?', *Liberation*, No. 36, 1959 and 'Concepts of Apartheid', *Liberation*, No. 39, 1959.

9. 'Strategy and Tactics', (ANC), op. cit.

10. 'Strategy and Tactics', (ANC), op. cit.

11. *The African Communist*, 1st Quarter 1963, pp. 24–70.

12. Quoted in Oliver Walker, *Kaffirs Are Lively*, Victor Gollancz, 1948, p. 22.

13. A. Zanzolo, 'The Theory of the South African Revolution', *African Communist*, 1st Quarter, 1963, p. 22.

14. Published by A.N.C. External Mission.

15. ibid.

16. V. I. Lenin, 'What Is To Be Done?', *Collected Works*, Vol. 5, Lawrence and Wishart, p. 384.

Chapter 3: The Resistance

1. Quoted in Edward Roux, *Time Longer Than Rope*, University of Wisconsin Press, 1966, p. 40.

2. ibid., pp. 14–15.

3. Monica Wilson and Leonard Monteath Thompson (eds), *Oxford History of South Africa*, Vol. 1, Oxford University Press, 1969, p. 347.

4. Cornelis W. De Kiewiet, *Imperial Factor in South Africa*, Frank Cass, 1965, p. 220.

5. Donald R. Morris, *The Washing of the Spears*, Sphere Books, 1969, p. 283.

6. H. J. and R.E. Simons, *Class and Colour in South Africa 1850–1950*, Penguin, 1969, p. 123.

7. Ibid., p. 290.

8. Zanzolo, op. cit., p. 21.

9. A detailed description of these events and their significance is contained in Govan Mbeki, *South Africa, The Peasants' Revolt*, Penguin, 1964.

10. 'Strategy and Tactics', (ANC) op. cit.

11. A. Lerumo, *Fifty Fighting Years*, Inkululeko Publications, 1971, p. 96.

12. Report of Joint Planning Council, quoted in Edward Feit, *South Africa, The Dynamics of the African National Congress*, Oxford University Press, 1962, p. 27.

13. Report to SACP Plenary Session of Central Committee, *African Communist*, 3rd Quarter 1968, pp. 9–10.

14. 'Strategy and Tactics', (ANC), op. cit.

15. *Contact*, 1 November 1958.

16. 'Frelimo Faces the Future': Interview, *African Communist*, 4th Quarter 1973, p. 51.

Chapter 4: Perspectives of Armed Struggle

1. Clausewitz, *On War*, Pelican Edition, 1968, p. 223.

2. V. I. Lenin, 'Lessons of the Moscow Uprising', in William J. Pomeroy (ed.), *Guerrilla Warfare and Marxism*, Lawrence and Wishart, 1969, p. 79.

3. Bashir Hadj Ali, in Pomeroy, op. cit., p. 259.

4. V. I. Lenin, *Collected Works*, Vol. 31, Lawrence and Wishart, p. 85.

5. V. I. Lenin, 'Address to Communist Organisations of the Peoples of the East', *Collected Works*, Vol. 30, Lawrence and Wishart, p. 162.

6. Sheridan Johns, 'Obstacles to Guerrilla Warfare – a South African case study', *Journal of Modern African Studies*, No. 2, 1973, p. 272.

7. Nelson Mandela, *No Easy Walk to Freedom*, Heinemann, 1965, p. 171.

8. Amilcar Cabral, *Portuguese Colonies, Victory or Death*, Tricontinental, April 1971, pp. 143–4.

9. Basil Davidson, *In the Eye of the Storm: Angola's People*, Allen Lane, 1972, Penguin, 1975, pp. 233–6.

10. *African Communist*, 2nd Quarter 1963, p. 6.

11. V. I. Lenin, 'Guerrilla Warfare', *Collected Works*, Vol. 11, Lawrence and Wishart, p. 220.

12. Vo Nguyen Giap, in Pomeroy, op. cit., p. 205.

13. Central Committee of the SACP, *African Communist*, 4th Quarter 1971, p. 29.

14. *The Memoirs of General Grivas*, Longman, 1964, p. 22.

15. *Rand Daily Mail*, 22 March, 1975.

16. Leo Kuper, 'Non-Violence Revisited', in Robert I. Rotberg and Ali A. Mazrui, *Protest and Power in Black Africa*, Oxford University Press, 1970, p. 797.

17. Fatima Meer, 'African Nationalism – Some Inhibiting Factors, *South African Sociological Perspectives*, pp. 121–57.

18. Herbert Adam, *Modernizing Racial Domination: The Dynamic of South African Politics*, University of California Press, 1971, p. 116.

19. J. Bowyer Bell, *The Myth of the Guerrilla: Revolutionary Theory and Malpractice*, New York, 1971; and 'The Future of Guerrilla Revolution in Southern Africa', *Africa Today*, Winter 1972. Also Lewis H. Gann, 'No Hope for Violent Revolution: A Strategic Assessment', *Africa Report*, 17 February 1972.

20. Johns, op. cit., pp. 296–7. Johns' is perhaps the most informative discussion of the period in question.

21. Declaration of ANC Executive Committee, 17–20 March 1975.

22. *Sechaba*, September 1973, p. 19.

23. F. Engels, 'Ludwig Feuerbach and the End of German Classical Philosophy', Chapter 4, in Marx/Engels, *Selected Works* (3 volume edition), Progress Publishers, Vol. 3, p. 363.

Part Three:
From Rhodesia to Zimbabwe

Anthony R. Wilkinson

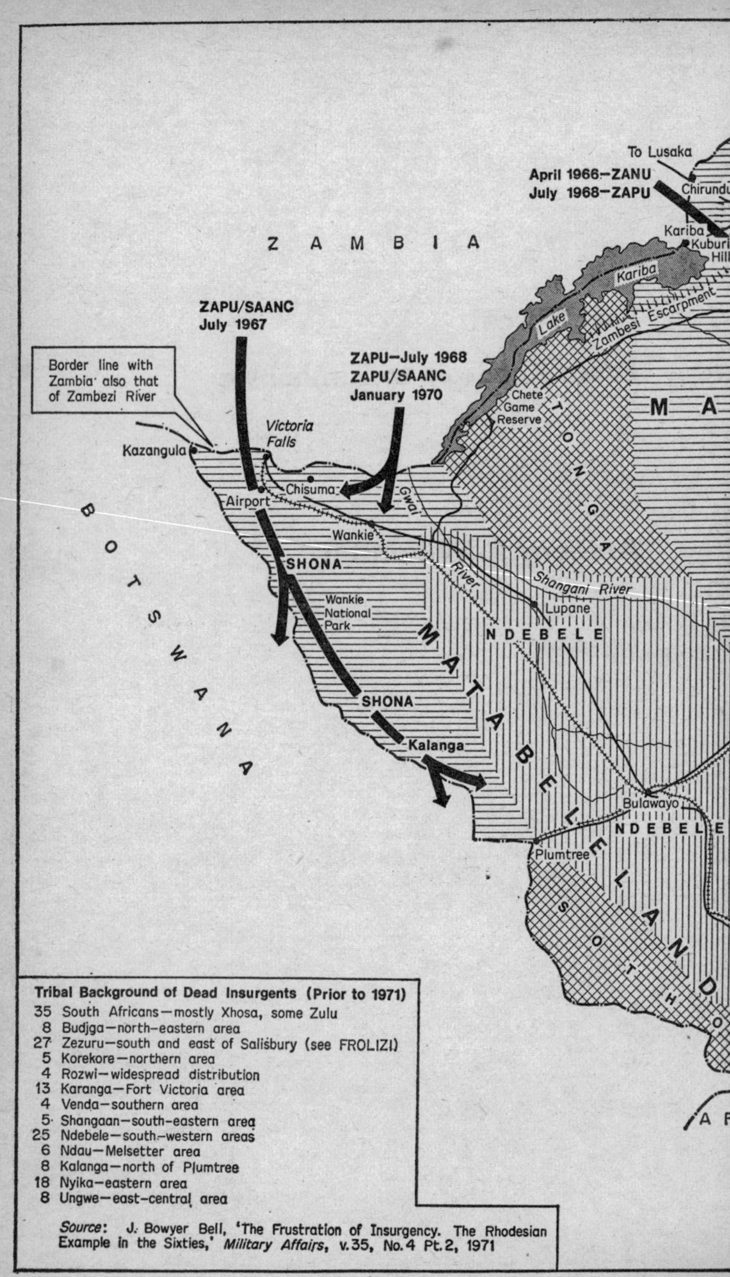

To Lusaka
April 1966–ZANU
July 1968–ZAPU
Chirundu
Kariba
Kuburi
Hills
Z A M B I A
Kariba
Lake
Zambesi Escarpment
ZAPU/SAANC
July 1967
Border line with
Zambia also that
of Zambezi River
ZAPU–July 1968
ZAPU/SAANC
January 1970
Chete
Game
Reserve
M A
Victoria
Falls
Kazangula
Chisuma
Airport
Gwai
T O N G A
Wankie
B O T S W A N A
SHONA
River
Shangani River
Wankie
National
Park
Lupane
NDEBELE
M A T A B E L E L A N D
SHONA
Kalanga
Bulawayo
NDEBELE
Plumtree
S O T H O
A F
Tribal Background of Dead Insurgents (Prior to 1971)
35 South Africans—mostly Xhosa, some Zulu
8 Budjga—north-eastern area
27 Zezuru—south and east of Salisbury (see FROLIZI)
5 Korekore—northern area
4 Rozwi—widespread distribution
13 Karanga—Fort Victoria area
4 Venda—southern area
5 Shangaan—south-eastern area
25 Ndebele—south-western areas
6 Ndau—Melsetter area
8 Kalanga—north of Plumtree
18 Nyika—eastern area
8 Ungwe—east-central area
Source: J. Bowyer Bell, 'The Frustration of Insurgency. The Rhodesian Example in the Sixties,' Military Affairs, v.35, No.4 Pt.2, 1971

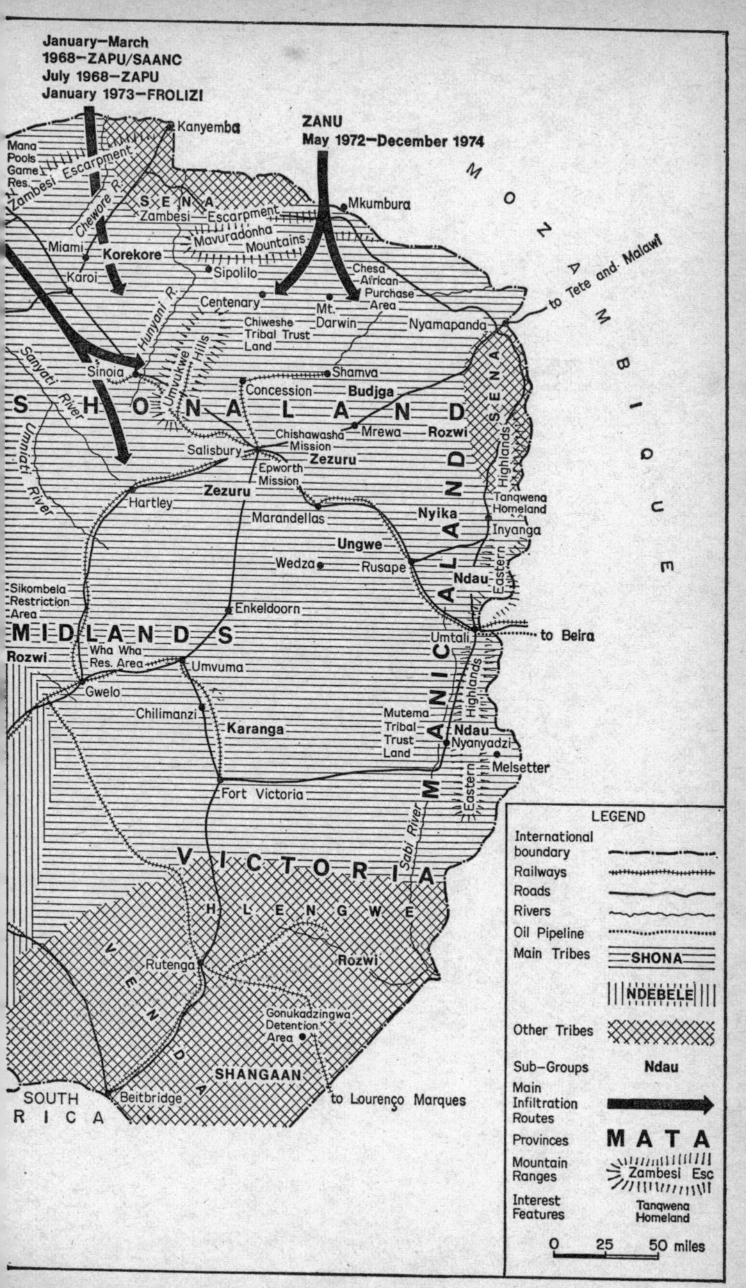
January–March
1968–ZAPU/SAANC
July 1968–ZAPU
January 1973–FROLIZI
ZANU
May 1972–December 1974
Kanyemba
Mana Pools Game Res.
Zambesi Escarpment
Chewore R.
SENA
Zambesi Escarpment
Mavuradonha Mountains
Mkumbura
MOZAMBIQUE
Miami
Korekore
Karoi
Sipolilo
Chesa African Purchase Area
Centenary
Mt. Darwin
Chiweshe Tribal Trust Land
Nyamapanda
to Tete and Malawi
Hunyani R.
Sanyati River
Umvukwe Hills
Sinoia
Shamva
Concession
Budjga
SHONALAND
Umniati River
Chishawasha Mission
Mrewa
Rozwi
Salisbury
Epworth Mission
Zezuru
Highlands
Hartley
Tanqwena Homeland
Marandellas
Nyika
Inyanga
Ungwe
Wedza
Rusape
Eastern
Ndau
Sikombela Restriction Area
Enkeldoorn
MIDLANDS
Umtali
to Beira
Rozwi
Wha Wha Res. Area
Umvuma
MANICALAND
Gwelo
Chilimanzi
Karanga
Mutema Tribal Trust Land
Nyanyadzi
Melsetter
Fort Victoria
Sabi River
VICTORIA
HLENGWE
VENDA
Rutenga
Rozwi
Gonukadzingwa Detention Area
SHANGAAN
SOUTH AFRICA
Beitbridge
to Lourenço Marques
LEGEND
International boundary
Railways
Roads
Rivers
Oil Pipeline
Main Tribes
SHONA
NDEBELE
Other Tribes
Sub-Groups
Ndau
Main Infiltration Routes
Provinces
MATA
Mountain Ranges
Zambesi Esc
Interest Features
Tanqwena Homeland
0 25 50 miles

Introduction

Chou En-lai, when visiting Somalia in February 1964, stated that 'revolutionary prospects throughout the African continent are excellent'. Ten years later, following the Lisbon coup of 25 April 1974, nationalist liberation movements in Angola, Mozambique and Guinea-Bissau called an end to their protracted insurgency campaigns against an estimated 150,000 (by 1974) troops which had been committed to the maintenance of Portuguese rule in these territories. Throughout the past decade Rhodesia has also experienced recurrent bouts of insurgency which have varied in their effectiveness. During the latter half of the 1960s, incursions from Zambia by several groups of insurgents were contained by Rhodesian security forces. Since the end of 1972, however, the nationalist insurgents have not only intensified their military activity but have also widened their area of operations to a point where very considerable strains have been imposed on the counter-insurgency capacities of the Rhodesian Administration.

South Africa has remained almost unscathed by such activity. Yet an announcement in June 1974 that the army was to take over responsibility from the police for all security matters in South-West Africa (Namibia), reflected an increasing preoccupation with military security in the Caprivi Strip, where there have been sporadic encounters with insurgents operating out of bases in Zambia. Moreover, the Lisbon coup and Portugal's withdrawal from Angola and Mozambique have altered the strategic balance in southern Africa by removing two of the lesser props to white rule and rendering a third, Rhodesia, much less viable as a buffer state.

Rhodesia's political and geographical position has given her a particular strategic importance in the confrontation between

White and Black in southern Africa. Until the changed situation in Mozambique, Rhodesia, together with Botswana, provided the most direct physical access into the Republic of South Africa, regarded by her enemies as the power-house for the whole system of white supremacy. Recent events suggest that white Rhodesia, unlike South Africa, has neither the human nor the material resources to sustain for any considerable time the luxury of racial privilege dependent on a system of social, economic and political discrimination. Yet Britain, unlike Portugal in the case of Angola and Mozambique, is in no position, as the responsible colonial power, to persuade or to force the white settler community to come to terms with the pressures of black nationalism.

Given these factors, it may be helpful to trace the development of political violence in Rhodesia from the emergence of modern black nationalism to the present and then to assess the Rhodesian situation in the wider context of southern Africa. By relating the history of the conflict to aspects of established insurgency and counter-insurgency thinking, it is possible to identify recognizable stages in this development.

Che Guevara wrote in *Guerrilla Warfare*:

> People must see clearly the futility of maintaining the fight for social goals within the framework of civil debate . . . Where a government has come into power through some form of popular vote, fraudulent or not, and maintains at least an appearance of constitutional legality, the guerrilla outbreak cannot be promoted, since the possibilities of peaceful struggle have not yet been exhausted.[1]

The years 1957 to 1965 in Rhodesia corresponded to such a constitutionalist phase, when representations first to the ruling white minority, and then to Britain, as the responsible power, failed to produce the elimination of racial discrimination and a transition to majority rule. Internal nationalist pressure and British influence did, however, lead the white community in Rhodesia to concede a reasonably moderate, multi-racial constitution in 1961. After some initial hesitation, this was rejected as inadequate by the nationalists. After 1961, nationalist policy was aimed at forcing British intervention to implement an acceptable constitution. Britain's failure in November 1965 to prevent the Rhodesian Front Government's illegal assumption of independence was a severe setback to this policy, and 1966 saw the first military encounters arising from the decision to embark on a campaign of insurgency warfare; although nationalist strategy appeared to be influenced by expectations of British or United Nations intervention as late as 1968.

In *On Protracted War*, Mao Tse-tung identifies and analyses a three-stage progression towards total revolutionary warfare. During the *strategic defensive* phase, the emphasis is on the political mobilization of the population, before the initiation of guerrilla warfare which should be limited to small defensive operations designed to protect the guerrilla bands and their bases. At this stage the guerrillas avoid becoming involved in positional warfare. A condition of *stalemate* is achieved by retaining the tactical initiative; and a quick victory is denied to the incumbent régime, whose forces suffer from falling morale. The guerrilla units are thus enabled to expand and consolidate; and towards the end of this stage it becomes possible for the first regular units to be formed as the *strategic counter-offensive* is reached. The national revolutionary army is then sufficiently strong to engage the forces of the incumbent régime in conventional positional warfare, supplemented by guerrilla activities.

John Pustay, in *Counter-Insurgency Warfare*, refers to a similar process when he describes insurgency as

> that composite conflict phenomenon which can be defined as the cellular development of resistance against an incumbent political régime and which expands from the initial stage of subversion-infiltration through the intermediate stages of overt resistance by small armed bands and insurrection to final fruition in civil war.[2]

Mao Tse-tung was fortunate in not having to face the problems involved in building up a guerrilla force from scratch. He was able to use sections of the population already possessing some degree of military experience and political motivation. He did not, therefore, need to pay much attention to the initiatory stages of the *strategic defensive*. Fidel Castro and Che Guevara, on the other hand, were not so fortunate. Che Guevara refers to these difficulties in his chapter on 'Organization in Secret of the First Guerrilla Band':

Almost all the popular movements undertaken against dictators in recent times have suffered from the same fundamental fault of inadequate preparation. The rules of conspiracy, which demand extreme secrecy and caution, have not generally been observed. The governmental power of the country frequently knows in advance about the intention of the group or groups.

In Rhodesia, the period from the nationalist rejection of the 1961 Constitution to the 1965 unilateral declaration of independence (UDI) was characterized by what Pustay describes as 'subversion-infiltration'; and this was successfully contained by stringent legislation and effective police action based on advance intelligence about nationalist plans. During 1966–8 the nationalists appear to have attempted to move into the intermediate stage of 'overt resistance' without sufficient preparation. The premature use of large, externally based insurgent columns in what amounted more to a form of 'positional' warfare than to small-scale actions by guerrilla bands made the job of the numerically superior and more mobile security forces a good deal easier, and their counter-insurgency operations were generally successful. Insurgent activities since 1972 suggest that this bitter experience led to a reappraisal by the nationalists of their tactics and strategy, which have more recently shown a greater attention to careful political preparation of the local population and the adoption of classic guerrilla 'hit and run' attacks by small, locally-based groups.

In the main, official Rhodesian statements on security force and insurgent casualties are certainly closer to reality than the sometimes impossibly extravagant claims made by the nationalists. It would be extremely difficult for the Rhodesian authorities to conceal – at least from the small white community – such losses as the insurgents have claimed to have inflicted. These claims do, of course, have a propaganda effect which may or may not be counter-productive. They have certainly reinforced the contempt in which many Whites hold the nationalists.* Also, if they were true, the Rhodesian Air Force would now have fewer aircraft than is in fact the case.

*For example the Commander of the Armed Forces, Lieutenant-General G. P. Walls, in an address to the annual convention of the Rhodesian

However, security force communiqués do not necessarily provide a clear picture either. The location of a particular incident is rarely revealed except in the most general terms. Neither are the circumstances of 'accidents' involving security personnel, vehicles and aircraft always fully explained. A complaint from a correspondent in the *Rhodesia Herald* on 10 April 1974 about the non-disclosure of a landmine incident prompted the Ministry of Information to reply that 'for security reasons it is not Government policy to give details of every single incident that occurs in the operational areas'.

Words like *terrorist* and *freedom-fighter* are inevitably contentious; the use of the terms *insurgent* and *counter-insurgent* can be used simply in a generic sense with no intended value-judgement. In order to avoid confusion, the various appellations used in this argument are defined as follows. *Guerrilla*: an insurgent more or less firmly and permanently based inside the territory controlled by the régime he intends to overthrow; *security forces*: the counter-insurgent equivalent of guerrillas, including the Army, Air Force, Police and civilian reserves based in, and operating in, the territory in support of the incumbent régime. François Chenu makes a useful functional distinction between *commandos* and *guerrillas*. Commandos operate from across a border and initially, at any rate, independently of the local population.[3] The term commando is also used in reference to agents of an incumbent régime operating against targets in territories giving sanctuary to insurgent organizations.

An outline of political violence in Rhodesia may help to illustrate some of the specific problems. as well as the general prospects, facing both the insurgent and the counter-insurgent forces. By reference to such theoretical models of insurgency warfare, it might be possible to recognize broadly the different stages in a particular conflict, although in reality there is often no clear demarcation between each stage. In Rhodesia for instance, it

---

Command MOTH on 21 October 1973 at Wankie, stated that: 'There are claims by the terrorists which are so transparently false that they not only brand the terrorists as obvious liars, but any who believe them, or base their assessments on their propaganda, lay themselves open to ridicule and contempt.'

can be seen that there were some incidents of 'infiltration-subversion' between 1961 and 1965 when the ends of nationalist policy were still primarily constitutional. Equally, since 1972 an avowedly non-violent nationalist organization within Rhodesia, the African National Council, was seen to be pressing for a negotiated solution, alongside the 'overt resistance' of small guerrilla bands from the exiled nationalist organizations.

1 The Failure of Compromise Politics

1957–61

The collapse of the Central African Federation in 1963 marked the end of cautious attempts by the Prime Ministers Garfield Todd and Sir Edgar Whitehead to limit racial discrimination in Southern Rhodesia. For example, the Public Service Amendment Act No. 42, in 1960, opened up the civil service on a non-racial basis; the Pass Laws (Repeal) Act No. 50 in 1960 eased the 'pass' system which regulated the lives of Africans; and the Land Apportionment (Amendment) Act No. 54, also in 1960, modified regulations affecting urban Africans. Nevertheless, the white-dominated Federation had been bitterly resented by black nationalists in all three territories. The Southern Rhodesian African National Congress (SRANC), formed in September 1957 by an amalgamation of the old Bulawayo-based Congress and the more militant Youth League in Salisbury, articulated the disaffection of the black population, both rural and urban, at their almost total subjection to the small resident white community. It made direct representations to the government, demanding changes in such unpopular legislation as the 1951 Native Land Husbandry Act. This was a well-intentioned measure designed to prevent soil erosion and other wasteful effects of applying traditional African farming methods to land which was subject to increasing pressure of population – both human and livestock. However, its thoughtless implementation – in particular, with the destocking of cattle and the introduction of individual land tenure – failed to take into account the unsettling effects of these novel practices on a tribal society in which land was owned, or at least used, communally, and where cattle were the basic measure of wealth and prestige.

Disturbances in Southern Rhodesia coincided with incidents

in Northern Rhodesia and violent protests in Nyasaland. Alleging SRANC complicity, the Southern Rhodesian Government declared a State of Emergency and on 26 February 1959 banned the SRANC; arresting some 500 of its members and detaining over 300. In 1960 the pent-up frustrations of the black population, especially in the larger towns, exploded in the worst outbreaks of violence, referred to as 'Zhii' by Blacks, since the late nineteenth century Shona and Ndebele risings, eighteen Africans being shot dead by the police. The significance and meaning of this violence has been analysed by Francis Nehwati:

> The word 'Zhii' has no precise equivalent in English. Its nearest meaning in English is 'devastating action', 'destroy completely', 'reduce to rubble'. It takes its origin from the sound caused by the fall of a huge rock. Any object so crushed is beyond retrieval. 'Ngizakabulala Zhii' (Ndebele) or 'Ndicakuwuraya Zhii' (Shona) means 'I will kill you and reduce your remains to powder'. Zhii is a very drastic act, an act which is reserved for an arch enemy. It is never invoked in minor situations . . . This was the feeling during the riots in Bulawayo in 1960, hence these riots are known and referred to as Zhii.[1]

Most Whites were reluctant to acknowledge, or failed to appreciate, that much of this violence was the result of years of accumulated frustration and tension suffered by the black population. The standard view of the white community was that nationalist 'agitators' were the unwitting dupes, if not the conscious agents, of Communist powers intent on gaining a foothold in Central Africa. Severe measures were introduced to control the outbreak of violent protests. These included the Unlawful Organizations Act and the Preventive Detention Act in 1959; and the Emergency Powers Act, the Vagrancy Act and the Law and Order Maintenance Act in 1960.

With the SRANC declared illegal, a new organization, the National Democratic Party (NDP), was started in January 1960. The SRANC attempt to achieve basic constitutional reforms which would provide Africans with a significant share in the government of Southern Rhodesia had failed. While the SRANC policy had been one of exerting domestic pressure on the régime, the NDP attempted to combine internal opposition with intensive lobbying of British Ministers, in the hope that Britain might use her authority to impress on white Rhodesians the necessity for coming to terms with the black majority.

On the face of it, this NDP policy seemed appropriate. The international impact of the Sharpeville shootings and Macmillan's 'wind of change' speech had indeed shaken Africa. Many outside observers and politicians believed that the Salisbury Government would soon give way to the same kind of internal and external pressures which were being effectively applied in Nyasaland and Northern Rhodesia, as well as elsewhere.

Indeed, for a short while, it seemed that Black and White had reached some measure of accommodation when Joshua Nkomo, the leader of the NDP delegation to the 1960–1 Constitutional Conference, initially accepted the multiracial 1961 constitutional proposals. These provided, according to Sir Edgar Whitehead, for a transition to a black parliamentary majority within fifteen years. The NDP in a press statement declared:

> We feel that the new provisions have given us a certain amount of assurance that the country will not pursue policies which mean that Africans would be perpetually unable to control their country . . . Above all, we are to have a new constitution which is an achievement resulting from the pressures of the NDP, a thing never before thought of in this country.[2]

But although the NDP delegates publicly accepted the new constitution, they had, throughout the negotiations, harboured serious reservations about some of its provisions relating to the franchise and parliamentary representation. And at home and abroad, most NDP officials rejected the proposed constitution *in toto*. Nationalists in other African countries were also highly critical. Leopold Takawira, a former President of NDP and then in charge of Pan-African and External Affairs in London, with the support of another former President, Michael Mawema, cabled to Nkomo:

> We totally reject Southern African constitutional agreement as treacherous to future three million Africans. Agreement diabolical and disastrous. Outside world shocked by NDP docile agreement. We have lost sympathy of friends and supporters . . . Demand immediate reversal of present position.[3]

Nkomo and his three fellow delegates were compelled to turn their backs on whatever measure of agreement had been reached at the conference. It is interesting to note the subsequent careers of these delegates, after the split which occurred in the nationalist movement in mid-1963. Joshua Nkomo headed the Zimbabwe African Peoples' Union (ZAPU), successor to the NDP, and was subsequently detained until his release in December 1974. The Reverend Ndabaningi Sithole led the breakaway Zimbabwe African National Union (ZANU). He was also detained and in February 1969 was sentenced to six years' imprisonment for allegedly plotting to assassinate the Rhodesian Prime Minister and two of his cabinet colleagues, but was among the nationalist leaders released in December 1974. Herbert Chitepo later became Director of Public Prosecutions in Tanzania; and as Acting Chairman of ZANU, had since 1966 been responsible for directing ZANU's military operations. On 18 March 1975 he was assassinated at his home in Lusaka. George Silundika became Publicity and Information Secretary of ZAPU.

This acceptance and then rejection of the proposals may have been a tactical error. Had the NDP rejected them at the outset, the movement would not have been laid open to accusations of lacking militant integrity. On the other hand, had they been accepted, Whitehead's multi-racial United Federal Party, with African support, might have been returned to office in December 1962, instead of the white-supremacist Rhodesian Front which achieved a somewhat unexpected victory. This might have given Blacks opportunities for increased political and social leverage within the white power structure; which might have been an advantage, even if extra-constitutional methods later became inevitable.

If the 1961 Constitution failed to meet the minimum aspirations of the black nationalists, it was as much as, if not more than, most Whites were prepared to concede. In the context of white-controlled southern Africa, it had appeared to be a significant concession; and the referendum of 26 July 1971 showed that the white electorate were prepared to accept the proposals by 41,940 votes to 21,826. However, it now seems clear that the result reflected more a determination to be independent of Britain than an expression of faith in progress towards a multi-racial society. This view is based on a 1965 survey which showed that of those who had supported the 1961 constitution, 45·1 per cent did so because they favoured its multi-racial character; and 54·9 per cent, because it was then thought to offer the best available terms short of total independence, precluded by Southern Rhodesia's constituent status within the Central African Federation. Electoral support for white-supremacist parties jumped from 47·2 per cent in 1958 to 56·5 per cent in 1962 and reached 79·3 per cent in 1965: a level which has been maintained ever since.[4]

Growing political agitation on the part of the black community and the belief of the white electorate that it had been betrayed by the British Government over the implementation of the 1960–61 constitutional proposals had both helped to harden white attitudes further. The two British White Papers (Cmnd 1399 and Cmnd 1400) were accepted by the white electorate in the referendum. The sense of betrayal arose from the subsequent insertion of Section 111, not included in the original White Papers, into the 1961 Constitution. This reserved additional powers to the British Government. Whether it was simply a misunderstanding or a deliberate deception on the part of the British Government, with the aim of outmanoeuvring the Whites and their aspirations for independence, there is no doubt that the affair was a major psychological factor in the process of retrenchment which has since characterized white Rhodesian politics.[5]

The nationalists and their sympathizers had overlooked the fact that Britain wielded little real power in Southern Rhodesia, unlike the territories administered directly from the Colonial Office; even if she retained a limited capacity to influence events, as for instance during the 1960 Constitutional Conference.

1962–5

As it became increasingly obvious that no fundamental reforms would be conceded by the Southern Rhodesian Government, nationalist policy aimed instead at creating a breakdown of law and order sufficient to induce British military intervention and the imposition of an acceptable constitution. One leading nationalist official later admitted that the decision to use political violence was taken as far back as 1960,

> although not for the purpose of guerrilla warfare but the purpose of carrying out acts of sabotage which were considered relevant to bring forth fear and despondency to the settlers of Rhodesia in order to influence the British Government and the settlers in Rhodesia to accede to the popular revolutionary demands of the people in Zimbabwe.[6]

Further evidence for this came from an early ZANU recruit, Hassan Chimutengwende, trained in Ghana in 1965. He maintained that the main emphasis of the scheduled nine-month course (reduced to six because of the imminent threat of UDI) was on sabotage techniques, and that 'very little time was spent on teaching us to use rifles and sub-machine guns on the grounds that we were not to engage in positional warfare'.[7] When Kwame Nkrumah was President of Ghana, there were secret training camps at Damongo in the northern region, at Half Assini, Mankrong and Obenemasi.

Both the nationalists and the Rhodesian Front had turned away from negotiations; the nationalists trying to force British intervention, and the Rhodesian Front strengthening the already formidable Law and Order (Maintenance) Act by making the death sentence mandatory for attacks involving petrol bombs, fire and explosives. Petrol bombs had already become an increasingly familiar feature of attacks, as the January–February 1970 issue of *Zimbabwe Review* points out: 'It was during the course of this Conference (i.e. 1960–61) that for the first time home-made petrol bombs were used by the freedom fighters in Salisbury against settler establishments.' In fact, most victims were Blacks who were either identified in some way with the government or who had simply failed to demonstrate their allegiance to the NDP.

During 1962 six Blacks died as a result of petrol bomb attacks. One of them, Kaitano Kambadza, was a police reservist. A petrol bomb severely damaged the home of Bernard Bomba, Secretary of the Young Federals branch of the multi-racial United Federal

Party; and that of Mr P. E. Chigogo, Treasurer of an African branch of the UFP, was similarly damaged. Samson Zawe, National Chairman of the liberal Central African Party, also survived a petrol bomb explosion at his home.

On 9 December 1961 the NDP was banned but reconstituted itself on 17 December as the Zimbabwe African Peoples Union (ZAPU), which involved the same people and followed the same policies as the NDP this was banned, in turn, in September 1962. The Rhodesian Government later published a White Paper, *Report on the Zimbabwe African Peoples' Union*, giving details of political violence between January and September 1962, which included thirty-three petrol bombings, the burning of eighteen schools and ten churches, and twenty-seven attacks on communications. During 1963 there was mounting evidence of external material assistance and training given to the nationalists. One prominent nationalist later confirmed that 'the decision to start bringing in arms and ammunition, and to send young men away for sabotage training dates from mid-1962, before ZAPU was banned.'[8] In September 1962 an organization, the 'Zimbabwe Liberation Army', began publicizing its existence by distributing leaflets. ZAPU denied any official connection with the organization; although, in fact, this group of about a hundred men was headed by 'General Chedu' – a triumvirate of two members of the ZAPU executive and a Youth Leader. Sabotage was organized, including the burning of dip tanks and a forest in the eastern districts, dislocation of railway lines and attacks on white-owned stores. However, these activities only hardened white attitudes and failed to elicit decisive action from the British Government.

The nationalists' continued lack of success within Rhodesia led to a crisis of confidence in 1963, dissident party officials having become increasingly critical of Nkomo's style of leadership. Difficulties within Rhodesia had led Nkomo to concentrate his political energies on the much more sympathetic and apparently fruitful international environment. However, some party officials considered that nationalist interests would be better served by Nkomo's presence in Rhodesia. His decision to establish an Executive-in-Exile resulted in an official split on 9 August

1963, when the dissidents, led by the Reverend Ndabaningi Sithole, formed the Zimbabwe African National Union (ZANU). Nkomo immediately announced the formation of the Peoples' Caretaker Council (PCC) which, although not technically a political party, nevertheless identified itself with the banned ZAPU, and provided a legal alternative, inside Rhodesia, to ZANU.[9] The initial split can be put down to personality and policy differences, but later conflicts between and within the two organizations assumed tribal and ideological dimensions which seriously inhibited the advancement of the nationalist cause.

In 1964 there was a serious outbreak of widespread political violence, and the great majority of the victims were black. Intimidations, stonings, burnings and gang warfare by 'Zhanda' (vigilante) groups were widespread. Blacks who, rightly or wrongly, were suspected of supporting the white administration or of belonging to the rival party, were the main victims. On 13 February, Ernest Veli, accused of belonging to ZANU, was stabbed to death by a group of PCC supporters. Moses Mundene, a PCC supporter, was killed by a group of ZANU members on 18 June. On 14 September a black police reservist, David Dodo, was beaten to death by two members of the PCC for giving evidence at a criminal trial. A sub-chief in the Rusape district was shot by PCC members on 10 October after they had set fire to huts in his village.[10]

Both organizations were banned on 26 August. The counter-productive effect of widespread, uncontrolled violence must have made some impression on both parties, and attempts to restore some measure of planning were made: no doubt partly in response to the ever-present threat of UDI. Evidence that PCC/ZAPU had begun to think in terms of organized violence is provided in *Zimbabwe Review*, which noted that at a session of PCC members in February 1964 it was decided to 'divide the whole country into command regions or fighting zones'.[11]

ZANU leaders had reached a similar conclusion. They had not been successful in gaining support from ZAPU followers, either through persuasion or intimidation, and decided to concentrate on a positive campaign of violence against the Whites;

intending both to impress black opinion and to lower white morale and eventually to achieve a complete breakdown of law and order. Sixteen different methods of sabotage were listed and five general areas encompassing the main roads from Salisbury to Bulawayo, to Fort Victoria, to Umtali and to Sinoia, as well as key targets in Salisbury itself, were included in a master plan entitled 1.16. Road blocks, attacks on white farms, destruction of livestock and crops, the disruption of electricity supplies and telephone communications, and petrol bomb attacks were planned, but thwarted by Rhodesian Intelligence.[12]

A ZANU group, 'Crocodile Commando', which did succeed in evading the police net, achieved notoriety with its attack on the Oberholtzer family. This group set up a roadblock, nineteen miles from Melsetter, two days after an unsuccessful raid on Nyanyadzi police camp. The first car, containing black motorists, was allowed to pass, but the Oberholtzer's vehicle was attacked. Mrs Oberholtzer, describing what had happened to her husband told the Court that:

> As he stopped, he got out and they threw stones at him. I can remember seeing four Africans around the car. They came up to him and I saw one raise a knife above his head and stab down at my husband. It was so quick and all in a rush that I did not see how many times he stabbed. It was quite a long knife. Stones were coming from all round. I could not see very well. They broke the windscreen with stones. I got a stone on my jaw.

The group then attempted to set the car alight but fled when the lights of an oncoming car appeared.[13] Petrus Oberholtzer died the same night.

Mrs Oberholtzer's version was later contradicted by Davis M'Gabe, at the time ZANU representative in Ghana. He alleged that the attack had taken place immediately after the raid on Nyanyadzi police camp, and that Oberholtzer had tried to stop the group's retreat. He continues, 'As they withdrew, a white farmer named Oberholtzer, with a carload of kids, sought to play hero and capture the group. The invading group tried to reason with him but in the end they had to deal with him. His family was not harmed.'[14]

One of the significant aspects of the attack was that the intended victims were to be white, and not black. 'Crocodile Commando' was inexperienced and undisciplined; but to use M'Gabe's title, it marked 'The Beginnings of Guerrilla Warfare'. Shay also states, in his account, that 'for the police, it was a time of action. They had recognized this as the forerunner of guerrilla warfare.'[15]

The nationalists trained and armed recruits in 1964 and 1965. Between September 1964 and March 1965, about forty ZANU members went to Ghana for training in guerrilla warfare, sabotage and the manufacture of explosives. And while in Tanzania, they were instructed to attack white farms in Rhodesia and to disrupt the May 1965 General Election. In April they crossed into Rhodesia, but thirty-four of them were quickly captured. Meanwhile, ZAPU had also been active. Between March 1964 and October 1965, fifty-two recruits took courses at different training centres; four in Moscow, one in Nanking, and one in Pyongyang, North Korea. They entered Rhodesia from Zambia, and twenty-four were soon arrested.

Although the nationalists created widespread disturbance, the resulting disorder was not such as to lead to British, or United Nations intervention. Referring to the nationalist aim of lowering white morale, a white Rhodesian historian commented that:

> the impending break-up of the Federation and the increasing truculence of the African nationalists led to a loss of confidence in the country's future. Fearing economic collapse and the chaos that could result from racial strife, thousands of Europeans left the country to seek homes elsewhere. But the majority of Rhodesians stayed.[16]

This assessment is borne out by comparing the figures on migration patterns with those on the incidence of political violence. But white confidence gradually returned, and led to a massive electoral victory in May 1965 for the National Front, and the unconstitutional assumption of independence in November of that year. The nationalist reaction to UDI is described by M'Gabe:

> For all those who cherish freedom and a meaningful life, UDI has set a collision course which cannot be altered. 11 November 1965, marked a turning point of the struggle for freedom in that land from a constitutional and political one to a primarily military struggle.[17]

Table 2: (a) Contravention of the Law and Order (Maintenance) Act
(b) European Migration Figures, 1960–75

Year	*Contraventions of the Law and Order (Maintenance) Act*	*European Migration Figures* *Immigrants*	*Emigrants*	*Net Flow*
1960	n.a.	8,000	7,000	+1,000
1961	901	8,000	10,000	−2,000
1962	1,112	8,000	12,000	−4,000
1963	961	7,000	18,000	−11,000
1964	4,435	7,000	15,710	−8,710
1965	2,319	11,128	8,850	+2,280
1966	724	6,418	8,510	−2,090[a]
1967	310	9,618	7,570	+2,050
1968	101	11,864	5,650	+6,210
1969	57	10,929	5,890	+5,040
1970	130	12,227	5,890	+6,340
1971	396	14,743	5,340	+9,400
1972	636	13,966	5,150	+8,820
1973	Period of intensified and sustained insurgency.	9,433	7,750	+1,683
1974		9,649	9,050	+599[b]
1975		12,425	10,500	+1,925[b]

[a] The net outward flow in 1966 is probably accounted for by the uncertainty surrounding UDI in November 1965.

[b] These would almost certainly have been negative figures, had it not been for several thousand Portuguese refugees from Mozambique and Angola following the April 1974 coup, which artificially boosted the immigration rate.

Source: Monthly Migration and Tourist Statistics, Central Statistical Office (Salisbury) and Annual Reports of the Commissioner of the British South Africa Police.

2 Insurgency and Counter-Insurgency 1966–70

The Rhodesian authorities took country-wide security measures, and the general uprising which the nationalist leaders hoped would follow UDI failed to occur. However, inflammatory broadcasts from Zambia, Tanzania and Egypt elicited some response; and there were many incidents of arson, stonings, crop-slashing and mutilation of livestock. Workers, particularly in Bulawayo, protested by taking part in industrial action, and at Wankie Colliery sabotage attacks were carried out by a ZAPU action group. The leader of this group, Mazwi Gumbo, stated later at his trial:

> Workers at the colliery were dissatisfied with the Company because it turned a deaf ear to our grievances. When UDI was declared, we became even more angry. We realise that only one people can rule a country. It should be the Africans.[1]

Some of the violence may have been directed by survivors from the group of insurgents who had returned to Rhodesia after training abroad. Hassan Chimutengwende described how he had 'stayed at large for eight whole months in Rhodesia, moving from village to village'; explaining to villagers that

> the British Government had said that it would intervene militarily only if 'law and order' broke down in Rhodesia. For that reason I urged them to do lots of burning and crop cutting, and was able to advise them. The 'gospel of action' which I preached was passed on by the others.[2]

During 1966 the conflict became more serious, when security forces clashed with some small groups of insurgents which had infiltrated from Zambia. The first officially acknowledged clash occurred at the end of April, when seven members of a ZANU commando unit were killed after being surrounded by police on a farm near Sinoia. A ZANU communique issued from Dar-es-Salaam on 30 April claimed that twenty-five members of the security forces had been killed and thirty wounded, in addition to the destruction of two helicopters; although in fact there were no security force casualties. The presence of a helicopter which had been effectively used as a gun-ship during the attack was an important factor. The insurgents had planned, but failed, to cut the Kariba power-line, which supplied seventy per cent of the country's electricity, and subsequently attack the blacked-out town centre and police station at Sinoia. A notebook found on one of the bodies showed that its owner had been trained at Nanking Military College in the previous November and December.

An earlier crossing had occurred at the beginning of April when another ZANU group of fourteen split into three sections. One section of two men headed for the Fort Victoria area; and another of five men had orders to sabotage the Beira-Umtali oil pipe-line and attack white farmers. All seven were arrested before they were able to complete their mission. A third section of seven men headed for the Midlands; and it is possible that their purpose was to make contact with their President, Sithole, who was under restriction at Sikombela, near Gwelo. This group may have been responsible for the attack on a farm near Hartley on 16 May. The farmer, Hendrik Viljoen, and his wife were killed by automatic fire.[3] The group responsible for this attack consisted of seven members, two of whom were away on a recruiting mission at the time of the incident. One of the two, Gombachuma, was a former policeman who had been discharged from the force. He was later sentenced to twenty-eight years' imprisonment. The group had been based in the Hartley area and was in contact with some of the local population. After the attack it split up; and although all but one of its members were eventually caught, three succeeded in staying in the Mount Hampden district, outside Salisbury, until arrested in September 1966. This group, although eventually given away, had had some measure of success in maintaining contact with, and receiving assistance from, the local population. One of the men, Edmund Nyandoro, told the court which sentenced him to death for the Viljoen murders in the following February, that he had been trained in Egypt, Tanzania and China.

In September the existence of another guerrilla unit was discovered near Lupane, south-east of Wankie, where a local headman had been shot by one of the group for reporting the presence of the insurgents. From expertly concealed hideouts the guerrillas had approached local villagers for supplies and recruited two local men as permanent members. The original group of eight had been trained in Algeria. Seventeen villagers were later charged with assisting, or receiving training from, the insurgents.[4]

Nationalists were also active in establishing cells in urban areas. One such cell was claimed to be at the University in Salisbury, where ZAPU had been in contact with three lecturers. Their liaison activities, it was alleged, included reporting on the deployment of security forces, the distribution of grenades, and the selection of white-owned farms, near Tribal Trust areas, for guerrilla attacks.

In the first half of 1967, Rhodesian Intelligence was aware of a build-up in arms and men across the Zambezi. In addition to some isolated incidents, several caches of arms were discovered. On 26 May four ZANU commandos attempting to infiltrate into Rhodesia in a pantechnicon had been killed in a gun battle near Chirundu. In view of such incidents, security forces were expecting further activity of some sort. By the end of July a joint force of Rhodesian ZAPU and the African National Congress of South Africa (SAANC) had already crossed the Zambezi, without being detected, between the Victoria Falls and Kazangula, and headed for the Wankie Game Reserve.

The composition of this force marked a significant development in the racial confrontation in southern Africa. A military alliance between the two organizations was announced on 15 August by James Chikerema, acting President of ZAPU and Oliver Tambo, Deputy President-General of SAANC. At the trial of James Edward April (alias George Driver) who was one of the insurgents, a fellow insurgent and witness, originally from Natal, revealed the plans of the group, which he claimed numbered seventy men. According to his statement, 'The force was under orders to split into three groups, one to move to the northern part of Rhodesia, the second to the southern part, and the third to the northern Transvaal.'[5]

In a series of engagements in August and September, both sides sustained heavier casualties than before; the security forces claimed thirty-one insurgents dead and a similar number captured, for the loss of seven members of the security forces and about twice that number wounded. The SAANC later claimed that in the first few days of battle fifty-four members of the security forces had been killed. For their part, the security authorities conceded that the morale and training of some insurgents had reached a high level.

Despite the eventual containment of the joint incursion, it became obvious that this operation, and the possibility of future incursions on a similar scale, threatened to stretch the capacity of the small Rhodesian security forces to an unacceptable degree, and South African para-military police units were therefore sent to assist the Rhodesian forces. It was a move which both outraged the nationalists and greatly embarrassed the British Government which still acknowledged legal responsibility for Southern Rhodesia.

Apart from an international outcry at 'the invasion of Rhodesia by South African troops', a debate resulted between the different nationalist organizations over the correct tactics and strategy to be followed. ZANU, highly critical of the military alliance between ZAPU and SAANC, argued that:

> In guerrilla warfare we must strive to spread the enemy forces so that we can wipe them out one by one. The greatest help we can get from ANC is for ANC to wage intensive guerrilla warfare in South Africa. If ANC can pin down the whole South African force within South Africa, then Zimbabweans shall be left with Smith alone without South African aid ... as it is now, the ANC and PCC-(ZAPU) alliance has made it easy for Smith and Vorster to unite and concentrate their forces to slaughter Zimbabweans.[6]

ANC's rival in South Africa, the Pan-Africanist Congress (PAC) also deplored the combined military operation and declared that: 'You cannot hope to gobble up a regular army, all at once in a conventional style war, as our brothers tried to do, and still claim to be waging guerrilla warfare. It is wholly unacceptable both in theory and practice.'[7]

These disputes between rival nationalist organizations touched on some of the basic problems (of a theoretical as well as practical nature) confronting the black liberation movement in its search for a viable strategy which could achieve the general objective of overthrowing white supremacy in the sub-continent. Conceptually at least, there seemed to be two contending approaches to this task involving different appreciations of the interlocking geo-political system of white-controlled southern Africa. The ZANU statement, quoted above, illustrated the thinking behind one of these approaches – essentially that there should be concurrent resistance in all the white-ruled territories leading to the progressive weakening and eventual disintegration of the whole system. In its most simplistic form this argument tended to overlook the wide disparities in the strength of the white regimes and to ignore the problems of access for externally-based insurgents. These were difficult in the case of Rhodesia (until the Portuguese began to lose control in Mozambique) and appeared almost insurmountable as far as South Africa was concerned (although the advent of nationalist régimes in Mozambique and Angola has opened up a new range of possibilities).

An alternative approach was outlined by Joe Slovo when he pointed out that 'the enormity of the task facing ANC guerrillas within South Africa itself gave rise previously to suggestions that the liberation of southern Africa should be approached as a project to be achieved in geographic stages – first Mozambique, then Angola and in the end South Africa' although he adds that 'this strategy appears never to have found favour in the ANC or any of the other liberatory movements'.[8] However, a variant of such a 'domino' type strategy, familiar in the literature on South-East Asia, has found support in influential quarters. In private discussions with black South African leaders during the meeting of the newly-formed Organization of African Unity (OAU) at Dakar in 1963 the former Premier of Algeria, Ahmed Ben Bella, outlined a plan, which was described as being 'based on the straightforward military notion of knocking off the weakest enemy and moving step by step towards the strongest'.[9] More recently at the meeting of the OAU Liberation Committee in Kampala during May 1972, President Idi Amin of Uganda supported the idea of 'setting and programming territorial targets' for the liberation movements. He also suggested that regional defence commands, subject to the overall direction of an OAU High Command, should be formed which would be responsible for liberating adjoining territories. Such a scheme, particularly if it was intended that African states should provide conventional backing to insurgent forces in the field, would require an organizational sophistication, logistic capacity and a quality and depth of command and control which are well beyond the present and immediately foreseeable scope of both the liberation movements and the OAU. However, the changing strategic balance caused by the collapse of Portuguese rule in Africa makes it more conceivable that one day a politically isolated and geographically exposed South Africa could be faced with such a contingency.

Hypothetically, one can envisage an OAU-sanctioned force, financed by Arab money and comprising soldiers from a black state or states in possession of considerable military muscle (such as Nigeria or Zaire), providing conventional backing to the operations of a Soviet and/or Chinese-armed guerrilla movement. The prospect of such a threat is still remote for South Africa but not quite so implausible with regard to Rhodesia. An operation of this kind against Guinea-Bissau was at least considered during secret discussions at the summit meeting of African leaders in Rabat during June 1972. Reporting on the Conference, Legum wrote that the strategy which had been

> evolving in secret for some time is that the immediate priority should be Guinea-Bissau, where the liberation movement led by Amilcar Cabral has already seriously weakened Portugal's hold.
>
> The possibility of striking decisively at Guinea-Bissau has been greatly strengthened by the public commitment of Nigeria's leader, General Yakubu Gowon, to contribute towards this operation. Nigeria has the military and economic resources to give some reality to such an operation against the Portuguese and President Sekou Touré is willing to allow Guinea to be used as a base for a combined African operation . . .
>
> They believe that the collapse of Portuguese rule in Africa would

greatly weaken the flanks of Mr Ian Smith's régime in Rhodesia and enable the African Liberation movements to intensify their pressures against him as well as along the South African frontiers, especially in South-West Africa (Namibia).[10]

In a thoughtful analysis written shortly before the Lisbon coup of April 1974 Ben Turok appeared to accept the partial validity of both these contending perspectives although he was primarily concerned to develop a strategy for the liberation of South Africa itself. Well aware of the debilitating effects of the exile condition; of the danger that reliance on expectations of *deus ex machina* solutions easily becomes an excuse for inaction; and of the problems of access to South Africa, Turok argued:

> It is often said that southern Africa is a single theatre of struggle – and so it is, with the successes of the armed struggles in Mozambique, Angola and Zimbabwe making an important psychological impact. *But no movement can predicate the stepping up of its struggle at home on successes elsewhere*, particularly when these struggles are themselves likely to develop slowly and distances to the south are great.
>
> There is an even greater imperative for focussing on South Africa itself. It is the heart of the white redoubt in the sub-continent and it is unthinkable that colonialism could be sustained in any of the neighboring countries if South Africa itself was liberated. There is in any case an obligation on the movement to ease the passage of others by draining the strength of the octopus at the center.
>
> Nevertheless what happens to the north is in many ways crucial. If the lines of communication of South Africa's forces become stretched over the whole of southern Africa, they will have serious logistical problems. The area is vast, the population overwhelmingly Black and the terrain to the north favorable for guerrilla warfare. Futhermore, the political consequences on an international level of South Africa's further military involvement will be serious. But, for the present, we must restrict our vision to the internal situation.
>
> At this stage the major impact o f armed struggles to the north is psychological. The capacity of Black guerrillas to hurt White troops and even to make a physical dent in White power is impressive.

With the special difficulties which confronted the South African Liberation movement in mind Turok noted that

> the most recent pronouncements of the external movement, however, indicate that the emphasis is once again moving away from immediate

armed struggle and there is greater emphasis on rebuilding political structures at home. The urgent need seems to be for political organizers who can return home and take root among the masses rather in the way this was done in the early days by Cabral in Guinea. But the possibility of the infiltration of armed units has not been dismissed and the theoretical basis for this, the detonator theory which dominated the movement's thinking for some years, has not entirely been left behind. Its implementation, of course, depends on the possibility of returning armed men safely and setting them up with a chance of surviving.[11]

With independence now come to Mozambique the prospects for such infiltration into the north-eastern Transvaal and northern Natal must have improved considerably – particularly if the recent search for *détente* in southern Africa should break down. Turok also referred to several important developments taking place within South Africa which open up fresh possibilities for internal political action as distinct from externally-based insurgent operations. Most significant in this direction are: the rise of black consciousness as reflected in the militant black South African Students Organization, the Black Peoples' Convention and among the black clergy; black industrial unrest which has manifested itself in the series of strikes since the end of 1971; and, as Turok points out, 'perhaps of decisive significance for the future struggle is the possibility that in the Bantustans there may develop the kind of communal solidarity which enables armed guerrillas to set up bases'.

It would be fairer to say that the process of liberation in southern Africa has tended to reflect the simple realities of power politics and geography than to argue that it has proceeded according to any particular preconceived strategic model. It is only too obvious that the liberation movement has been least successful in South Africa which was not only more effectively insulated geographically but also immensely more powerful than the other white-ruled territories.[12]

The principle that success breeds success is very apparent in the experience of the various liberation groups. It is noticeable that the PAIGC movement in Guinea-Bissau, which was the most isolated of the white-ruled territories and where the armed struggle had been most successful, received by far the largest amount of external material support. Aid to the liberation movements in the former Portuguese territories has been consistently greater – and it is difficult to avoid the impression that this was largely because their prospects of success seemed better than those of the Rhodesian and South African liberation movements. At the OAU conference in Rabat during June 1972, referred to above, it was decided to concentrate resources on the anti-Portuguese movements. The strategy for the liberation of southern Africa was accordingly outlined in a document – the *Accra Declaration on the New Strategy for the Liberation of Africa* – which was released after the OAU Liberation Committee's meeting in Accra in early 1973. With the decolonization of the Portuguese territories achieved, the next step was outlined in the *Dar-es-Salaam Declaration on Southern Africa* which emanated from the OAU Council of Ministers' meeting in April 1975. It referred to 'the Accra Strategy of 1973 concentrating on the liberation of the Portuguese colonies' and continued

> The victory over Portuguese colonialism which vindicated the Accra Strategy led Africa . . . to make use of the victories achieved by the freedom fighters of Mozambique, Angola, Guinea-Bissau and Cape Verde, São Tomé and Principe for the advance of the freedom march further south with particular emphasis on the liberation of Zimbabwe and Namibia.

In keeping with OAU policy, the Liberation Committee, during its meeting in May 1975, recommended that the largest allocation of its funds should go to the reconstituted and enlarged African National Council in Rhodesia – nearly $500,000 in material and administrative assistance. The Committee also approved $1·5 million to run OAU training centres in Tanzania and Zambia which would be used primarily to train guerrillas of the former ZANU, ZAPU and FROLIZI but since united under the reconstituted African National Council.[13]

Apart from an element of ill-concealed pique, ZANU criticism of the joint ZAPU/SAANC operation in 1967 may have been inspired by the genuine fear that the two organizations were adopting a 'domino' approach to the task of southern African liberation. Matthew Nkoana, a PAC member, criticized the tendency of some ZANU and PAC followers to find fault, as a matter of petty principle, with any action of their rivals. However, he admitted that some of the accusations were justified including

the valid criticism that some of the initial battles in the Wankie area in August and September last year assumed the character of modern positional war as opposed to guerrilla warfare ... and the equally valid criticism that the men ventured into enemy territory without any advance planning of operations.[14]

Both these points are significant. The superior mobility and size of the counter-insurgent forces in operations of a 'conventional' type resulted in large groups of insurgents being surrounded with comparative ease. The air support afforded to the ground troops was also a crucial factor. (On 22 August the Rhodesian Air Force had, for the first time, attacked insurgent positions with rockets and napalm.)

The lack of any overall political objective apart from confrontation was apparent from the joint ZAPU/SAANC communiqué issued after a week of fighting. 'It is the determination of these Combined Forces to fight the common settler enemy to the finish, at any point of encounter, as they make their way to their respective fighting zones.'[15]

On 19 September the Rhodesian Parliament passed a bill providing for a mandatory death penalty for any person found in possession of 'arms of war ... unless he can prove beyond reasonable doubt that he had no intention of endangering the maintenance of law and order in Rhodesia or a neighbouring country'. The exiled nationalists were not deterred. The August/September incursion had been into Matabeleland; ZAPU, a primarily Ndebele-orientated organization, had expected that the Ndebele and the Kalanga (a Shona sub-group largely absorbed by the Ndebele) would be favourably disposed towards the insurgents. Now, possibly in a bid to outdo the Shona-orientated ZANU, the ZAPU leadership decided to launch a joint ZAPU/SAANC force into northern Mashonaland.

After preliminary reconnaissance at the end of 1967, insurgent columns successfully established between January and March

1968 a series of six base camps some twenty miles apart, leading in a southerly direction towards the farming area of Sipolilo. Their objective was the recruitment and training of local tribesmen for an armed uprising. Meanwhile the insurgents were under strict orders to avoid contact with the security forces and successfully avoided detection until they were moving to Camp Six. Their presence was discovered by a game ranger who had been investigating the uneven distribution of game caused by insurgent activity. In a series of engagements, fifty-eight nationalist commandos were killed (forty-three ZAPU and fifteen SAANC) and a similar number captured; for seven members of the security forces killed and several wounded. ZAPU and SAANC spokesmen reversed these casualty figures and also claimed that four helicopters had been shot down. Nationalist leaders in a broadcast from Zambia in mid-March claimed that guerrillas had overrun Miami, 126 miles north-west of Salisbury. Journalists a few days later could find no evidence of so much as a single shot having been fired there. The January–March infiltrations which had begun so successfully ended in costly failure, for reasons similar to those that had caused the failure of the 1967 operations. Large concentrations of insurgents were at a serious disadvantage against mobile ground troops supported by aerial bombing, and there was insufficient local support in an area which was rather sparsely populated. In one case two insurgents were arrested by a chief's messenger. Although there were a few successful contacts, an anonymous contributor to the SAANC pamphlet on guerrilla warfare admits that local support was sometimes unreliable. 'A lot of people,' he said, 'were being used by the enemy, especially pensioned policemen, teachers and some of the wealthier farmers.'[16] Nevertheless, security authorities recognized the seriousness of the situation, in which over one hundred insurgents had been operating undetected in the country for three months.[17]

In late March, PAC, which had been critical of the ZAPU/SAANC alliance, was itself engaged in a combined operation through Mozambique with COREMO (Comité Revolucionario de Moçambique). The intention was to sabotage the Beira-

Umtali oil pipe-line on the way to South Africa. In June the PAC/COREMO group was intercepted by Portuguese forces near Vila Pery, between the Rhodesian border town of Umtali and Beira. Four insurgents were killed and three captured, for the loss of three Portuguese troops. Documents found on the group leader, Kibwe Kondlo, revealed that the plan was code-named 'Operation Crusade', involving twelve PAC members and a COREMO escort of five men. Whatever the merits, or otherwise, of military alliances, the exiled PAC and SAANC guerrillas all faced the same problem of access into South Africa. The shortest route lay through Rhodesia, which was regarded by South African insurgents as being of general strategic importance. In the explanation of *Sechaba*:

> What has to be clearly understood is that Rhodesia (Zimbabwe) is not only the gateway to the citadel of fascism – South Africa – but it is now, more than ever before, the most essential link in the entire imperialist strategy of maintaining the Zambesi frontier as the advance battle line in defence of colonial interests in southern Africa.[18]

The prompt assistance given to Rhodesia at the time of the mid-1967 incursions, which had included SAANC fighters *en route* to the Republic, underlined South African concern for the security of her borders with Rhodesia and Botswana. Recent developments in the former Portuguese territories have stressed rather than diminished South Africa's interest in keeping the conflict in Rhodesia down to manageable proportions. Even before the Lisbon *coup* of April 1974, it had become apparent to the more percipient South African politicians that South Africa's continued military and economic support for an unviable white régime in Rhodesia could lead to an escalation of the fighting, drawing South Africa into a generalized regional confrontation.

In July 1968 ZAPU and SAANC were again active. A force of ninety-one men, divided into three groups, crossed at various points on the border with Zambia. On 12 July twenty-five crossed at the junction of the Gwai and Zambezi rivers, bound for Hartley; a second party of thirty-eight entered at the confluence of the Chewore with the Zambezi on the same day;

and on 13 July twenty-eight crossed up-river from Chirundu, also making for Hartley. The actions which followed, involving both Rhodesian and South African units, were considered as models of counter-insurgency tactics backed by advance intelligence reports. According to security force claims, thirty-nine insurgents were killed and forty-one captured, with eleven unaccounted for.

'Operation Griffin' against the third group of twenty-eight was regarded as one of the most successful demonstrations of counter-insurgency tactics and is therefore worth examining in greater detail. The security forces arrested a man who had become detached from the main party, which had itself inadvertently circled back on the Zambezi, to a point seven miles south of its original crossing place. The rugged terrain, especially of the Kuburi Hills, had made it impossible to follow a direct route and the group had lost its way. The straggler revealed details of the size, equipment and direction of his group. Fast-moving tracker units were put on its trail. The security forces, knowing the general direction of the group, were able to leap-frog ahead and prepare a series of ambushes, in which twenty-four of them were killed, three captured and one escaped. In this action the South African Police suffered their first combat casualty in Rhodesia with the death of Constable du Toit; four other South African policemen and two Rhodesian troopers were wounded.[19]

The 1966–8 confrontations had taken place against a background of Rhodesian attempts to negotiate a British recognition of her *de facto* independence; on HMS *Tiger* in December 1966 and again on HMS *Fearless* in September 1968. The exiled nationalist movements, it seemed, still hoped that a decisive military defeat of the security forces would precipitate a sufficient breakdown of 'law and order' for British or United Nations military intervention to follow. However, by the time of the *Fearless* negotiations in 1968 (see Appendix I) which marked a British retreat from the 1966 *Tiger* terms, they had apparently given up such hopes:

It may now be dangerous to the development of the liberation struggle to predicate that struggle on the basis of Britain as the sovereign administering power or to call for *her* troops in this situation. *Any*

British troops in Rhodesia now could be solely there to frustrate the armed forces of liberation.[20]

There were no armed clashes in 1969 with commando groups from across the border. The severe military defeats of the previous three years, and the final disillusionment over Britian's attitude necessitated a reappraisal of nationalist tactics and strategy. In a television interview shown on Granada Television on 1 January 1970 – which led to a dispute over the ZAPU leadership – James Chikerema, Acting Chairman of ZAPU, remarked that

> ... this is really a protracted struggle – we do not intend to finish in a matter of two, three, four or five years – this is a protracted struggle ... The type of war we fight depends on – on changes of tactics and I can tell you that we've changed our tactics ... We will combine both where they meet us and intercept us – we will stand and fight ... where they don't see us we will go to our own areas and infiltrate ourselves into the population and organize our masses.

Although ZAPU by early 1970 was near to a leadership crisis, there was some attempt to put the revised nationalist strategy, however makeshift, into action. On 17 January a South African Police camp at Chisuma was attacked by some fifteen insurgents. Six policemen were wounded; and one insurgent was, it seems, accidentally shot by his comrades. The police camp suffered considerable damage, and the operation seems to have been planned in some detail. Before the attack, two of the guerrillas, disguised as labourers temporarily employed by the South Africans, had actually surveyed the layout of the camp. A simultaneous assault on Victoria Falls airport damaged buildings with machine-gun fire. Another section of the same insurgent group attempted, without success, to sabotage the nearby railway line. Nationalist officials claimed that these actions had resulted in eight South Africans and five Rhodesians being killed, two helicopters and a light aeroplane destroyed, and the disruption of communications.[21] Apart from these two main attacks, there were other less dramatic encounters between guerrillas and security forces, in one of which a soldier from the Rhodesian African Rifles was killed. In another incident, nationalist commandos fired at a radio station on the banks of Kariba to protest against the assumption of Republican status by Rhodesia (in March 1970). In Britain a ZAPU official issued a statement which declared: 'The creation of a white man's republic in their land does nothing except to emphasize the continuing challenge, a challenge that demands the speedy escalation of the politics of violence.' Court trials during 1970 and 1971 also provided considerable evidence of small-scale infiltration and underground activity.[22]

3 Divisions Abroad: Solidarity at Home

The severe military setbacks of 1967 and 1968, coupled with the inevitable problems and frustrations of exile, not surprisingly had adverse effects on the morale of the nationalist rank-and-file, while the leadership also fell into considerable disarray. As John Marcum points out in analysing the effects of the exile condition on the nationalist organizations:

> If these movements were ever to attain revolutionary goals, however, they had to do much more than simply survive. Their leaders and militants had to overcome the initial shock of displacement and had to deal successfully with a broad range of environmental, existential and technical problems.[1]

Failure to dislodge their common enemy, the white settler régime, tended to exacerbate tensions and divisions both within and between ZAPU and ZANU. The presence of the feuding and indisciplined nationalists also threatened Zambia's own security. The Zambian Government had been seriously embarrassed by the faction-fighting and by the publicity which had been given to the nationalists' practice of kidnapping black Rhodesians living in Zambia as recruits for their armies. The nationalists, for their part, justified such strong-arm activities on the grounds that most countries have military conscription in time of war, and that Zimbabwe is no exception. The Zambian authorities had on several occasions intervened to release these 'recruits'; but when Zambian nationals were also drafted, the situation had developed to a point which no state could tolerate. In October 1968, fifty-two members of ZAPU and ZANU were arrested in connection with kidnapping activities and deported to Tanzania. If nationalist groups, which were weak and divided, posed threats to Zambia's internal security, the prospect of harbouring an effective liberation movement on her soil also carried the danger of external attack, as the South African Minister of Defence underlined in April 1968. Speaking to the House of Assembly, he stated that countries harbouring terrorists 'must realise that provocation can lead to hard retaliation, in the interests of peace and self-respect'.

Towards the end of 1969 and during the early months of 1970 the leadership crisis in ZAPU deepened. In October 1969 James Chikerema, Vice-President of ZAPU, had permitted a *World in Action* television team to film a nationalist unit on the banks of the Zambezi without either obtaining permission from the Zambian Government or informing his own colleagues. His action brought to the surface the growing rift between the ChiShona-speaking members of the leadership (Chikerema and George Nyandoro, Secretary-General of ZAPU) and the Sindebele-speaking group mainly represented by J. Z. Moyo (Treasurer), T. G. Silundika (Publicity) and Edward Ndlovu (Assistant Secretary). Moyo issued a document at the end of February 1970 (see Chapter 1: note 6) in which he criticized Chikerema's leadership for being too autocratic, assessed the deteriorating situation in ZAPU's military camps and suggested improvements. In his 'Reply to Observations on Our Struggle', Chikerema admitted that all was not well in ZAPU's military wing:

> Yes, Comrades, the Party and the Army is in dismay. It has no Commander. It has no administration. It has no team spirit. It is corrupt, and therefore not sincere to its objectives . . . The Army has been divided into tribal factions. The Party is divided into tribal factions and clannish empires. There are cadres that are more equal than others in both the Party and the Army.

He also admitted that the Zambian Government had 'rightly' objected to his unilateral authorization of the filming, for which he apologized. However, he refused to give way on his claims to the leadership of ZAPU, accused the Ndebele faction of planning to oust him, and announced that he intended to take full control of all party functions. Moyo and his colleagues almost immediately challenged Chikerema's interpretation of his right to the leadership and emphasized its collective nature. In March 1971 over twenty leading Shona officials were kidnapped by dissident elements of the party's military wing who had apparently become dissatisfied over pay and conditions of service. The Zambian police intervened and a large number of ZAPU men were taken to a specially prepared camp at Mbaloma in Central Province. It was reported that 163 were held at Mbaloma, thirty-four at Kasama and five at Chipata. On 24 April 1970 the *Times of Zambia* had prominently featured a story about a gun battle between rival Shona and Ndebele factions of ZAPU in which three Ndebele and six Shona were injured and four were reported missing. Chikerema's decision to start unity talks with ZANU widened the split even further; and in August President Kaunda, exasperated and embarrassed by the military failures and faction-fighting of the Rhodesian nationalists warned that they would defeat Zambia's willingness to accommodate them unless they got together.[2] The Zambian Government showed that its warning was to be taken seriously when 129 ZAPU dissidents were deported to Rhodesia, where they were immediately arrested and some later even received death sentences in the Rhodesian courts.

Despite all this, ZANU announced at the beginning of August that talks with ZAPU were to be stopped because of the difficulties of negotiating with an organization which was so hopelessly divided. This decision also marked a split in the ZANU leadership; and the members of the Central Committee who had supported the continuation of the search for unity, in particular Nathan Shamuyarira, were expelled. In October the Front for the Liberation of Zimbabwe (FROLIZI) was formed and headed by Shelton Siwela, a ZAPU veteran of the fighting in the Zambezi valley. Chikerema and Nyandoro from ZAPU and Shamuyarira and Godfrey Savanhu from ZANU, were on the FROLIZI Council. Both ZAPU and ZANU however, refused to recognize the merger, claiming that it was an unrepresentative clique of the Zezuru clan. ZAPU's Deputy Secretary denounced FROLIZI as a 'haven of refuge for political rejects'. Instead of creating a unified movement, the effect was to create three competing nationalist groups instead of two.

As a result of the divisions between and within the exiled

nationalist groups, there were no major incursions into Rhodesia during this period. ZAPU had planned to infiltrate 112 men across the Zambezi in March 1971, but they had refused to go. Meanwhile, however, the situation within Rhodesia itself was far from static. During 1971 there was a noticeable upsurge of disaffection at various levels of African society: most dramatically shown in demonstrations by university students, trainee teachers and even schoolchildren, after the Ministry of Education announced a new salary structure, which in effect discriminated against the great majority of black teachers. 124 pupils from Tegwani school were convicted and punished for having participated in an illegal procession through Plumtree. Placards with slogans such as 'People's Liberation, a free Zimbabwe or Death' and 'Rightly Rhodesia is Ours', were said by the magistrate to have 'verged on the subversive, if in fact they are not subversive'.[3]

The Government's determination to introduce and enforce discriminatory legislation aggravated existing resentment. In particular the implementation of the Land Tenure Act, which replaced the Land Apportionment Act, caused considerable bitterness, especially among long-standing black communities threatened with eviction from areas designated as 'white' under the Act. The Government's attention was particularly directed at the 'Tangwena' and 'Mutema' communities in eastern Rhodesia and the two mission communities at Epworth and Chishawasha near Salisbury.

The history of the Tangwena people illustrates the way in which white settler interests have been asserted at the expense of the cultural and physical survival of traditional African communities. The land claimed by the Tangwena, which included their ancestral burial grounds, consisted of a ten-by-five mile stretch of territory along Rhodesia's border with Mozambique and encompassed some of the richest agricultural land in the country. The tribe at present has some 3,000 members; with many dispersed elsewhere. In 1905 the British South Africa Company sold a quarter of a million acres, which included a large part of Tangwena territory, to the Anglo-French Matabeleland Company, without consulting the African inhabitants of the area. In 1944 the Matabeleland Company ceded 58,000 acres to the Gaeresi Ranch Company (Private) Limited.

In 1962 the Rhodesian Front came to power and in 1964 advised landowners to evict African squatters from their land. In 1965 the inhabitants of five villages on the Gaeresi Ranch ignored a request to leave by the manager of the Company. In 1966 they were ordered to leave by the Government; and, when they again refused, their chief was charged and convicted under the Land Apportionment Act for occupying 'European' land. The Tangwena appealed successfully against the conviction in the High Court, on the grounds that they had been in occupation of the land before 1905. However, in 1969, Clifford Dupont, the Officer Administering the Government, issued a Proclamation under Section 86 of the Land Apportionment Act, ordering the Tangwena to leave the ranch by 31 August of that year. The Government offered the Tangwena alternative land, but they again refused to move, and in September police were sent to evict them. In the process, houses and property were destroyed, and the Tangwena fled into the surrounding mountains where they have been ever since. In July 1974 there were about 350 women, nearly ninety men and over 150 very young children living and hiding in the mountains under increasingly harsh conditions. In 1970 the Government impounded all the Tangwena cattle and followed this up with a series of prosecutions against individuals and organizations which supported the Tangwena struggle to regain the right to live on their traditional lands. Several raids and searches by the police and troops, supported with helicopters, have been carried out and the border area with Mozambique patrolled since ZANU had begun to take advantage of the unsettled conditions in Mozambique's Tete province, caused by expanding FRELIMO activity, to infiltrate north-eastern Rhodesia.

The struggle of the Tangwena against the Government raises several points. Most importantly, it shows how the question of land distribution and ownership is fundamental to the white-black conflict in Rhodesia. It shows how white settler interests are asserted in a manner which overrides, and displays a complete lack of understanding for, the cultural values and physical needs of the black communities. Finally it shows that a courageous commitment to a non-violent campaign of resistance has totally failed to make any headway against an insensitive and implacable government. There is no evidence that the Tangwena community itself has become actively involved in the recent ZANU offensive in the north-east; but it would be surprising if, after the treatment they had received from the administration, some individuals had not by now been recruited into the guerrilla forces.[4]

Political violence increased during 1970 and 1971 (see Table 2), and there were several incidents involving security. In April 1971 three Rhodesian soldiers were killed when their vehicle detonated a landmine while crossing a river-bed on the Mozambique border north of the Mavuradonha Mountains. In a trial at the end of the year, it was revealed that seven schoolboys had been recruited by their teacher to go to Zambia 'for training as freedom fighters' and had attended a course in mid-May which included an introduction to the use of weapons, political lectures, and film shows at the Chinese Embassy in Lusaka. At the end of the three-day course, the boys had been told that they would have to go to Tanzania for long-term military training, but they had refused to do so. They were each given suspended sentences of five years' hard labour and were corporally punished on their return to Rhodesia. At his trial the teacher, Martin Mwale, who was accused both of attending a training course himself in 1970 and of recruiting the pupils, stated that he had become involved because he 'was highly critical of the Government and saw no hope for the black man except through violent revolution'.

In July a large cache of arms including rifles, machine-guns, grenades, ammunition and explosives was discovered at a warehouse in Salisbury's light industrial area. The store foreman had arranged for the cases to be smuggled in from Zambia on lorries, and, it was alleged, an accountant at the Bible Society in Salisbury was to be responsible for their distribution to ZANU cells in the city. The scheme was discovered by an African detective. At the end of August Rhodesian security forces clashed with a group of FRELIMO guerrillas who had crossed from Mozambique into Rhodesia, south-east of Mucumbura.

A Rhodesian communiqué stated that one member of the security forces had been wounded, seven FRELIMO killed and one captured.

It was against this background that a further round of Anglo-Rhodesian negotiations took place. Lord Goodman, operating in a discreet go-between capacity during 1971, finally succeeded in finding the basis for an agreement between the two governments. The British Foreign Secretary, Sir Alec Douglas-Home, claimed that the terms fell within the Five Principles, which he had himself first enumerated as Prime Minister in 1964. On 25 November a White Paper containing the proposals was made public. The settlement clearly represented a British retreat from the *Fearless* position of three years before. The White Paper itself stated that the new constitution would be a modified version of 'the constitution adopted in Rhodesia in 1969', which had been founded on explicitly discriminatory lines (see Appendix). Ultimately the success of the settlement terms depended on the implementation of the fifth principle: that the British Government would need to be satisfied that any proposed basis for independence was acceptable to the people of Rhodesia as a whole. The Pearce Commission accordingly visited Rhodesia on 11 January 1972 to 'ascertain directly from all sections of the population of Rhodesia whether or not the proposals are acceptable'.[5]

The agreement, and the impending visit of the Pearce Commission, marked a period of relative freedom for political activity, which was used by the African National Council (ANC), formed in mid-December 1971, to mobilize (black) opinion against the proposals. Bishop Abel Muzorewa, the ANC Chairman and then regarded as one of the most moderate members of the ANC Executive, described them in a letter to *The Times* on 11 February 1972 as 'both an insult to the African people and a prescription for a bloodbath'. It was no accident that the initials of the new body were the same as those of the African National Congress under which the nationalists had been united in the late 1950s. The importance attached to this reminder of pristine unity was also reflected in the composition of the Executive, carefully balanced between former ZAPU and ZANU officials, many of whom had been recently released from detention.

Perhaps one of the most ominous new factors for the Rhodesian Administration was the indication of potential discontent among some members of the Rhodesian African Rifles. Two of the Commissioners noted that:

> A group of African members of an Army security unit, including N.C.O.'s, rejected the proposals (with one exception) largely from reasons relating to a feeling of unjust and racially biased treatment by the Government, although they were obviously being treated as a privileged group.[6]

On several occasions in the past, nationalists have cast doubts on the loyalty of the Rhodesian African Rifles. They have claimed that deserters had taken refuge in Zambia and that numbers of black soldiers were imprisoned at a camp near Salisbury, in 1968, for refusing to go to the Zambezi valley. Although such claims are difficult to substantiate, there may well be some truth in them. As recently as December 1973, it was reliably reported that six black NCOs at Nkomo garrison – named as Davis, Verengayi, Philemon, Patrick and Pedzisayi – had been charged with mutiny, tried by court-martial and gaoled for twenty-five years.[7]

The Army has depended heavily on the loyalty and the acknowledged professionalism of its black soldiers; and there is no doubt that the Rhodesian African Rifles (RAR) has a strong sense of corporate identity, reinforced by the practice of recruiting largely through family connections and from the Karanga people who live around Gutu and Chilimanzi in the Fort Victoria area. But, whatever the truth in allegations of disaffection, the black members of the Rhodesian security forces must find their position increasingly invidious as the conflict intensifies. In August 1974 the Rhodesian GOC remarked: 'it must be appreciated that the terrorists are using all possible means to "get at" African soldiers, policemen and airmen': though he went on to declare that, despite these pressures, they had been performing well.[8]

The implications of these developments within Rhodesia were not lost on the nationalist parties abroad. Both ZAPU and

ZANU recognized the opportunity for a fresh offensive in the new conditions created by the ANC's successful mobilization of black opinion against the 1971 settlement proposals. In January demonstrations in Shabani, Gwelo, Salisbury, Fort Victoria and Umtali took place and deteriorated into serious confrontations with the police that resulted in several deaths. There seemed to be fairly widespread fears among urban Blacks that their views might not be heard by the Commissioners, or that the Pearce Commission itself might be no more than a whitewashing exercise for the British and Rhodesian Governments. In the circumstances, some degree of violence was probably inevitable. The ANC leadership, despite its commitment to the non-violent expression of opposition, was unable to prevent some physical intimidation from taking place or mass protests from becoming violent. The Rhodesian Administration for its part did not hesitate to apply administrative sanctions and restrictions on some individuals and groups who worked to oppose the settlement terms.

In the event, the Pearce Commission found widespread discontent among urban and rural Africans at all levels. In May 1972, it concluded:

> We are satisfied on our evidence that the Proposals are acceptable to the great majority of Europeans. We are equally satisfied, after considering all our evidence, including that on intimidation, that the majority of Africans rejected the Proposals. In our opinion the people of Rhodesia as a whole do not regard the Proposals as acceptable as a basis for independence.

The Commission considered that the main reasons for the emphatic black rejection included a profound distrust of the Government; the failure to consult African leaders at any stage in the negotiations; and a persistent, if unrealistic, belief in the extent of Britain's ability to continue influencing events in Rhodesia.

4 The Zimbabwe Nationalists take the Initiative

Despite efforts by the exiled nationalist groups to take the credit, the formation of the African National Council and its mobilization of opposition to the proposed 1971 settlement appears to have been an essentially spontaneous internal initiative. There was, however, a general recognition that previous tactics had failed and that there was a need for a new approach. As early as mid-1971 the Chairman of ZANU, Herbert Chitepo, had told a Danish journalist, Jasper Soe: 'It is useless to engage in conventional warfare with well-equipped Rhodesian and South African troops along the Zambezi.'[1]

More recently, at one of ZANU's biennial conferences held in September 1973, Chitepo admitted that too much emphasis had been placed on military activity at the expense of political matters. Elaborating on his 1971 statement, he confirmed that a change of strategy had taken place between 1969 and 1972:

> We have since tried to correct this tragic error by politicizing and mobilizing the people before mounting any attacks against the enemy. After politicizing our people it became easier for them to co-operate with us and to identify with our programme.[2]

The military views of ZAPU, too, had undergone some changes.

As a first step, an attempt was made to restore some measure of unity in the nationalist movement. At the Organization of African Unity (OAU) Liberation Committee meeting at Benghazi in January 1972, both ZANU and ZAPU made declarations of their intentions to unite. And the OAU, hoping to encourage this process, stated that its liberation funds would only be given to a united front. These hopes appeared to have made some headway when on 23 March at Mbeya in Tanzania, ZAPU and ZANU signed a protocol establishing a Joint Military Command (JMC), which was to be 'responsible for planning and conducting the revolutionary war in all its aspects'. Although FROLIZI was not a party to the United Front, both the JMC and FROLIZI, which was recognized to exist 'at the military level', received financial support from the OAU Liberation Committee. The April 1972 issue of *Zimbabwe News* commented that 'the formation of the United Front has given ZANU and ZAPU the chance to jointly study the question of correct ideology calmly and seriously'. However, the JMC failed to get off the ground. According to Maxey 'this was probably because ZANU was fairly advanced in its programme of infiltration of the north-east of Rhodesia, which had begun before the JMC was formed. To have tried to have involved ZAPU at that stage would have put the programme back'.[3]

In March 1973 persistent efforts by the OAU conciliation committee succeeded in persuading ZAPU and ZANU to form a Joint Military and Political Council, although this proved to be no more effective than the old JMC. Both organizations proceeded independently with their offensives. The rapid intensification of the insurgency and the resulting increase in the number of incidents over the past three years makes it impossible to describe events in detail.[4] The events described below have therefore been selected to illustrate the nature of the conflict in Rhodesia.

During 1972, ZAPU commandos had introduced a new tactic – the landmine – to the conflict along the border with Zambia. Rhodesian security forces had been expecting such a development following the extensive use of mines in Mozambique and the Caprivi Strip. In August, a farmer from Karoi was injured when his car hit a mine in the Mana Pools area. An attempt was made to sabotage the railway close to the Victoria Falls. In October, an army vehicle struck a mine in the Chete Game Reserve near Lake Kariba: a Rhodesian Army sergeant was killed, and a trooper wounded. On 8 January 1973 a South African vehicle detonated a mine on a track near the Zambezi in north-western Rhodesia: two South African policemen were killed, and three South Africans and two Rhodesians wounded.

In response to this last incident, the Rhodesian Government closed the border with Zambia (see below, pp. 276–80).

Whilst ZAPU was launching its mine offensive along the Zambian border, ZANU was in the process of opening up a new front. Taking advantage of the disruption in Mozambique's Tete district, caused by FRELIMO's expanding activity in the area, ZANU insurgents infiltrated into north-eastern Rhodesia, making use of FRELIMO supply routes and bases. Although probably still unaware of the extent and depth of ZANU penetration in the area, Ian Smith nevertheless felt obliged to warn a relatively ignorant, if rumour-ridden white public. The security situation, he declared, in a radio interview on 4 December, was 'far more serious than it appears on the surface, and if the man in the street could have access to the security information which I and my colleagues in Government have, then I think he would be a lot more worried than he is today'. And, on the following day, Defence Headquarters issued the first detailed communiqué since August 1971, admitting that security forces had clashed with armed nationalists:

> Continued vigilance on the part of the Security Forces in the border areas within the past fourteen days has led to the death and capture of a number of terrorists who recently infiltrated Rhodesia with the intention of subverting the local population and establishing bases and arms caches. A considerable quantity of arms and explosives of Communist origin has been captured.

In November, while patrolling in the Mzarabani Tribal Trust Land which lies between Centenary and the Mozambique border, security forces intercepted a large column comprising eighty porters, each carrying weapons and leading a donkey similarly loaded. Despite the fact that ZANU personnel had spent the greater part of 1972 in carefully preparing a political base for the military offensive which was to follow, this clash with the security forces probably forced them to begin military action sooner than they would have chosen. In any case, ZANU's military wing, the Zimbabwe African National Liberation Army, opened its campaign with a series of attacks on isolated white farmsteads in the Centenary area. The first of these took place on 21 December 1972 at Altena Farm in

Centenary, belonging to the de Borchgrave family and then occupied only by the farmer's four children and their grandmother. One of the children was injured. The family then moved for protection to neighbouring Whistlefield farm, owned by the Dalgleish family, which on 23 December also came under attack. Mr de Borchgrave and another of his children were injured. Stores on the farms were raided, and an army vehicle on the way to Whistlefield farm was blown up in an explosion which killed one member of the security forces and injured three others. On 28 December, a security force communiqué announced that another army vehicle had been blown up and three soldiers wounded. A ZANU communiqué covering the period stated that fifteen soldiers had been killed in a battle seventy-five miles from the Mozambique border. ZANU also claimed that Whistlefield farm had been used by security forces as a command post after the Altena attack and that twenty-five of them had been killed in the attack on the farm on 23 December. On the same day they claimed to have destroyed an army vehicle, killing thirty-one soldiers. On 22 December a security force communiqué had announced that as a result of a combined operation with Portuguese forces on the Rhodesia–Mozambique border, two guerrillas had been killed.

Soon after these initial raids against white farms, the guerrillas appeared to be well-established in the Chiweshe Tribal Trust Land, which was of considerable strategic importance for their operation. The population and terrain of the area provided good cover for the guerrillas, who were then able to carry their operations into the surrounding farming areas of Centenary, Umvukwes and Mazoe.

Security authorities described how:

> Once across the frontier the guerrillas are guided by local tribesmen as they move southwards by night in single file. Their routes follow river lines or well-worn paths, in order to avoid detection by trackers. Porters, changed regularly along the route, carry supplies which are used later to set up arms caches and medical supplies nearer the intended target. Generally these convoys amount to no more than a few dozen but there have been occasions when a score of guerrillas were accompanied by over a hundred porters. Not only is the party

fed by the population, but local assistance is called on to help cover the tracks of larger groups by driving livestock in their wake the following day. About ten or twelve miles may be covered in a single night; during the daytime the convoy will rest close to water and near a *kraal* which will supply food. Great care is taken to conceal all signs of the resting place before moving off. The arms are hidden by guerrillas in small quantities over a large area, using bushes, rocks and crevasses. If they are left for any length of time they have to be protected from ants. Chinese anti-vehicle mines were originally cased in wood until it was found that termites ate away at these cases. Grain and mealie meal are hidden in caves, and some *kraals* have stored their grain at such a distance that the guerrilla can help himself. Frequently food is stolen from European farms and stores.[5]

It seems from the pattern which emerged from these and subsequent attacks on farmsteads in the Centenary, Mangula and Shamva districts that the guerrillas first obtained from local villagers the names of unpopular farmers in the area and selected their farms for attack. They surrounded and then raked the house with automatic fire, lobbing grenades through the windows and blasting the buildings with rockets or explosives before leaving with a parting burst of automatic fire. Security units coming to the scene were often delayed by landmines planted in advance on approach roads, so giving the guerrillas time to disappear into the darkness.

In addition to the change in tactics from the open confrontation of previous years, the guerrillas had succeeded to a significant degree in securing the support of local tribesmen. Farmers were placed in a situation where their house-servants or farm labourers may have been subject to the influence of the guerrillas. One farmer from Centenary, with experience of the Mau Mau in Kenya, remarked that 'the atmosphere among farmers here is very similar, except that we know these chaps are using highly sophisticated modern weapons. I would call it Mao Mao rather than Mau Mau.'[6]

Also reminiscent of the Kenyan emergency has been the use of traditional spirit mediums to stir up feelings among local tribesmen against the Administration. The guerrillas were able to secure the support of several mediums, one of the most significant being that of Nehanda – a previous medium of

Nehanda had played a central role in the 1896 war of resistance against the white pioneer settlers. References to ancestral spirits and to the '*Chimurenga*', as the wars of the 1890s are called, have been common and provide inspiration for many nationalists. One man, for example, stated in court that he had felt he could not sit idly by while 'four million people were suffering. You snatched away our country unlawfully ... we are going to fulfil the aims of the war we abandoned in 1897'.[7] Chimutengwende remarked that before infiltrating back into Rhodesia in 1964 after their training in Ghana, 'each freedom fighter then swore a solemn oath never to give away useful information to the enemy and never to betray the spirit of Chaminuka, our great nineteenth century Shona prophet'.[8]

In a message to the Zimbabwe African National Liberation Army (ZANLA) smuggled out of Connemara prison where he was detained until December 1974, Sithole, as President of ZANU and Commander-in-Chief of ZANLA, exhorted his followers in a similar vein:

> I greet you in the name of our brave and gallant heroes of the Chimurenga of 1896–7 who fell in the great cause of liberating this our wonderful country from foreign rule ... In the names of Mkwati, Nehanda, Kagubi, Mashayangombe, Makoni, Kumzi, Nyandoro and others in Mashonaland, and I greet you in the names of Somabulana, Mlugugulu, Dhliso, Siginyamatshe, Mpotshwana and others in Matabeleland who master-minded and prosecuted the first Chimurenga in Zimbabwe. The heroes of the first Chimurenga were defeated not because they had no fighting spirit but because the enemy had guns and our men only spears. They lacked that which makes men the same size ... The fighters of the second Chimurenga of Zimbabwe now also have guns – the thing that makes all men the same size – and we are confident that those who defeated us in the first Chimurenga will be defeated without fail.[9]

A prime objective of ZANU's operations would seem to have been the undermining of the myth of white invulnerability. On 8 January 1973 guerrillas attacked the District Commissioner's office at Mount Darwin – a symbol of white authority – fired at the local club, and dynamited a nearby bridge. According to a ZANU account, twenty-five members of the security forces were killed in a 'packed officers' mess', and twenty soldiers were killed in the bridge incident. A few days later two government land inspectors were killed, and a third, Gerald Hawkesworth, was captured. Hawkesworth was paraded as a ZANU prisoner-of-war in front of villagers on the way out of Rhodesia to Tanzania. His capture and eventual release in December 1973 received wide publicity and was of considerable propaganda value to the nationalist forces.

Although the security authorities had been aware of nationalist activity in the north-eastern border area before Christmas 1972, the Administration certainly appeared to have been thrown off balance by the suddenness of the attacks and the significant degree of support the guerrillas had secured among the local population. The Rhodesian Front MP for the Sinoia/Umvukwes area stated in the House of Assembly in March 1973: 'There is no doubt that . . . the forces and people of the Centenary area were caught by surprise . . . at the outset there was certainly a lack of co-ordination between the Army, Police, the Air Force and the Police Reserve.'

With ZANU and ZAPU already active in the field, FROLIZI felt obliged to take some action in support of the militant claims it had made since its formation. Towards the end of 1972 or the beginning of 1973, FROLIZI shifted its training camp and seventy recruits to eastern Zambia near Feira, where the boundaries of Rhodesia, Zambia and Mozambique share a common point. On 17 February two groups of six men each crossed the Zambesi into Rhodesia.[10] Three of the twelve men were Coloured: as far as is known, this was the first occasion on which members of the Coloured community had entered Rhodesia as insurgents.

By the end of February one of the groups, led by a man referred to simply as 'Moses', had arrived in the Mukwichi Tribal Trust Land which is near the small town of Miami. Having established a base in the area, they attempted to find local recruits. The second-in-command of the group, Christopher Gumborinotaya, had a name which indicated that he was originally a Korekore tribesman from the north-east; and he was probably familiar with the area, especially as his mother, whom he had visited on his arrival, lived in Mukwichi. The presence of the men was discovered after Moses and Gumborinotaya had visited an African store and had been ordered by two African District Assistants to produce identification papers. When they had failed to comply, the district assistants had attempted to arrest them but then fled when the FROLIZI men had fired at them with pistols concealed in their clothes. The follow-up operations by the security forces, which included 'sticks' of about half-a-dozen men each from the RAR, the BSA Police and the Police Reserve, resulted in two members of the FROLIZI group being killed, three captured, and one apparently escaping without trace by 16 March – a month after the initial crossing. One member of the Karoi Police Reserve Anti-Terrorist Unit was killed when he and his seven companions were ambushed by the FROLIZI men, who were forced to withdraw after a security force aircraft had been called up and given away their position.

The second group, which included two Coloureds and was commanded by Hatududuzi Naison Guvamatanga, a former school teacher, took a different route through Rhodesia. The group lost its way after the rain had damaged their compass and they ran out of food. They finally arrived on Groenvlei Farm near the small mining settlement of Mangula. When the farm was empty, they raided it for food and then set fire to it before leaving. In a car stolen from the farm, they drove to Sinoia, from where they hijacked another car, forcing two Africans to drive them to Hartley. Commandeering yet another car they made their way to Gatooma, where they held up a petrol pump attendant and seized the station's takings. From Gatooma they drove through Que Que and finally abandoned their vehicle near the tiny *dorp* called Umvuma and made their way to a farm in the Enkeldoorn district where they set up camp.

On 25 March the two Coloured men left to look for recruits in Salisbury, where they arrived two days later in the mainly Coloured suburb of Arcadia. They were recognized and reported to the police, who immediately set up road blocks around all the Coloured suburbs and sealed every exit from Salisbury. Unaware of the police search, the two men were staying in Ardbennie, another Coloured suburb, with the brother of one of the men.

Again their presence had been reported, and they were arrested on 29 March.

After parting from their two Coloured colleagues, the four black members of the group had made their way to Wedza and set up camp on Laughing Waters Farm belonging to an Afrikaner, Andries Joubert. Again the presence of the insurgents was given away after a clash with an African plain-clothes policeman in a store. Their camp had also been accidentally discovered by an African herdsman who reported his find to his employer. When Joubert arrived at the camp and was about to arrest its single occupant, Guvamatanga shot him from an ambush position. When security forces arrived later, Guvamatanga and his companion had disappeared. The local Afrikaner community was angered by the failure of the security authorities to forewarn local whites of the insurgent presence. In his article, Tony Kirk quotes the statement of Joubert's father to a *Sunday Mail* (Salisbury) reporter, which provides an insight into the reactions of the white community to the war:

> A few of us here have decided we have had enough. If the government can't do much for our security, then the older people are going to take up their rifles as we did in the old times – we shall do as we think right and just. We can't see that these terrorists should be able to kill while we have to stay at home and bury our young men that are shot. I think the old Boers had the right ideas. We should move into the Zambesi and clean the whole valley of these terrorists.

On 16 June Guvamatanga was finally spotted by an African policeman on a bus at Enkeldoorn and was shot and captured as he tried to escape.

A few observations on the FROLIZI incursion are pertinent. Their hopes of obtaining recruits and mobilizing the population had met with varying success. The Moses group succeeded in securing support from at least three *kraal* heads and their villages. The other group had less success, although it is worth noting that at least fourteen people were imprisoned for assisting or hiding the men. Equally significant, however, was the part played by black petty officials of the Administration. Kirk notes that 'at every turn the guerrillas encountered demands that they identify themselves' from District Assistants or plain-clothes policemen. Once positively located and surrounded, they had little chance of escaping from the security forces. Considering the conspicuous manner in which the Guvamatanga group travelled across the country, the venture was fortunate to have lasted as long as it did. The FROLIZI group's movements in the Midlands and its presence in the capital city seemed to have had a greater psychological impact on the complacent white population than the more remote insurgent activity in the north-east.

The urban areas had been relatively free of overt political violence, although there were occasional indications that the situation was not completely dormant. On 20 October 1973 a domestic servant, William Chikandamina, was seriously burned when an incendiary grenade he was carrying in the Borrowdale suburb of Salisbury exploded. And a few days before the 1974 General Election, a hand-grenade was thrown into a crowded Salisbury nightclub injuring six people. Although the risk of detection for the nationalists would be high, white Rhodesia would probably be extremely vulnerable to a campaign of sustained urban guerrilla activity. Kirk suggests:

> Many people have underestimated the value of this psychological effect in a guerrilla campaign in a developing country. The Rhodesian government, for instance, placed great importance on attracting foreign investment into the country and otherwise stimulating economic activity. To encourage businessmen it tried to project an image of a strong government and political stability. The initial upsurge in the liberation struggle in 1972 did not entirely destroy the image of stability ... But the presence of guerrillas in the country's largest city provided a telling contradiction to the government's determined optimism. Combined with the outbreak in the north-east, it shook business confidence and, had Rhodesia not possessed stringent controls on the movement of foreign exchange, would probably have led to a flight of capital.

A determined campaign of urban violence, despite the undoubted hazards for its perpetrators, would be likely to add considerable momentum to the rising emigration rate.

A variety of activities has characterized the ZANU offensive in the north-east. The attacks against white farmsteads have been mentioned already. As measures to protect the farmhouses themselves were effectively implemented, the attacks were directed more against farm equipment or outbuildings, including stores and the huts of farm labourers. The purpose of attacking isolated farming communities was probably to try and drive the farmers from the land; thereby not only damaging the important agricultural industry but also weakening the security of the rural areas where farmers perform vital Police Reserve functions. The attacks against black farmworkers' property – many of them aliens from Malawi or Mozambique – may have been calculated to produce a labour shortage on the farms by frightening away alien workers. This and the attraction of returning to an independent Mozambique has resulted in a serious labour shortage in the north-eastern farming areas. In the white agricultural sector in 1973, 130,235 employees out of a total of 255,886 were non-Rhodesians.

On the evening of 5 July 1973 a band of seventeen guerrillas with sub-machine-guns raided a Jesuit Mission School at St Alberts in the Muvuradonha mountains. They harangued the schoolchildren and staff and abducted 273 of them before splitting into separate groups and making for the Mozambique border nearly thirty miles away. According to the Zimbabwe African National Liberation Army (ZANLA) Chimurenga communiqué No. 4:

> A high powered team of high-ranking commandos and political commissars . . . address(ed) a political meeting at St Albert's Mission at the invitation of students, staff and local people. The high powered ZANLA team freely addressed the meeting for two hours . . . after the address . . . the people present unanimously reached an agreement that every able-bodied male and female present should go for military training. As the people marched, led by ZANLA officers, some got tired and others sick, and therefore decided to go back to the Mission. On their way back they were rounded up by rebel terrorist forces and taken to interrogation centres before being allowed to go back to the Mission. Meanwhile the enemy forces who tried to pursue the ZANLA fighters and the people, were blown up by mines which had been laid by ZANLA before the two-hour address. Two enemy troops were killed and six wounded and their truck destroyed by the explosion. The ZANLA mission was very highly successful.

This dramatic abduction of nearly 300 people was the largest single operation undertaken by the insurgents. However, it remains questionable how much the raid achieved for the guerrilla cause. Most of the children were aged between 7 and 16 and were hardly suitable material for recruits and, in the follow-up operation by security forces, the guerrillas were compelled to abandon them. One of the Mission staff who had insisted on accompanying the kidnapped children described what happened to them: 'After our capture we got lost very badly in the dense bush and finally about ninety children and myself found ourselves suddenly alone with a terrorist who was armed with a Communist-type weapon. He told us we were to keep still during the day and keep under cover.' Finally the guerrilla abandoned them saying 'I am tired of this whole thing. You can go back.' On the morning following the raid, security forces caught up with one of the groups and a guerrilla was killed in the battle. One 15-year-old girl was killed, according to the Rhodesian Government, as a 'result of an accident following the discharge of a firearm by an African member of a police unit'. It is possible that there had been some liaison between a few of the older pupils and the guerrillas. The planning and execution of the raid certainly suggested that some of the guerrillas were well acquainted with the layout of the Mission, and several of them may have been former pupils. One of them, according to Father Rojek, had wanted to assault him 'because I refused to admit him to Standard One some years ago'.[11]

In other attacks on schools, teachers have been singled out for execution, although the motives for the killings are not always apparent. On 25 August, for example, five insurgents went to Mangare School in the Kandeya Tribal Trust Land near Mount Darwin and compelled three teachers to watch while they beat to death the headmaster, a Mr Chipara, who also happened to be the brother of one of the teachers. Such attacks against individuals may be explained by some private antipathy towards the individual or because he is regarded as supporting the administration in which case execution of the victim is intended to serve as a deterrent to others in similar positions.

Other features of the ZANU campaign are illustrated by a security force communiqué of 6 June 1974:

> Terrorists have continued to focus their attention on stores, and several have been broken into during the past two weeks. One store was gutted after its contents had been removed, while the storekeeper was robbed of $600. An African owned bus was stopped along a road north of Mount Darwin and the driver was made to hand over the $175 in his possession.

Buses travelling in the north-east have detonated mines so often that they are referred to as 'minesweepers'. Bus hijackings have not only proved lucrative financially but have also been used to make political points. On one occasion, a group of eight guerrillas commandeered a bus in Dande village near the Mozambique border. They told the driver that he had ignored previous warnings that buses should stay clear of the area. Some of the guerrillas remained with the passengers and conductor to prevent anyone from calling the security forces, while the others took the driver and his bus into the bush where it was set alight. The driver was sent back to Dande with instructions to 'report everything that has happened; do not leave out anything'.[12] Individual passengers have sometimes been singled out for particular attention. On another occasion an insurgent, after hijacking a bus near Mount Darwin, kidnapped a local tribal official, Headman Kandeya, and shot him dead. Tribal officials associated in nationalist eyes with the Government's rural administration have frequently become victims of ZANLA execution squads.[13]

The increased number of raids on stores, bus hijacking for the cash takings and the kidnapping of civilians from mid-1973 suggested that the insurgents may have been experiencing supply and manpower problems, as the Administration's counter-insurgency measures became more effective. On 24 November 1974, newsmen were told by senior security officers that an estimated seventy-five per cent of the insurgent leadership had been killed since the launching of 'Operation Hurricane' at the end of 1972 up to July 1974. As a result the 'terrorists operating in the north-east are of low calibre. Their average age tends to be about 19 and some as young as 15 have been killed during operations. It is estimated that between 350 and 400 terrorists are now in Rhodesia'. By the beginning of the last week in November, 478 insurgents had been killed (twenty-nine in November alone), 149 black civilians had died and about 1,000 had been abducted. Another thirty-four people, including Whites, had been killed by land mines.[14] There did appear to be some evidence for security force claims that as original groups of highly-trained and disciplined insurgents were broken up or eliminated, they tended to be replaced by local recruits whose training had been much less adequate and whose activities sometimes amounted to sheer banditry. In March 1974, for instance, during the trial of a man charged with robbery in the Sipolilo area, the prosecutor noted that offences committed by Blacks masquerading as 'terrorists' were becoming more frequent.[15] The lack of discipline among some men purporting to be guerrillas is illustrated by the careers of Kid Marogorongo and Solomon Ngoni who had achieved notoriety in the area. They had been responsible for cutting off the feet of a Malawian woman and severing the upper lips of two Blacks, one of them a woman called Sarah Chinyani Masawi, with a bayonet and rusty pliers. In addition, they had raped several women including a 14-year-old girl and an expectant mother eight months pregnant. The breakdown of discipline represented by such activities can hardly have helped further the nationalist cause. ZANU does appear to have established some machinery, however summary and rudimentary, to maintain its authority. It is thought that Marogorongo and Ngoni might have faced execution at the hands of a ZANU court if they had not first been killed by security forces.

On 15 July a security force communiqué announced the deaths of two senior guerrilla leaders, Silas Murwira (alias James Bond) and Patrick Tavengwa (alias Mao) who appear to have had some charismatic appeal and to have been more effective insurgents than Marogorongo and Ngoni. Both had been trained in Tanzania by Chinese instructors: the former during 1968 and the latter between 1971 and 1972. Murwira had been active in the north-east since the beginning of December 1972 and had been involved in numerous actions, including the mass abduction of schoolchildren from St Albert's Mission in July 1973. Tavengwa moved into the north-east during November 1973 and was said by security authorities to have been responsible for 'five murders, four serious assaults against innocent tribesmen, an unsuccessful attack on a police post as well as several robberies'. In June and July 1974, the two had joined forces and taken part in several raids on white farms before they were killed by security forces.

One of the more effective tactics employed by the insurgents has been the land–mining attacks on security roads, although the results have often been indiscriminate. While security personnel and vehicles have frequently been victims, even more civilians, both black and white, have been killed or injured. For example, two Blacks were killed and twenty-nine injured when a civilian passenger vehicle detonated a mine in the Chiweshe Tribal Trust Land on 23 September. A day later, another African died when his truck hit a mine also in Chiweshe.

The most successful operations by the insurgent forces have usually resulted from hit-and-run ambushes which have caught security units by surprise. At the end of April 1973, the security forces suffered one of their worst setbacks when they lost five soldiers and another five were seriously wounded in a ZANLA ambush. Even so, three guerrillas were killed and others captured in the incident.[16] In another such attack on 8 March 1974, ZAPU commandos surprised a South African Police patrol on the banks of the Zambezi upstream of Victoria Falls, killing five policemen. A black policeman who had witnessed the ambush from a distance escaped, and security forces later traced the tracks of the insurgents to a point on the Zambezi where they had crossed back into Zambia. In an attempt to forestall any unease among South Africa's white public over the incident, the South African Minister of Police, speaking at the passing-out parade of Coloured policemen at Bishops Lavis Training College, stated that immediate

> instructions were given that 100 men should be drawn from Pretoria, the Witwatersrand and the West Rand area for a specific task on the border. In less than six hours after the instructions were issued in Pretoria, the 100 men were at the border, approximately 1,600 kilometres from where they were called up, fully equipped with weapons, sleeping bags, camping equipment, etc., and ready to undertake their task.

When insurgent groups found themselves in a position where they were forced to engage in set battles with security forces, they were invariably at a serious disadvantage, given their numerical inferiority, their vulnerability to aerial observation and attack, and the greater mobility of airborne security forces. It was announced on 20 May, for instance, that twenty guerrillas had been killed in some of the heaviest fighting of the war in the north-east. Sixteen guerrillas from two different bands were killed, including several leaders, in a battle which lasted throughout a weekend. The security force communiqué stated:

> The operations which involved intensive air and ground action reflected a high degree of co-operation between the forces taking part. These include regular Police, Army and Air Force personnel as well as Police Reserve and Police Anti-Terrorist Units (P.A.T.U.), national servicemen and territorial units. Two minor casualties were suffered by the security forces.

Quantities of arms and ammunition were also recovered.

Another clash with guerrillas which occurred on Wednesday, 14 August, between Mount Darwin and Bindura illustrated the tactics of the security forces very well. Early on the Wednesday morning a group of insurgents was sighted and reported to the Joint Operations Command Centre (J.O.C.C.). Within twenty minutes helicopters, each carrying a 'stick' of Rhodesia Light Infantry soldiers, were on their way to the spot. As the men were dropped the guerrillas, who had concealed themselves in the surrounding countryside, opened fire. While the troops were being deployed on the ground, the helicopter pilots helped direct the battle by locating pockets of insurgents from the air. The insurgents, outnumbered and exposed, decided that there was no point in trying to make a stand and attempted to disperse. But their attempt to escape was thwarted with the arrival of fixed-wing aircraft, which had been called in to bomb and strafe them. Eight insurgents were killed, while Major E. C. Adamms of the security forces also died in the engagement. The comment of a Special Branch officer underlined the difficulties experienced by insurgent groups in such conditions, no matter how determined their resistance: 'They put up a good fight but if we meet these chaps face to face as we did in this instance we will beat them every time.'[17]

Although airpower has played a crucial role in the successes of Rhodesian counter-insurgency operations, the Air Force has not come through unscathed. Over the past three years, at least five helicopters, several light aircraft and a Canberra bomber have crashed for one reason or another. One or two helicopters have also certainly been badly damaged by ground fire. The Canberra which crashed on 6 April 1974 may, it is believed, have fallen victim to the explosion of its own bombs. According to the Ministry of Defence, the bomber was on a routine 'Canberra low-level sortie' at the time of the accident. ZANU however, claimed that it had been shot down by ZANLA ground fire during a battle near Mudzengerere village in the Centenary district.[18] Two light aircraft crashed on the 14 and 20 of April, according to a security force statement, 'in a remote border area'. However, there is good reason to believe that the first plane was shot down by FRELIMO, possibly with a Soviet *Strella* ground-to-air missile over Mozambique about seventy miles north of Mkumbura which is on Rhodesia's north-eastern border. The FRELIMO communiqué stated:

> A 'Dornier' reconnaissance plane was shot down in Fingoe. The pilots were killed. Documents found on one of the bodies identified him as DURRETT Patrick Rickman, born September 24, 1947 [1954?]. He carried a Rhodesian driver's licence No. 90978 – Airforce. We also salvaged a FN rifle No. L–451 and a first aid kit.

The communiqué was published alongside a photograph of the driving licence.[19] The Ministry of Defence statement confirming that Flight Lieutenant B. C. Weinmann and Senior Aircraftsman P. R. Durrett had been killed in the crashed aircraft also mentioned that it had been tampered with prior to being found by security forces. If it was not a case of mistaken identity, the FRELIMO claim that it was a Dornier is interesting as the Rhodesian Air Force was not known to have such aircraft. There is the possibility that it had been acquired from the Portuguese, who had received several shipments of DO-27s from West Germany for extensive use in the African wars. The second light aircraft apparently crashed while searching for the first.

The location of the crashed plane raises the question of Rhodesian military operations outside the country. During 1971, these amounted to little more than informal liaison with Portuguese forces across the border. In April, three Rhodesian soldiers had been killed when their vehicle detonated a mine in a river-bed on the border after returning from a visit to a Portuguese post. During 1972, Rhodesian authorities became increasingly alarmed at the inability of the Portuguese to contain FRELIMO's expanding activity in Tete, and the Rhodesian Prime Minister expressed these fears on his visit to Lisbon in October 1972. Irritated by these insinuations the then Portuguese Prime Minister, Dr Marcello Caetano, replied in a broadcast on 15 November that 'some of our neighbours with less experience do not conceal their fears and in this way play the game of the enemy. They have been told more than once there is no reason for their great apprehension.' Nevertheless, despite the Portuguese Government's susceptibilities, Rhodesia gained something out of the Portuguese. In April 1973 the Commander of the Portuguese forces in Mozambique, General Kaulza de Arriaga, disclosed that there was a 'gentleman's agreement' between Rhodesian and Portuguese security forces that either side might cross the border in 'hot pursuit' of FRELIMO or ZANU guerrillas. And in an interview in the November 1973 issue of the *Rhodesian Farmer*, the Rhodesian Prime Minister elaborated further on the issue:

> It is a well-known international convention which says that if you have terrorist incursions in your country, and if you are chasing them, and are in hot pursuit, then you are entitled to go across international borders in hot pursuit. This is the agreement that exists between us . . . Obviously we don't want to immediately stop at an imaginary line and let people get away with murder.

In fact this simply gave public recognition to what had been going on for some time. For example, a report in the *Sunday Times* (11 June 1972) by Philip Jacobsen mentions several fierce engagements said to have involved Rhodesian troops in Mozambique, including one incident in which at least five guerrillas were killed by a Special Air Service unit. The detention and secret trial of the journalist, Peter Niesewand, after his report of

Rhodesian military involvement in Mozambique, illustrated the sensitivity of the Rhodesian authorities to the issue. During the trial Mr J. F. Fleming, Secretary for Law and Order, was called as a state witness and acknowledged the fact: 'I am saying that Rhodesian forces were there (i.e. in Mozambique), but we were embarrassed by reports saying we were there.'[20] By the end of 1973 the scale and frequency of Rhodesian operations in Mozambique had grown very considerably since 1971. Max Hastings reporting in the London *Evening Standard* stated that 400 men of the Rhodesian Light Infantry had joined the Special Air Service units in carrying out sweeps against insurgent bases in Mozambique. The helicopter-borne troops were dropped for operations which lasted up to two or three weeks. Hastings quoted one RLI NCO who said: 'When we are on the Rhodesian side of the border, we are in action perhaps about once a fortnight. But in Mozambique we are in contact virtually every day.'[21]

Corroboration of these news reports of Rhodesian security forces' increasing involvement in Mozambique's Tete district came from a secret report by middle-ranking Portuguese Army officers which was published only a few days before the Lisbon coup of 25 April 1974. It stated:

> Contrary to official denials, there exists a close collaboration in the military field between the Portuguese Army and Rhodesian troops, who include mercenaries from South Africa and other countries. This has been verified for the past four years all along the border with Rhodesia, in the districts of Tete and Vila Pery, but since the beginning of last year the collaboration has intensified with the permission given to the airborne troops from Rhodesia to operate in a very large area, north and south of the Zambezi, up to (and in certain cases beyond) the meridian that passes through the village of Carinde, in the Zambezi, 100 kms inside Mozambique territory. These operations, co-ordinated with the Portuguese military operations, consist of speedy paratroop actions in specified areas and the liquidation of any human lives (there being no military or civilian prisoners) and a return to their bases in Rhodesia.[22]

David Martin, who visited Tete with FRELIMO met some 1,500 refugees fleeing from north-west Tete where Rhodesian troops had been operating. He was told by one refugee that Rhodesian troops had crossed the Zambezi in inflatable boats during the night of 21 July 1973. Five days later, after clashing with a small band of FRELIMO guerrillas, villages in his area were attacked by bombers and jet-fighters, and troops were landed by helicopter.[23]

5 Counter-Insurgency Measures

The Rhodesian administration has responded to the upsurge of insurgency since 1972 with a variety of economic, administrative and military counter-measures.

THE BORDER CLOSURE[1]

On 30 August 1972 a white farmer was injured in a land-mine explosion in the Mana Pools National Park. The incident led to the first of several warnings by the Smith régime to Zambia:

> Since it is within the scope and power of the Zambian authorities to prevent terrorists operating from their country, the Rhodesian Government feels that it must make it clear beyond all doubt that, if the Zambian Government fails to recognize its responsibilities in this matter, the consequences would rest squarely on their shoulders.[2]

Then, on 13 November, after the mine incident in the Chete Game Reserve at the end of October, in which a Rhodesian soldier was killed, the Rhodesians again warned the Zambian authorities. A senior Rhodesian official told the Zambian Secretary for Transport, Mr P. A. Siwo, that if the Zambian Government continued to allow 'terrorists' to operate against Rhodesia, road and rail traffic between the two countries would be halted. Two incidents on 8 January finally led the Government to carry out its threat. One was the landmine explosion near the Victoria Falls in which two South African policemen had died, and the other was the attack on Mount Darwin by ZANU guerrillas. An official Rhodesian statement on 10 January said that the border would remain closed until 'satisfactory assurances from the Zambian Government that they will no longer permit terrorists to operate against Rhodesia from their territory' were received. However, the full effect of the blockade was weakened by the announcement of exceptions for south-bound Zambian copper and north-bound mail and medical supplies. The supply of power to Zambia from Kariba was also unaffected.

The Rhodesian Government's handling of the border closure was widely criticized both inside and outside the country. In Zambia, a three-hour cabinet meeting was held on the evening of 9 January to discuss the crisis. Zambia had taken the previous Rhodesian threats seriously and used the time available to draw up contingency plans. President Kaunda in effect turned the tables on Mr Smith by accepting the closure as permanent. On 11 January, a spokesman for the Ministry of Power, Transport and Works announced that Zambia would no longer send her copper through Rhodesia, despite its exemption from the blockade: thereby denying Rhodesia a valuable source of foreign exchange. Immediate action was taken to establish alternative routes for Zambian traffic, and on 12 January a high-level meeting of government and copper mining officials, private transport organizations and diplomats was called to plan an emergency operation. For President Kaunda, the border closure and the resulting sympathy for Zambia's plight seemed to present an opportunity to reorientate the country's communications and economy away from dependence on the white south. As he stated: 'The blockade is a blessing in disguise. It gives us a golden opportunity to correct Zambia's false start.'[3]

In addition to being snubbed by Zambia, Rhodesia also managed to antagonize her closest allies, South Africa and Portugal, neither of whom were consulted prior to the closure. South Africa and Portugal both regarded the move as a potentially dangerous and unnecessary escalation of the conflict, as well as being harmful to their own economic interests. The South African Prime Minister, outlining his attitude, stated that: 'South Africa was not a party to this decision on the part of Rhodesia.' And he pointedly added, 'we do not initiate boycotts and we do not reply to sanctions with counter-boycotts'.[4] Once again, as in 1965, the Republic had been forcibly reminded that Rhodesia could be a serious barrier to her long-term objectives of improving relations with black states to the north.

The Rhodesian Government was also strongly criticized from various quarters in Rhodesia. The extreme right-wing groups regarded the Government's response, particularly the exemption of copper, as too weak and called for military action against insurgent bases in Zambia and the severance of power supplies from Kariba. The closing of the border was described by Pat Bashford, President of the liberal, multi-racial Centre Party as a 'tragic error' which 'not only damages the Rhodesian economy at a time when we can least afford it; it also does considerable harm to the trade of our friendly neighbours'.[5]

The size of the loss of revenue for Rhodesia Railways can be seen from the estimate of the monthly journal *Africa* (March 1973) that Rhodesia Railways' receipts from traffic with Zambia were over Rh. $16 million in 1971. The newly-formed Rhodesia Party 'doubted the wisdom' of the move and expressed the same fears as the Centre Party. In the face of all these adverse reactions the Government backed down. An official statement on 3 February declared: 'As a result of messages received the Rhodesian Government is now satisfied that their objectives in closing the border have been achieved. Accordingly the border will be reopened from 6 a.m. tomorrow.'[6] President Kaunda denied that he had given any assurances and confirmed that the border would remain closed, adding: 'How do I know Smith will not turn on the blockade again? It would be stupid of us to depend on some abstract assurances.'[7]

This reaction must have taken the Rhodesian Administration by surprise and certainly exposed the naivety of its thinking. In an interview shortly after the closure, Mr Smith described some of the 'new nations' around him as having 'no experience of responsible management' – in contrast, of course, to Rhodesia. He went on to say:

> I know the Bantu pretty well, and I believe that this is the sort of thing that they understand, when you say to one of them, look, friend, are you trying to throw your weight around, because if you are, you are going to come off second-best. He will say, right, we know where we stand.[8]

This kind of attitude is apparent in many of the régime's policies within Rhodesia, as well as in relations with neighbouring black states.

One of the effects of the border closure – intended to curb insurgent activity – was, on the contrary, to have removed the necessity for any understanding which may have existed between the Zambian Government and insurgents in Mozambique that there would be no attacks on the Beira–Umtali railway. Once the railway was no longer handling Zambian copper exports – and a substantial quantity of her imports – it became a prime target. It was in fact attacked for the first time by FRELIMO guerrillas on the last day of 1973.

The closure was also unsuccessful as a means of intimidating Zambia into taking action against insurgent groups based in her territory. Incidents along the border continued and tension increased. On 16 January, a Rhodesian patrol was fired on by Zambian soldiers between Kariba and Chirundu. A Rhodesian police launch was damaged by fire from the Zambian bank two days later. On 19 January, a South African patrol boat was fired on under Chirundu bridge, and on 11 February a Rhodesian angler was killed and his two companions injured when their boat was machine-gunned below Chirundu.

The Zambian authorities in turn accused Rhodesia of planting mines along the Zambian side of the border. On 15 February, only minutes before the arrival of a special United Nations mission at a site near Chirundu, to investigate the situation, a plastic anti-personnel mine injured two women, a teenage girl and two children. During 1973, at least twenty Zambians died as a result of mine incidents. Several Zambians were arrested and charged with treason for assisting Rhodesian agents to plant the mines. Rhodesian authorities denied any association with the explosions and went out of their way to point out that the explosions had occurred near to known 'terrorist' camps. The truth is difficult to establish. While it is possible that Rhodesian insurgents may have been behind some of the incidents, perhaps in order to sustain Zambian hostility towards Rhodesia, it is just as likely that there was some substance in the Zambian claims. In June 1968, a bridge over the Luangwa river near the Zambia–Mozambique border was destroyed; and, in 1969, shortly after the first Ndola/Dar-es-Salaam oil pipeline became operational, it was put out of action by saboteurs who blew up a pumping station near Iringa in Tanzania. The general view in Lusaka was that commandos from the white south had been responsible. It is possible that such incidents might have been the work of self-styled saboteurs like the 'Red Fox', whose private mission was to blow up ZAPU headquarters in Lusaka. The 'Red Fox' was a Rhodesian electrician, Harold Boyes, who was arrested at Kitwe in February 1969 and released in March 1971 after two years in prison. He revealed that his organization consisted of himself, a Rhodesian M.P., and two Salisbury businessmen, but stressed that it was a 'completely unofficial organization, it had nothing to do with the Government in any way'.[9]

The situation on the border was, therefore, already very tense when a further event focussed international attention on the area. On 15 May, Zambian troops opened fire on a party of American and Canadian tourists who were exploring a gorge below the Victoria Falls. Two Canadian girls were killed and an American man injured. It emerged that the major responsibility for the incident was that of the Zambian soldiers, whose conduct both before and during the affair was, according to reliable reports certainly questionable. Nevertheless, it remains to be explained as to why the Rhodesian authorities, who were certainly aware of the tension along the border, had not taken precautions to keep tourists away from areas of danger. The upsurge of insurgent activity in general, and the Victoria Falls shootings in particular, had an adverse effect on tourism – a major foreign exchange earner. According to official statistics, the number of holiday visitors to Rhodesia dropped from 339,210 for 1972 to 243,812 in 1973: a fall of almost thirty per cent. In 1974 the figure was lower still at 229,570.

MILITARY MEASURES

Even before the onset of renewed nationalist military activity from the end of 1972, the Rhodesian security forces were already experiencing shortages of finance and white manpower. In June 1973, the GOC stated in his Annual Report that Army morale was 'satisfactory' but that poor conditions of service and pay were giving cause for concern: 'Urgent measures are needed to halt the exodus of experienced men from the regular Army and to attract more recruits.' There was a similar situation in the Air Force and BSA Police.

The increased security burden also showed up the inadequacy of the existing structure and roles of National Service and the Territorial Force. The Defence Act of December 1972 introduced a number of measures in an attempt to remedy the situation. The period of National Service was increased from 245 to 365 days, and at the same time liability for service was extended to include personnel formerly exempted for minor medical deficiencies. In November, the catchment area for the weekly parades of Territorial Force members was enlarged from a seventeen to a thirty kilometre radius from all the main towns. This included both residents and, a new category, those employed within the prescribed areas. In March 1973, the Minister for Law and Order announced that men would be able to do their National Service in the BSA Police as well as in the Air Force and Army. In June the Minister of Defence announced that powers would be taken to deal with draft-dodgers which would require all employers to provide details of their employees between the ages of 17 and 30. It was hoped that the extra manpower resulting from the tightening of the conscription net would help to relieve the pressure on members of the Army Reserve or 'Dad's Army', most of whom were aged between 38 and 48 and who had been called up in August 1973 to release younger men for more active operational roles.

In February, plans were announced for a massive increase in the security forces, so as to shift the conduct of the war from the 'defensive' function of border control to a more 'offensive' role. The National Service intakes were to be doubled. Men over 25 who had no military commitment and had been in Rhodesia for more than five years were to be liable for one month's service annually and used 'principally for protective military duties'. At the same time it was announced – in order not to frighten off prospective immigrants – that immigrants would be given a five-year period of grace (later reduced to two years) although they would be able to volunteer for service sooner if they wished.

In April, a new joint recruiting centre was set up in Salisbury, and lump sum payments were offered to National Servicemen – up to Rh. $1,590 – in order to encourage them to stay an extra year. In May, another pay increase was announced, which was especially designed to persuade National Servicemen to remain in the Army, with the long-term aim of forming another RLI battalion. In March, the pay of Coloured and Asian National Servicemen was brought into line with their white colleagues in an attempt to counter rising resentment at this discrimination. A report on 31 March in the *Rhodesia Herald* listed a number of grievances. Non-whites cannot achieve any higher rank than NCO even if they are highly qualified and merit commissions. Non-white doctors, for instance, have not been called up, since doctors are automatically commissioned. One Salisbury Asian remarked: 'Officers must be saluted and Europeans cannot countenance saluting a non-white.' Non-white servicemen also complained of being refused service at hotels and restaurants while serving at Karoi and Kariba. One conscript told the reporter: 'We are turned away from the very places we are supposed to be defending.'

As a result of these measures, Mr P. K. Van der Byl, the Minister of Defence, felt able to tell the Rhodesian Front Congress in September that the Defence Forces were up to strength. It was anticipated that the field strength of the security forces could be doubled by mid-1975. In February, the Government had appointed Mr J. L. de Kock as a Deputy Minister in the Prime Minister's Office with the special responsibility for the co-ordination of the military and civilian aspects of security operations against insurgents in the country. The civil administration has become increasingly involved in the counter-insurgency effort – participating at the various levels of the Joint Operations Committees (JOCs) and establishing new security infra-structures in the affected areas. A senior Army spokesman told journalists on a visit to a Joint Operations Headquarters in December 1973: 'We will win this war with the co-operation of the local population . . . it is the civilian forces who face the greatest battle in winning the hearts and minds of the people.'

ADMINISTRATIVE MEASURES

If the border closure failed to achieve an easing of the security situation along the Zambian front, it was even less successful in halting the spread of guerrilla activity in the north-east. Accordingly the Government introduced a series of regulations and administrative measures in an attempt to reassert its control in the area.

On 19 January 1973, the Emergency Powers (Collective Fines) Regulations empowered Provincial Commissioners to impose collective fines on communities in which it was suspected that a member or members had assisted, or failed to report the presence of, guerrillas. Soon after the regulations came into effect it was reported that tribesmen of Chikukwa Kraal in Chiweshe had had their cattle seized by police and soldiers after they had failed to report the presence of guerrillas.[10] The concept of collective punishment was carried even further when more than 200 tribesmen from Masiwa Kraal in Madziwa Tribal Trust Land south of Mount Darwin, were moved some 750 km. south to a completely alien physical and tribal environment near Beitbridge, 'as a punishment for assisting terrorists and for rehabilitation purposes'.[11] Cattle belonging to the tribesmen were sold and their crops and huts were destroyed by security forces in order to prevent guerrillas from obtaining food and shelter. According to the Government, the inhabitants of the *kraal* had allowed a guerrilla group to use it as an operations base and had also collaborated with the guerrillas in the killing of several Africans in the area. The policy of collective punishment, which was justified on a very dubious interpretation of Shona custom, was attacked by the Rhodesia Party opposition:

> Hundreds of people, women and children, may now be punished by a single civil servant for the offence, or suspected offence, of one man, without any recourse to the impartiality of our law . . . This is a terrible admission of failure and smacks of panic. Rather than combat the terrorist cause it can only serve to advance it. Reprisals against innocents have been and will always be a major cause of escalation in civil or guerrilla warfare, and this measure is exceedingly unwise.[12]

As the Administration increased the pressure on the local

population, in an attempt to deny support for the guerrillas, the guerrillas themselves also adopted tougher tactics. After a guerrilla leader, named Maranke, had been killed by security forces in Chiweshe in 1973, the guerrillas suspected that they had been betrayed by some local people. They responded by exacting reprisals against suspects, some of whom were 'tried' and executed in public.

In order to create 'no-go' corridors along the border area and to deprive the guerrillas of contact with the population, the Administration embarked on a crash programme, code-named 'Operation Overload', to resettle tribesmen into 'protected villages', sited at strategic locations throughout the north-east. The first 'no-go' areas were established in the north of the Centenary district, and 'protected villages' were set up at Hoya, Sowe and Maraabui. Hoya, for example, housed about 1,500 people, mostly women and children and elderly men. According to officials, the younger men were either working in the urban areas or had been 'kidnapped' by the guerrillas. Some twenty-five miles from the Mozambique border, Hoya comprises fifty-five acres of cleared bush surrounded by a high wire-mesh security fence. The accommodation is built on concrete slabs with corrugated-iron roofing and cement-washed hessian walls. The District Commissioner told journalists visiting the area that 'until we can get the battle for the hearts and minds of these people into full gear, we are doing only a holding action. We must have a presence with these people and control to make our task easier.'[13]

In February and March 1973, Chiweshe Tribal Trust Land had been sealed off. All schools, clinics, grain mills, churches, shops and businesses were closed while security forces conducted a search through the area. The population was gathered into large screening centres and their identities checked. This task was facilitated by having available such legislation as the African (Registration and Identification) Amendment Bill, which had been tabled in November 1972 and required all Africans over the age of 16 to carry an identification certificate at all times. In June 1974, a stricter regulation was passed which stated that in certain specified areas all Africans over 12 years old had to be in possession of such a document (colloquially known as a *situpa*). In July, 46,960 people from 187 *kraals* in Chiweshe were moved into twenty-one 'protected villages' and, by the end of October, over 16,000 tribesmen from the Madziwa Tribal Trust Land had also been settled in such villages. The whole Chiweshe operation took less than three weeks, and the quality of the re-settlement camps, although varying considerably, left much to be desired. The new village settlements are regarded by the authorities as permanent institutions, which it is hoped will provide growth points for the development of the Tribal Trust Lands in the north-east. According to the Estimates of Expenditure for the year ending 30 June 1975, a total of Rh. $2,615,000 was earmarked for the establishment of 'protected villages' and 'no-go' corridors. The figure for the previous year was Rh. $435,000. In line with this scheme, irrigation projects, roads and rural markets are being set up. However, the operation bears all the hallmarks of a hastily improvised policy rather than any carefully planned social and economic strategy of pre-emption. Conditions at the villages, particularly those affecting sanitation and water supply, range from serviceable to appalling, as a number of letters to the *Rhodesia Herald* underlined. Conditions were particularly bad at Nyachuru 'protected village' in the south-west of Chiweshe, where resistance to the move had been strong. One letter stated:

> I was appalled by the conditions prevailing when I drove through the whole village the other day, and I was ashamed for the person who excused the whole situation by the need for speed as a tactical experience... How can we expect any co-operation when we expect families to be removed from their homes, herded into villages which are wire-enmeshed, have no shelter, no sanitation, and are expected to sleep in the open at this time of the year? It is inhuman.[14]

In early 1973, the Rhodesian Prime Minister had admitted that one reason for the lapse of security in the north-east had been the lack of grass-roots communication and that the civil administration was spread too thinly. More bluntly, this could have been described as sheer neglect. In a move to strengthen the Administration in these more remote areas, four new districts were created in the north-east and eastern highlands.

Announcing this in February, the Minister of Internal Affairs named the new districts as Centenary, Rushinga and Mudzi (both in the Mtoko area), and Mutasa, north of Umtali – all bordering on Mozambique. He also announced plans for the establishment of local African militia which would include specially-trained District Assistants (DAs) to function like military NCOs By September 1974, over 1,000 such DAs had been given basic military training. In June it was announced that European men would be able to do their National Service with the Ministry of Internal Affairs. They were to be giv n military training and then posted to the re-settlement villages, where they would supply 'backbone' to the local African militia and the DAs.

Priority was also given to improving existing and constructing new security roads in the affected areas.

In February 1974, emergency regulations were published allowing the Government to recruit residents of the north-east for forced labour if it was 'in the interests of public security'. The regulations stated that those eligible for compulsory work would be aged between 12 and 60 years of either sex and would be paid at a rate fixed by the authorities. The kind of tasks involved were the construction and maintenance of roads, bridges, fences and dams. Other provisions enabled the authorities to control the provision of food and the movement of livestock, as well as to detain people up to sixty days instead of the previous thirty, and to inflict corporal punishment on anyone who behaved in a contemptuous manner towards the District Commissioner and his staff. It was announced on the radio on 8 February that these measures would be 'particularly useful in the protection and administration of protected villages'.

One technique used by the authorities has been the distribution of information through pamphlets dropped throughout the area from the air. One such leaflet dropped in the Chesa Purchase area in February 1973 declared that: 'the speed with which you inform the police and soldiers is the speed with which your schools, grinding mills and beer halls will be opened'. And in addition to the distribution of warning leaflets with pictures of dead guerrillas – a technique used in previous operations – the

Administration has even purported to have enlisted the support of tribal mediums. One pamphlet, translated from the Chishona, read:

> Mhondoro, your tribal spirit, has sent a message to say that your ancestral spirits are very dissatisfied with you. Besides Chiwawa (an important spirit) has abandoned the man whom he used as his medium because this man has helped the terrorists. As a result of this, there has been no rain, your crops have died and there could be great famine. It is only the Government which can help you, but you have to realize your obligation to help the Government also.

Other leaflets distributed in English, ChiShona and Sindebele have offered rewards for providing information to the authorities. These ranged from 'not less than $5,000 for information leading to the death or capture of a senior terrorist leader' to 'not less than $300 for each full box of small arms ammunition, grenades, anti-personnel mines or for each light weapon'.

Also in the general attempt to secure co-operation from tribesmen in the affected areas, the Government enlisted the assistance of Blacks who supported the existing Administration. For example, in April 1973 the Provincial Commissioner led a group of seven senior Chiefs on a tour of the north-east to demonstrate their support for the Government. On 7 November, the Government-sponsored *African Times* headlined the fact that 'over 1,000 chiefs, headmen and *kraal* heads throughout the country expressed overwhelming support for the government in its fight against terrorism'. Mr Samson Chibi, Secretary-General of the African Progressive Party, addressed a number of meetings at various centres in the north-east on behalf of the African Anti-Terrorist Group. At one meeting held at Bindura and attended by over 3,000 people, Mr Chibi declared: 'It is pretty obvious that the terrorists have no hope of winning, but if allowed to continue they can bring untold harm and suffering to innocent people.' He called on them to report suspected 'terrorists' to the authorities immediately and added that the recent policy of rewards for information 'was a step in the right direction'.

Despite, or perhaps largely because of, the combined effect of these various measures, the Administration appears to have succeeded only in alienating local tribesmen in a huge arc along the border areas stretching from Miami around to Umtali. As short-term measures to exert physical control over the population, they may prove fairly effective; but, in the longer term, they are more likely to promote a resentment which can only increase the moral influence of the nationalist guerrillas.

THE USE OF FORCE

The use of intimidation and terror is a familiar feature of civil or insurgency-type warfare and is invariably practised to a greater or lesser extent by both sides in any such conflict. In Rhodesia, the undoubted brutality of assaults against individuals in both the white and black communities, in which civilians have been maimed or killed, has given rise to a sense of moral outrage on both sides. This situation raises the distinct, but related, questions of whether, in terms of morality, the ends justify the means; and whether, in practical terms, the means are likely to achieve the end.

Whites in Rhodesia fail to recognize that guerrilla warfare is essentially the weapon of the weak against the strong. The black nationalists believe that the whole system of white supremacy has to be attacked where it is considered weakest; and they can see no more reason for following so-called 'rules of war' which would put them at a disadvantage, than could the Boers, in their own guerrilla war at the turn of the century. The Boers, too, had refused to 'fight like gentlemen', in conspicuous uniforms on an open battlefield, much to the initial incomprehension and indignation of the British Army.

In civil and guerrilla warfare, it is often difficult and sometimes impossible to distinguish between military and civilian personnel on both sides, since civilians are likely to be engaged in support roles of one kind or another. For example, many of the white farmers belong to PATU units which form part of the security forces, while their wives manage radio stations so as to release their menfolk for more active duties. It may be equally confusing for security forces, fighting against people who appear to be innocent peasants by day but who become guerrillas by night. In such circumstances accidental as well as deliberate atrocities are almost inevitable. The massacres at My Lai in Vietnam by American soldiers and at Wiriyamu in Mozambique by Portuguese forces are well known instances. According to allegations by two Spanish priests of the Burgos Order, Fathers Martin Hernandez and Alfonso Valverde Leon, Rhodesian troops were implicated in the killing of civilians during operations in the vicinity of Mucumbura in September 1971. The priests were arrested in Rhodesia on 31 December 1971, handed over to the Portuguese, and subsequently charged with having aided FRELIMO and having publicized reports of the massacres by Portuguese and Rhodesian troops. They were released after twenty-two months in detention without trial, and expelled from Mozambique. Although neither had actually seen the killings take place, they had helped bury the bodies. The events they described may not have been unrelated to the two incidents (mentioned above) in which three Rhodesian soldiers had been killed by a mine in April while crossing a riverbed on the border, and the attack in August by FRELIMO guerrillas on a Rhodesian border village, as this extract from the report of the Burgos fathers suggests:

24.4.71 – An African chief was killed by men from FRELIMO because he was considered to be an accomplice of the Portuguese Government. He had been warned three times. On the same day a mine exploded near the river Mucumbura. Three Rhodesian soldiers were killed and two badly wounded. The FRELIMO guerrillas had set a mine beween the two frontiers to keep Rhodesia from intervening in the war against Portugal.

During the last days of August 1971 the men of FRELIMO went to a village in Rhodesia, on the frontier with Mozambique, to kidnap an African named Bauren. It seems that this man had been giving a lot of information to the Rhodesian government about the Mozambique guerrillas. When the guerrillas arrived at Bauren's hut, he was not there and so they decided to take away some object they found there to show him they did not agree with his position as a man 'bought' by colonialism.

They did not burn his hut nor harm any of his family. Bauren notified the Rhodesian government that FRELIMO guerrillas had been into Rhodesia, and reprisals began immediately afterwards.

1.9.71 – a big force from Rhodesia entered Mozambique, remaining here for a week pursuing the guerrillas. All the villages they visited were in Mozambique and in the area of our mission in Mucumbura.

3.9.71 – in the village of Deveteve, the Rhodesian soldiers killed David, the son of George. It was evening and he was going out to bring in his cows. As he went along the path he was shot dead. The soldiers took him to a nearby hillock and left him there after cutting off his hands and feet. Three days later he was found and buried by villagers from Mandwe. David was one of our best Christians in Mandwe and was married with four children.

We arrived on the day of the funeral and went to meet the Rhodesian soldiers to obtain an explanation from them. They themselves recognised it had been an error ('. . . a very unfortunate thing, Fathers. Sorry, we thought he was a terrorist . . .'). But they did not go to David's family to ask forgiveness.

5.9.71. – a squad of Rhodesian soldiers arrived in the village of Singa. They took with them the three eldest sons of Singa, the village chief, and told the old man he should not be scared and should go to where part of his family were hidden and bring them home.

Singa obeyed and went to look for his family. It was already night by the time they were coming back, talking peacefully, along the path. But another Rhodesian squad shot them when it saw them. Only two children managed to escape death. The following died instantly: the chief Singa, his son Adamo (10 years old), his daughter Ronica, recently married and pregnant, his three daughters-in-law Matiguiri, Rotina and Ester. Also two babies who were being carried on their mothers' backs – one the son of Matiguiri and the other of Ester.

When the soldiers realised what they had done, killed a poor old man and a group of mothers and innocent children, they tried to hide everything so no-one would know. They built a human bonfire with all the bodies and burnt them. But a very strong fire is needed to get rid of all the traces. There were remains of burnt flesh and charred skeletons, which were discovered on the following day by the Africans in the village.

We arrived at the village of Singa a week later and found all the villagers so full of fear and terror they had not even dared go and bury the burnt bodies. The two children who had managed to escape death accompanied us to the place where their family had been killed. Almost all the skeletons had been picked over by hyenas.

We took some photographs and sent the film to the bishop. Two days later the colonel of the district told us: 'Our Portuguese Government has heard that you took some photographs in Singa and has ordered you to hand over the roll.' We informed him that we had already given it to the bishop in Tete. We know now that the bishop had sent the film to be developed in Lourenço Marques and he fears he will never receive the photographs.

The wife of Singa, a very old woman, could only say one thing to us: 'I am alone, I am alone.' This old woman has indeed been left completely alone, with eleven children around her. These were the children of her daughters-in-law Matiguiri, Rotina and Ester. We did not know what to say to her when she showed us all the motherless children. The eldest was only 10 years old.

Many witnesses told us that between 1 and 7 September helicopters landed in Mucumbura with dead and wounded. We cannot give further details because we do not know the names of the dead. They were buried quickly by Portuguese soldiers in Mucumbura. The Rhodesian soldiers were all in villages some way from the mission and we do not know all that happened during that week of real terror in which the African people saw nothing but helicopers and armed men everywhere.

We also have evidence that about a dozen people were taken away to Rhodesia to be interrogated . . .[15]

In a war where both the insurgent and counter-insurgent forces are fighting to secure control over the civilian population, there is little room for individuals or groups to remain neutral. Where persuasion proves inadequate, the whole weight of an incumbent régime's legal, administrative and military machinery is used to enforce compliance. This has clearly occurred in Rhodesia. In February 1973, emergency regulations increased the maximum penalty for aiding guerrillas or failing to report their presence, from five to twenty years' imprisonment with hard labour. In July the Minister for Law and Order, Mr Lardner-Burke, said that he believed still tougher penalties were needed

. . . because it is obvious that some people living in the affected areas have not yet got the message that the Government means business when it says it is going to eliminate terrorists . . . I want to make the point that it is not enough to remain neutral, it is no good for people to close their eyes and say to themselves – this is between the terrorists and the Government.[16]

When the bill was introduced in September, death was proposed as the maximum penalty for harbouring guerrillas, for failing to report their presence, for undergoing terrorist training and for encouraging anyone or recruiting anyone to undergo such training. In February 1974 further emergency regulations were announced which, among other things, enabled magistrates' courts to be set up in the affected areas when it was considered necessary and without prior notification in the *Government Gazette*.

A different kind of intimidation is illustrated by a Ministry of Information Press Release (27 November 1974) entitled 'Fire Power Demonstration' –

> An awe-inspiring display of fire power by air and ground units of the Security Forces in Rhodesia was witnessed on Tuesday by nearly 1,000 tribesmen and their wives drawn from many *kraals* in the operational area. The demonstration was one of several which have been mounted in recent weeks to demonstrate the effectiveness and arms superiority of the Security Forces over the terrorists. Only last weekend, four terrorists, including a notorious section leader, were killed by Security Forces in the area where the demonstration was held. Among the audience at Tuesday's demonstration was a heavily manacled African man who is alleged to have collaborated with the terrorists by giving them food and shelter. Another African man told the crowd how he had defected from the terrorist ranks and walked many miles to rejoin his people and assist the authorities in their fight against terrorism. The demonstration began with a talk by a burly warrant officer from the Rhodesian African Rifles on the various weapons used by the terrorists – automatic rifles, land mines and stick grenades. He urged the crowd to report the presence of strangers to the local authorities or police and to hand over any terrorist weapons and ammunition they should find. The talk was followed by an impressive demonstration of army support units being dropped from helicopters minutes after a contact had been made. Live ammunition was used in the attack. This was followed by a low-level attack by strike aircraft on the target area using machine guns and bombs. The demonstration ended with a high speed rocket attack by aircraft of the Rhodesian Air Force and a spine-tingling low-level sweep over the startled crowd.

Rhodesian security personnel, in common with most administrations which have at one time or another been confronted by insurgency warfare, have practised what a Rhodesian judge criticized as 'methods of strenuous interrogation' – a euphemism for psychological and physical torture. In a document, dated 15

August 1974, several Church leaders expressed their concern that public ignorance and official inaction had allowed such activities to continue with impunity:

The public has been made fully aware of the assaults by armed insurgents and we too deplore the atrocities committed. What they are not aware of is the frequency and seriousness of assaults committed by some members of the security forces and the effect these are having upon the civilian population in the tribal areas, caught as they are between two contending forces and menaced by both.

The Church leaders attempted unsuccessfully to have the matters fully investigated by the authorities who took the view that any incidents that may have occurred amounted to no more than mistakes or misadventures which are inevitable in any military campaign. In their response to this attitude the Church leaders statement continued:

Our concern is not with such misadventures; we fully concede that unfortunate incidents are difficult to avoid. Our information points to something much more serious, namely the deliberate use of illegal and inhumane acts of force when questioning civilians, even those against whom there is no prior evidence of complicity with the enemy.

Accordingly, no action having been taken by the responsible Ministers, the document which contained a selection of ten cases of assault against apparently innocent tribesmen, was sent to a chosen group of 'responsible citizens who are leaders in the community' asking them to use their 'influence to secure an immediate termination of the inhumane methods that are being used to elicit information from the civilian population. Not only are they unworthy of our country, but they are also alienating the people upon whose support we depend for success in the campaign against terrorism'.[17] The nature of these assaults is illustrated by the following case taken from the report:

Draft Statement No. 31.
In the course of investigating a land mine explosion in January, 1973, in the Silverberg area, a number of people were arrested. Among them was Michael Ndaramba who gives the following account:

'On 4 January the police came to Jackson's home. All men in the village were arrested and taken to the camp, including myself. When we arrived at the camp we were told to line up: Walter from Bulawayo, myself, Francis from Salisbury, Jackson, and Dick, another brother.

Then Paul Manibata came out of the shed and was asked to identify the man who had been with him when the land mine exploded. He started at one end and went along the line. He pointed at Francis who who was at home on a short holiday from Salisbury. Francis was taken into the shed and we were told to wait outside. Francis was beaten by the police. We could hear him crying. After Francis had been beaten, Paul Mandibata said that he had made a mistake: not Francis, but Jackson, had been with him when the land mine exploded. Jackson was then led into the shed and continually beaten. We could hear him crying for a long period. That was the last we ever saw of Jackson.

After a while we were told to return home. We were asked to carry Francis who had been beaten so badly on his feet and about his body that he was unable to walk. We sent a child to fetch a wheelbarrow so that we could carry him home, about one mile from the camp.

On 12 January we were told that Jackson was dead. This message was brought by the police who came in a helicopter and landed in our village. They asked me who I was. I said: "I am Michael Ndaramba." They asked: "What is your relation to Jackson?" I said: "He is my younger brother." Then they said: "We have come to tell you that Jackson is dead." I asked them where Jackson had died. They replied: "You have nothing to do with that." I said: "I want to go and see where he died and where his body is so that I can take his body home and bury him." They replied: "You are not allowed by the law. You should come to the camp, that is where you may hear whether they will agree to your burying Jackson's body."

Despite repeated requests the body was never returned to the family, nor was the family informed that any inquest was to be held into the death or of the outcome of investigations.

Subsequently lawyers were contacted in Salisbury who made inquiries through the Ministry of Law and Order. The Minister of Law and Order declined to hold an inquest or to return the body of Jackson to his family. The lawyers were informed that Jackson had been taken in a helicopter by the police and during the flight had turned his head to make an indication and collapsed forward dead. When the helicopter landed he was taken to a police doctor who confirmed that Jackson was dead. According to the post-mortem Jackson had a fracture of his neck which had interfered with his spinal cord leading to death.

The lawyers learned from the Minister that the body was buried at the police camp, but subsequently the Minister told the Chairman of the Commission for Justice and Peace that Jackson's body had been cremated.

Such cases, although apparently becoming more frequent, are still the exception rather than the rule. Security authorities do not actively condone such behaviour and the importance of behaving correctly towards the local population is in fact stressed in training. Incidents in which innocent civilians have accidently been killed by security forces are sometimes reported 'with regret' in communiqués. For instance:

Security force Headquarters today (June 25) advised that, subsequent to an engagement with a group of terrorists in the north-eastern border area recently, three African male civilians were killed in an ambush, and another injured. These civilians were moving at night in contravention of the curfew which had been widely publicized in this and other curfew areas. Next-of-kin have been advised and the injured man treated in hospital. Police routine enquiries are being completed and the papers will be submitted to the magistrate in due course. Security Force Headquarters sincerely regret this occurrence but emphasize that tribesmen living in curfew areas ignore the curfew regulations and warnings given at their peril.

Nevertheless, whether genuine accidents or deliberate assaults, there does seem to be a strong tendency – on the part of the authorities and the white public – for such incidents to be overlooked, explained away, completely dismissed as untrue or as exaggerated out of all proportion, or to have them played down for fear of angering white opinion and lowering the morale of the security forces – all reactions which have been observed commonly enough elsewhere and are not confined simply to white Rhodesians. The Minister of Law and Order, Desmond Lardner-Burke, replied on 9 April 1974 in the Senate to the calls for an official inquiry into the alleged misconduct of some members of the security forces: 'My attitude is that a commission of inquiry is not necessary. Indeed, in my opinion, it could be harmful to the morale of the security forces. It is not for the security forces to prove their innocence; it is for those who make these allegations to prove their guilt.'

Control of non-regular personnel is more difficult than it is over soldiers subject to regular army discipline. For this reason some of the assaults have probably been perpetrated by civilian personnel, acting in a temporary para-military capacity, against individuals suspected of being implicated in attacks against friends or family in the local white community. In his series of articles for the *Evening Standard* (21, 22, 23 August 1973), Max Hastings quoted a remark by the wife of a farmer, also a Police Reservist, in the Sipililo area. Referring to a suspect who had been captured locally, she said:

> There were two brothers down in the native reserve who were responsible for a lot of the trouble in this area. A few weeks ago one of them was captured and everyone thought they would get information out of him that would sort things out here. But while they were jumping up and down on him to get him to talk, somebody jumped too hard. He died. So they never did found anything out from him.

The use of terror by insurgents may be either the cause or the symptom of weakness. It can, for instance, increase a community's sense of dependence on the protective authority of an incumbent régime; alternatively, it might reflect the insurgent's inability to win over the population or to inflict significant defeats on the counter-insurgent forces. Insurgents often feel compelled to resort to terror tactics as an alternative to the administrative apparatus and legal sanctions which are available to an established government. Insurgents frequently use the technique of selective assassination in an attempt to assert their authority and to serve as a deterrent. The victims are individuals who are known to be, or are suspected of, supporting the incumbent régime. A pamphlet issued by the Ministry of Information – *Anatomy of Terror* (May 1974) – outlines in graphic detail this kind of case as well as assaults motivated by other less rational considerations. On 28 January 1974 in the Madziwa area three District Assistants were 'seized, beaten up, ridiculed and bound by the side of the road. Terrorists opened fire killing Regis. Others feigned death.' And on 10 May in the Mount Darwin district 'two members of a road maintenance unit in the Kandeya area were killed and four wounded when a terrorist ordered them to line up. He then opened fire with an automatic weapon at point blank range.'

The indiscriminate use of terror is invariably counter-productive in its longer-term effects, whether perpetrated by the insurgents or by security forces. On the other hand, when general terror has been carefully avoided, certain techniques of terror, such as selective assassination, have been successful in inviting government reprisals which then result in the alienation of the affected community from the government. Conversely, as Maxey points out in his discussion of the use of terror by an incumbent régime: 'It may produce information. If the person is not then allowed contact with other Africans, the hatred it causes may not be spread ... Fear of brutal punishment may well frighten a person into not doing anything likely to bring that punishment down. But this will really only be effective if the punishment is reasonably sure – i.e. if the means of detection and apprehension are effective.'[18]

Historically, rationalizations about the use of violence for political ends have depended on whether the community in question was itself responsible for such methods or suffered as a result of them. Many white Rhodesians, for instance, were prepared to accept the saturation bombing of German cities (indeed, one of them, Marshal of the Royal Air Force Sir Arthur Travers Harris, as Commander-in-Chief of Bomber Command 1942–5, master-minded strategic bombing operations, earning the nickname 'Bomber' Harris) or the dropping of atomic bombs on Japanese cities, because it was thought such action would bring an end to the Second World War, even though civilian populations were decimated in the process.* The early European settlers in Rhodesia considered the suppression of African resistance in 1893 and 1896–7 to be necessary if white political control, with all its supposed civilizing influences, were to be established. The scale and violence of the military actions taken against the Shona is illustrated by this description of the attack on Matshayongombi's *kraal* in 1896:

> The earlier hand-grenading had had its desired effect and early in the morning Matshayongombi himself appeared wounded at the mouth of

* It has been estimated that nearly half a million people were killed during the five years of the Allied bombing offensive; and that 70–80,000 died at Hiroshima with 70,000 injured, and 35–40,000 died at Nagasaki with 40,000 injured.

one of the caves and was mercilessly shot down. After the dynamiting many of Matshayongombi's people were entombed but 278, including 215 women and children, came out and surrendered during the next four days.[19]

In similar fashion, black nationalists now argue that the victims of the guerrilla attacks on white farms, which have outraged the white community, are the inevitable casualties of a war of liberation against the political descendants of those pioneer settlers who had laid waste the homes of Matshayongombi's people and many others in the wars of the 1890s. White-ruled Rhodesia was founded by force and for eighty years has successfully been maintained by the exercise of its economic and military superiority, or by the threat of it. Confronted for so long by the apparently overwhelming might of the white settler community many Blacks had acquired a conditioned response of subordination to white authority – which is a quite different condition from Mr Smith's oft-repeated claim that 'we have the happiest Africans in the world', although many Whites genuinely believe this to be true. It is a belief which conveniently accords with their interests and prejudices. Max Hastings quotes one farmer who took a more realistic attitude on this: 'You ask why we don't mount a "Hearts and Minds" campaign to keep the Africans loyal. What can we offer them? Our only hold on them is that they look to us, as their bosses, to pay and feed them. But once you start talking about equality – well, what would they need us for?' This kind of thinking is not representative of all, or even a majority, of white thinking but it does underline the generally acquisitive and exploitative nature of white supremacy in Rhodesia. Except for a small number of liberals who work actively for a non-racist society, even those Whites who accept theoretically the idea of black social, economic and political advancement are reluctant to make any practical commitment to this end. In a survey carried out in 1971 it was found that, although 78 per cent of the respondents considered development of the Tribal Trust Lands vital, 58 per cent of Rhodesian Front respondents, 16 per cent of those in the Centre Party and 34 per cent of the non-aligned would not agree to the European being more heavily taxed to accelerate the process.[20]

It is not altogether surprising then that the black nationalists have emerged from the experience of the past eighty years with the belief that 'might is right'. It has after all been taught to them by their white masters. Wittingly or not, Des Frost, the Chairman of the Rhodesian Front, subscribed to the maxim. In his address to the Party's Congress in September 1975 he attacked the ANC and criticized outside interference in Rhodesia's affairs:

> Rhodesia can take no more from this rabble who are masters of the art of leading from the rear. The ignorant and uninformed continually compare Rhodesia with previous colonies in Africa. They forget our forefathers fought and conquered Rhodesia twice, then bought it from the British South Africa Company and finally we told the British Government to take a running jump. What more do we have to do to prove to the world that we control Rhodesia and intend to continue to do so.[21]

The task, as the nationalists see it, is to demonstrate to their more fatalistic compatriots – by puncturing the myth of white invulnerability – that perpetual black subjection to the white man is not the inevitable and natural order of things.

6 Comparative Perspectives

In his review of Richard Gibson's book *African Liberation Movements: Contemporary Struggles Against White Minority Rule*, for the September/October 1973 issue of *Survival*, Ali Mazrui identifies three general types of colonial or ex-colonial situations. First, one can discern those territories, mostly to be found in West Africa, in which the colonial power rapidly came to regard its rule as temporary and its role as essentially that of a mentor guiding fledgling nations to independence. Secondly, there were those territories which contained a sizeable minority of white settlers and which were regarded, with varying degrees of commitment, as *extensions* of the metropolitan power. The third category is that of territories in which the presence of a large white minority amounts almost to indigenous status and which are no longer in any form of subordination to a metropolitan power.

Such a system of classification, while necessarily somewhat arbitrary, can nevertheless be of value for this analysis. In the first place, actual situations may correspond closely to a particular type. South Africa, for instance, exemplifies the third category, and the former Portuguese territories offer good examples of the second. Then, it is helpful to view other colonial situations from the intermediate positions which they occupy on this spectrum. The former Belgian Congo (now Zaire), as the following quote from Colin Legum's *Congo Disaster* indicates, falls between the first and second categories.

Long before the avalanche hit them, the Belgians had begun to recognize the need to take account of increasing pressures from other parts of Africa, as well as from their own missionary-trained *evolués*, the emancipated, Westernized middle-class ... support had grown for the concept of a Belgo-Congolese Community. It envisaged the permanent association of the Congolese with the Belgians: equal members within a single community ... In this way the Congo would find its eventual independence within the wider Belgo-Congolese Community. In its essence the idea bears a strong resemblance to the French policy for Algeria. Its distinguishing feature is that while the French insist that the Algerians *are* French, the Belgians recognize the separateness of the Congolese.[1]

Algeria was characterized by a metropolitan power which regarded the territory as a subordinate constitutional and economic unit of France (at least until the fall of the Fourth Republic); and by a large settler community of over one million with considerable local military power, which was used to resist the decision to grant Algeria independence: a situation representing features of the second and third categories. The characteristics of Northern Rhodesia (now Zambia), through its association with the white-dominated Central African Federation, and Kenya, which by 1960 had a fair-sized settler population of some 61,000 Europeans, suggest different points of location between the first and third categories.

Gary Wasserman, in an analysis of Kenya's colonial status, argued:

The demise of colonial rule in Kenya was not the same as the erosion of European farmer domination; nor were they necessarily interdependent. English colonialism in Kenya dealt both with the attempt to colonize Kenya with European settlers and with the maintenance of a system of authority called colonialism in the country. Regarding the latter, more important aspect of the term, the settlers were an important link – perhaps at times the most important – but certainly not the sole one. Colonial officials, commercial interests, tribal authorities, the Asian community and missionaries, were all vital supports to the system. The separability of the two aspects of the colonial system can be seen in Rhodesia where the settler dominated political system could survive without colonial authority, and in a Ghana where colonial authority existed without settler presence. The distinction becomes important in examining Kenyan colonial history. Although both colonial authority and settler dominance were finished off by independence in 1963, they were not always complementary before that ... in a sense, the colony created the colonists, rather than vice-versa.[2]

The experience of (Southern) Rhodesia over the past two decades can usefully be analysed by reference to the differing colonial legacies outlined in these three broad categories.

RHODESIA – A 'COLONY IN TRUST'?

As has been argued above (in Chapter 1), during the late fifties and early sixties African nationalists in Southern Rhodesia, as well as many observers and politicians overseas, tended to overestimate the relevance and applicability to the Southern Rhodesian situation of the kind of nationalist tactics and strategy which had proved effective in West Africa and increasingly successful in Nyasaland (now Malawi) and Northern Rhodesia. For example, an analysis in a nationalist journal considered that the NDP had committed a serious error in adhering to 'assumptions which proved hazardous':

> The liberation movements assumed that since all other British colonies were in that period achieving independence through forcing the British Government to a constitutional table, settlement of the Rhodesian problem was most likely going to follow the same pattern. Hence the attempt at constitutional solutions . . . in 1961.[3]

Britain's peculiar residual metropolitan relationship with Rhodesia was epitomised by the latter's unique and somewhat contradictory status since 1923 as a 'self-governing colony'. This helps to explain both the attempts of the Rhodesian Government to negotiate British recognition of its illegally assumed, but *de facto*, independence; and the persistent tendency of the African population to look to Britain for its salvation. Until the late 1960s, the exiled nationalist movements tended to think in terms of precipitating British intervention in Rhodesia on their behalf. And, from the end of 1971, an avowedly non-violent nationalist organization, the African National Council (i.e. prior to the merger of ZANU, ZAPU and FROLIZI under the reconstituted ANC), was seen pressing for a negotiated solution alongside the guerrilla activity of the exiled movements. It is significant that the only occasion on which the original African National Council registered any real impact on behalf of African nationalism (and then only in the negative role of forestalling the implementation of the November 1971 Settlement

Proposals agreed between the British and Rhodesian Governments) was when the rebel régime temporarily permitted a British presence in the form of the Pearce Commission. The way in which this vestigial metropolitan dimension has served to deflect the full force of black nationalism has been described by Kenneth Good:

> Settler colonialism in Rhodesia has taken full advantage from the existence of a constitutional mystification over the location of ultimate political power. The precise degree to which Rhodesia has been constitutionally independent of, or dependent on, Britain always remained uncertain . . . Britain has co-operated with Rhodesia in the maintenance of an important illusion, which has misdirected African nationalism away from Salisbury and towards London . . . This legal fiction has served as an important element in the settler colonialists' system of control.[4]

RHODESIA – AN INDEPENDENT SETTLER POWER?

When it was finally realized by the African nationalists themselves, as well as by outside observers, that Britain had neither the power nor the will to intervene effectively in Rhodesia, it seemed that the Rhodesian case might more correctly be understood in terms of independent settler power, as exemplified by South Africa. The system of white supremacy in Rhodesia, as Peter Harris has argued, comprises a 'coalition' of four main groups:

1. A growing sector of (white) resident-controlled capitalism. The owners of local wealth (including the self-employed and professionals), it has been suggested, constitute about 15 per cent of employed Whites.
2. A somewhat static but strategically important and hence influential sector of white landowners, amounting to 20 per cent of the economically active white population.
3. A large (perhaps 65 per cent) group of skilled and semi-skilled workers (including administrative personnel) who have limited economic influence but considerable electoral importance.

4. A not insignificant remnant of foreign capital, although its size is uncertain and difficult to identify.

On the viability of the system, Harris concludes;

The 'coalition' is effective precisely because each constituent group is dependent on others in some important sense . . . White landowners are dependent on the coalition for subsidies . . . but offer in compensation the political and military stability associated with land stabilization . . . White capitalists require support from the coalition in order to maximise the 'rate of exploitation' . . . the returns of which are secured out of the relative deprivation of black industrial workers and peasants . . . to subsidize white landowners and workers . . . the importance of white workers is felt initially at the level of their influence in the electoral system . . . but their long-term strategic role is important since they form a reliable industrial–administrative base for the system.[5]

Rhodesia has had to pay out many millions of rand every year[6] in subsidies (excluding the railway subsidy) in compensation for the loss of sales of commodities affected by sanctions. The guaranteed minimum price for tobacco, which has only recently been removed, is the most obvious example of such. It has been estimated that the Tobacco Corporation, which bought up the national crop and resold it to sanctions-breaking foreign buyers, made an average annual loss since UDI of about Rh$ 20 million, which was partly covered by the Rhodesian Government. Significant also are the extremely generous terms upon which farmers, who wish to purchase farms in the security-affected north-eastern areas, are able to obtain loans. To approved applicants, 100 per cent long-term loans on fixed assets (i.e. land and buildings) are available, at 7¼ per cent rate of interest. 100 per cent short- and medium-term loans at a similar rate of interest are also available for the cost of financing the season's crop and for movable assets such as tractors and farm implements. In September 1971, the Minister of Law and Order, Mr Lardner-Burke, stressed the importance of keeping people on the land: 'It is only when you have vacant farms that you are liable to suffer from squatter problems. This could lead to infiltration of terrorists or their supporters and could undermine the security of the country.'[7]

It is estimated that the cost of farm security measures will amount to Rh$2,200,000. Business contributes indirectly to the counter-insurgency effort through taxation. In August 1974, for instance, the Minister of Finance announced a 10 per cent retrospective surcharge on individual and company income tax to help pay for the security burden. Firms also contribute more directly by 'making up' the wages and salaries of employees doing National Service if their army pay is less then that in their civilian occupations; and by releasing employees for their Territorial Force and Civilian Reserve commitments, which may amount to one to three months annually.

The great disparities between White and Black in Rhodesia are maintained by the symbiotic alliance of these ruling white groups and through their control of such crucial mechanisms as the franchise, land allocation, labour legislation and practice, and education. The incomparably high standard of living which the whites have enjoyed has largely been made possible by the perpetuation of the enormous differential between white and black incomes.

Table 3: Average Annual Earnings in Rhodesian Dollars, 1965–74

Period	1965	1966	1967	1968	1969	1970	1971	1972	1973	1974
European, Asian and Coloured Employees	2,577	2,666	2,715	2,823	2,973	3,114	3,357	3,628	3,901	3,935
African Employees	249	259	269	278	287	305	324	337	359	398
Wage Differential	2,328	2,407	2,446	2,545	2,686	2,809	3,033	3,291	3,542	3,537

Source: Monthly Digest of Statistics, Central Statistical Office, Salisbury.

While it is true that black incomes have risen consistently since UDI, the more significant observation is that the gap between white and black incomes has steadily widened except for a slight narrowing of the gap in 1974.

The system of white supremacy has demonstrated a considerable degree of resilience in the face of international sanctions, guerrilla incursions and diplomatic isolation. This independence has been vigorously asserted by commerce and industry, the defence forces and the general white public, which has strongly resented external 'interference' in matters which are regarded as of domestic concern. However, it is worth looking more closely at the real nature of this independence and its economic, military and political components. Despite white Rhodesia's not unimpressive record of survival for nearly ten years against a formidable combination of internal and external pressures, Rhodesian independence may nevertheless contain the seeds of its own ultimate destruction.

Economic

Southern Rhodesia emerged from the break-up of the Central African Federation with a diversified money economy geared to the needs of the relatively small white population. Since 1964 the economy has expanded: apart from a temporary fallback, following the imposition of economic sanctions after UDI at the end of 1965. Agriculture, manufacturing and mining have been mainly responsible for the growth of GDP since then.

Table 4: Expenditure in Rhodesian Dollars on Defence, Internal Affairs, Police, Roads and Road Traffic, between 1971–2 and 1975–6, showing Percentage Increase

Period	*Defence Expenditure*	*Internal Affairs Expenditure*	*B.S.A. Police Expenditure*	*Roads and Road Traffic Expenditure*
1971/2 Rh.$	19,981,000	9,670,000	16,738,000	7,843,000
1974/5 Rh.$	45,119,000	25,663,000	29,958,000	24,301,000
1975/6 vote Rh.$	57,014,000	31,007,000	33,328,000	28,024,000
percentage increase in cash terms 1971/2–1975/6	280	320	199	357

Source: Monthly Digest of Statistics, Central Statistical Office, Salisbury.

Table 5: Migration of Economically Active European Professionals

Migration of Professional, Technical and Related Workers (Male and Female)

	1965	1966	1967	1968	1969	1970	1971	1972	1973	1974
Immigrants	1,172	688	979	1,366	1,250	1,391	1,600	1,593	1,122	1,106
Emigrants	1,095	1,107	887	760	957	943	921	969	1,310	1,384
Net Migration	+77	−419	+92	+606	+293	+448	+679	+624	−188	−278

Source: Monthly Migration and Tourist Statistics, Central Statistical Office, Salisbury.

The average growth in agricultural output at current prices since 1965 has been at a rate of 9·2 per cent a year. In the immediate post-UDI period, a combination of poor seasons and sanctions held back growth; but since 1969 output has expanded rapidly. The agricultural sector as a whole now contributes about 17 per cent to GDP. The existence of economic sanctions has forced farmers to diversify and has reduced the sector's former dependence on the fluctuations in the price of tobacco – the country's major export commodity until UDI.* The rapid development of the cotton industry, for example, not only helped to fill the gap caused by a sanctions-induced fall in tobacco production, but also proved the base for an expanding textile industry. Output from textile manufacturing, which included cotton-ginning, more than doubled between 1965 and 1969.

Manufacturing contributes most to GDP: about 23 per cent. Output in real terms has risen at an annual rate of 9·8 per cent; although the rate of expansion in 1973 fell to 7·4 per cent from 10·3 per cent in 1972. The rapid growth in this sector can largely be attributed to the enforced programme of import substitution. No doubt some of the firms now producing local products of items formerly imported have a degree of vested interest in the maintenance of the *status quo* which provides protection from foreign competition.

*In 1965 the tobacco crop was 246 million lb. but fell to 200 million lb. in 1967 and was fixed at 132 million lb. for the following years until it was increased to 145 million lb. for 1972. (In 1974 there appeared to have been a break-through in the export of tobacco, and the size of the crop was increased.

The mining industry has shown an annual average growth rate of 9·1 per cent in real terms. Success in this sector is probably attributable to the fact that it has been given priority in the allocation of foreign exchange for the acquisition of much needed capital equipment. Mining, along with transport, construction and public administration each contribute about 6 or 7 per cent to GDP, although mining makes a disproportionately large contribution to exports.[8]

While commerce and industry have been forced to make a virtue out of necessity, and have done so with considerable success, the business community has been almost unanimous in supporting past attempts to negotiate a political settlement which would result in the lifting of sanctions. The need for foreign markets, capital, and new plant and equipment has become particularly urgent during the last two or three years in most areas of the economy, but especially in the more capital-intensive sectors of mining and manufacturing. The greatest scope for growth and increased employment lies in the expansion of the manufacturing sector and it is this sector which is now most seriously impaired by sanctions. The expansion and development of the economy is particularly crucial for Rhodesia which has to keep pace with one of the world's fastest growing populations (3·6 per cent) over half of which is under the age of fifteen. In a study carried out at the end of the 1960s for the opposition Centre Party on the implications of the population explosion, it was concluded that Rhodesia would need annually an extra 30,000 houses, 150,000 acres farmed, 320 primary schools, 1,680 primary school teachers and 40,000 new jobs. Many of the 40,000 who enter the labour market every year are frustrated young school leavers and as the Centre Party study group warned 'this means a growing number of idle malcontents who are potentially dangerous. And the situation will worsen when today's babies grow up and something like 90,000 extra males come onto the labour market each year by 1990'.[9] The Ministry of Finance's *Economic Survey for 1974* showed that the Rhodesian economy faced its most serious problems since 1968. However, it also shows the relative failure to date of economic sanctions. A 10 per cent growth rate in 1974 took the post sanctions compound average rate of real growth to 6·75 per cent a year; and since 1967, the economy has managed to create 39,000 new jobs a year for the fast growing black population.[10] It is questionable whether this record can be sustained in the face of (a) the prospect of more effectively enforced sanctions now that Mozambique is independent; (b) the rising costs of countering a widened and intensified insurgency; and (c) the repercussions within Rhodesia of the economic and financial difficulties experienced by the world in general. The economic growth which has taken place in the modern cash economy over the past decade has been at the expense of the traditional subsistence sector and the political consequences of this neglect ultimately rebounded on the white population and the Government which represented it.

That the existence of widespread urban unemployment, increasing pressures on the rural areas and the implementation of discriminatory legislation has provided a fertile recruiting ground for the exiled nationalist movements has been reflected by the events since the Pearce Commission and the growing security problems of the Administration.

Military

Rhodesia has a small but nevertheless, in regional terms, relatively significant and efficient, defence capability. According to the International Institute for Strategic Studies' *Military Balance 1975–76* the Army consisted of 4,500 regulars and a Territorial Force of 10,000. These figures will have been raised considerably as a result of the measures taken in response to the worsened security situation. The Army has been forced to increase its manpower by improving conditions of service to attract white recruits; by doubling the size of National Service intakes and lengthening the period from nine to twelve months; by the recruitment of a second battalion of Rhodesian African Rifles (it was announced in July 1975 that the first Company was operational); and by a greater utilization of women and older men in non-combatant roles releasing younger men for active duties. Since 1966 the Rhodesia Light Infantry, the RAR and the Special Air Service Squadron have been organized on a counter-insurgency basis. On 30 January 1969 the Minister of

Defence announced that the number of paratroopers was to be doubled and that the RLI was also to be enlarged. The Rhodesian Armoured Car Regiment was formed on 1 July 1972 although it was based on the existing corps (the armoured cars are the South African *Eland* – a local version of the French *Panhard* which is made under licence in South Africa and possesses a 90mm. gun and two machine guns).

The Rhodesian Air Force has played a vital role in counter-insurgency operations. It comprises upwards of forty-five combat aircraft including squadrons of Hunter F5A-9 fighters (acquired in 1962); some ancient Vampire FB-9 jets and Provost trainers which can be used in COIN ground-attack and support roles; several B-4 and T-4 Canberras with bombing and reconnaissance functions; Macchi AL-60s in spotter and support roles; Douglas C-47 and a Beech Baron transport craft; Aeritalia/Macchi AM 3Cs; and a large number of tactical helicopters, French Alouette 11s and 111s. Many of these Alouettes are South African, operating under a contract between the two governments and have remained in Rhodesia despite South Africa's withdrawal. South African Super Frelon, Puma and Bell Cobra troop carrying helicopters have also been reported in operation in Rhodesia. This combination of strike, bomber, reconnaissance, fixed and rotary – wing transport capacities has proved most effective in counter-insurgency operations since 1966.

Although the Rhodesian security forces have shown considerable ingenuity in improvising with locally made equipment and in evading sanctions, in particular by acquiring additional helicopters, the long-term implications of the problems of replacement and obsolescence cannot be avoided. Reliance on sanctions evasion is both a risky and expensive business, as the exposure in July 1974 of Rhodesia's secret and unsuccessful attempt to purchase Jordan's second-hand fleet of thirty-one Hawker Hunters showed. The Jordanian Government, according to the reports, was to receive £14,600,000 for the planes, spare engines and armaments. However, the South African and Rhodesian negotiators refused to pay for some of the extra equipment which they had no interest in acquiring. Even so they were to have paid £16,250,000 for the reduced package, which they were finally to receive. Clearly, for the middlemen who arranged the deal it should have been a very profitable transaction.[11] More recently, it was reported that the Rhodesian Air Force had been involved in undercover negotiations with Venezuelan businessmen to buy 28 American Sabre interceptor jet fighters, which were on offer at £225,000 each.[12]

The possibility that guerrillas in Rhodesia may now have access to Soviet *Strella* ground-to-air missiles constitutes a potentially serious threat to the air superiority previously enjoyed by Rhodesian security forces. Quite apart from this possible new internal challenge to Rhodesian airpower, there is also the question of its continued effectiveness as a deterrent to attack by hostile aircraft from neighbouring states. In March 1973, a senior Air Force Commander told a meeting of the Rhodesian National Affairs Association that, unless a political settlement was reached which resulted in an end to sanctions, Rhodesia could not hope to match the more sophisticated aircraft being acquired by some black states in the region.

White Rhodesians have, for the most part, tended to be confident in their ability to defeat insurgents in the field. They point to the effective containment of armed incursions between 1966 and 1970; and, while acknowledging that the guerrilla offensive since the end of 1972 constitutes a more serious threat, they nevertheless take comfort from the high 'kill ratio' in their favour. When the Rhodesian Prime Minister announced a cease-fire on 11 December 1974, following the Lusaka Agreement (which failed to be implemented), 499 insurgents had been killed, as against 58 members of the security forces, while 164 civilians, nearly all black, had also lost their lives since the end of 1972. Whatever successes the security forces may have achieved in a purely military sense they have nevertheless been at a heavy social and economic price. This is clearly borne out by the phenomenal rise in expenditure on military and administrative counter-insurgency measures which were a direct response to the guerrilla offensive launched in 1972. The frequent call-up of civilians for reservist duties has not only had detrimental effects on the country's economy and administration, but has also been responsible for lowering the morale of Territorial

Force members who have been kept away from their families and their jobs for long and frequent periods. The former Chairman of the Associated Chambers of Rhodesian Commerce, Mr Mike Britten, suggested in an interview with the *Rhodesia Herald* in November 1973 that the main reasons for the shortage of professional (i.e. white) people were uncertainty about the future, a lack of opportunities, and the heavy commitments of 'military call-up' which was 'the overriding factor causing people to leave'. Writing in the same month, Herbert Chitepo outlined ZANU's strategy:

> The strategical aim ... is to attenuate the enemy forces by causing their deployment over the whole country. The subsequent mobilization of a large number of civilians from industry, business and agriculture would cause serious economic problems. This would have a psychologically devastating effect on the morale of the Whites, most of whom had come to Zimbabwe, lured by the prospect of the easy, privileged life promised by the régime.[13]

The most mobile sections of the white population are probably:

1. Young people, particularly students studying abroad, who have no binding family or financial commitments in Rhodesia. Although the age structure of immigrants has remained fairly constant over the last ten years, the percentage of emigrants in the 20 to 24 age group, which would include many students, rose consistently until 1974 when Government policy made it more difficult for young people to emigrate (see graph, p. 313). It is likely that many young people, who ostensibly or initially leave as tourists, are in fact leaving Rhodesia for good.
2. Recent immigrants who have not had time to establish binding commitments or emotional attachments to the country. Although complete up-to-date figures are not available, there does appear to be a high turnover of immigrants. (See Table 6.)

It is clearly not possible to identify with total certainty or precision the 'resistance threshold' of white Rhodesians – i.e. at what point or points, under the varying levels of insecurity which are conceivable in the future, which categories of and how many Whites would be prompted to leave the country. Two

20-24 AGE GROUP: PERCENTAGE OF TOTAL IMMIGRANTS AND EMIGRANTS

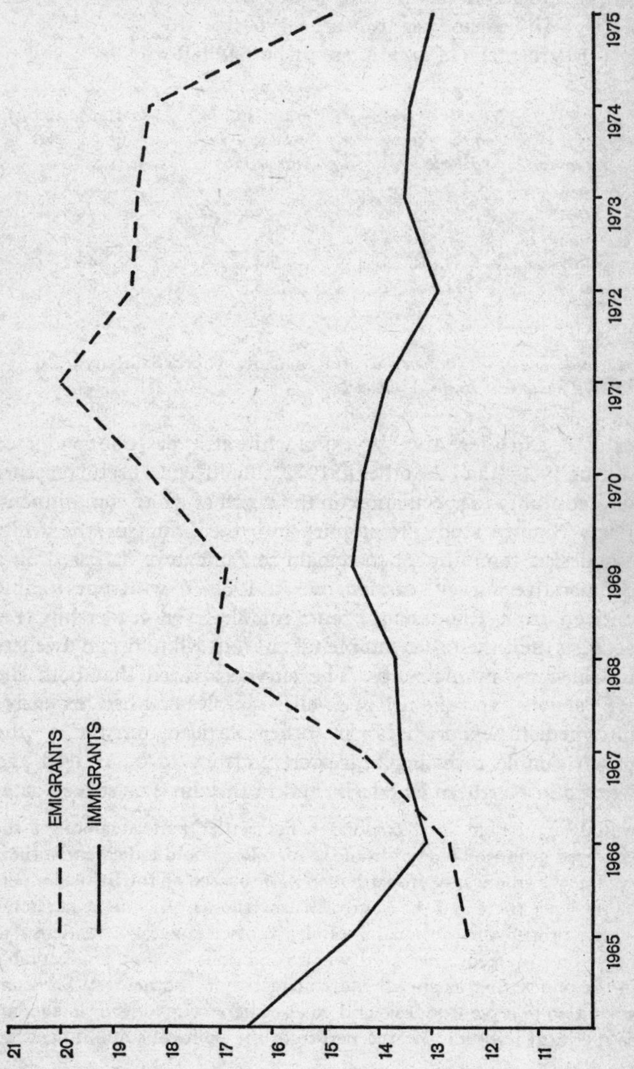

Table 6: Number of Immigrants, 1964–9
(a) Into Rhodesia
(b) Still in Rhodesia in March 1969
(c) Percentage of Immigrants who had left

Year	*Number of immigrants into Rhodesia*[1]	*Number of immigrants still in Rhodesia in March 1969*[2]	*Percentage of immigrants who had left*
1964	7,000	2,762	60·5
1965	11,128	3,886	65·1
1966	6,418	3,036	52·7
1967	9,618	5,470	43·1
1968	11,864	8,356	29·6
1969 Jan/Mar	2,698	2,472	—

[1] *Monthly Digest of Statistics*, Central Statistical Office, Salisbury
[2] *1969 Population Census, Volume 1*

valuable and interesting surveys of white attitudes, one conducted during 1968–9 and the other in 1971, should lend a useful measure of plausibility to speculation on the depth of white commitment. Barry Shutz's study 'to inquire into the limits of the white Rhodesian commitment to remain in Zimbabwe' is based on a comparative survey (carried out in 1968–9) with one sample derived from Rhodesian Front 'middle-level' leadership (i.e. activists) and the other sample taken from white urban dwellers in Salisbury municipality. The survey showed that both the RF 'activist' and the urban dweller samples had had 'extensive intermediate experiences' in other African territories (the urban sample revealing a greater tendency to have lived and worked in Northern Rhodesia) and in Britain. The survey data:

would suggest an inter-colonial white settler pattern amongst the surveyed groups. This syndrome of mobility would indicate that there is a linkage amongst white settlers in Africa based on the British imperial presence there and the South African colonial (fragment) keystone. These propensities towards mobility further suggest a tendency to move on to 'greener pastures' when conditions become unacceptable in the one setting or appear more attractive in another . . . The consideration to leave Rhodesia and go elsewhere at any given time looms as a critical indicator for the nature of the political commitment. In gross terms, 54% of the RF said that they had never considered leaving Rhodesia (before 1969), while 42·5% admitted that they had. Consideration to leave was not so high amongst the urban dwellers ... Fear of a white, perceived-as-liberal, 'sellout' government motivated over one-third of the RF activists to consider leaving Rhodesia at some time. An extension of this fear, the development of conditions for an 'African takeover', stimulated another 30%. Political considerations thus influenced nearly three-fourths of the RF activists who had pondered departure from Rhodesia ... The disparity between the responses of the two survey groups (as seen in Table 7) would appear significant. While a vast majority of the activists (70·4%) would leave Rhodesia with the eventuality or threat of African government, only 44·8% of the Salisbury urban-dwellers feel similarly, although it cannot be inferred that this group are necessarily more tolerant. Also rather interesting is the fact that over one-fourth of the Salisbury sample indicated that they would remain in Rhodesia under *any conditions* in contrast to the 8·3% of the RF activists who were so committed. Those responding in this way usually identified their commitment in terms of 'staying and fighting ... By country of birth, there is a propensity for South African-born activists to be somewhat more prepared to leave Rhodesia with the appearance of even a "white liberal" government (18·9%). At the same time, the South African-born chairmen also show greater inclination to stick it out at all costs (13·5%) than those born elsewhere (including Southern Rhodesia). It would seem then that the opinions of the South African-born activists tend to characterize the RF group as a whole, inasmuch as they see Rhodesia in the context of greater South Africa'.[14]

The author uses the concept of the 'fragment society' to explain the status of white Rhodesian nationalism. Examples of successful British 'fragment' nations are Australia, New Zealand and Canada. Shutz argues that 'Rhodesian fragment options for independence and sovereignty are severely limited. The elements of recency of settlement and unfavourable relative size would appear as meaningful obstacles to the sort of autonomy enjoyed by other British colonial offshoots', such as the successful 'fragment' nations mentioned above. This perceptive analysis comes to the suggestive conclusion:

The quasi-fragment character of white Rhodesian society begins to form. Although the Rhodesian whites are not the least inclined to return to Britain ... they do see the Republic of South Africa as a homeland . . . Like the British (i.e. English-speaking) South Africans, Rhodesian whites (almost totally English-speaking) appear ready to subordinate their own cultural traditions to another European fragment which has effectively maintained its domination over an increasingly threatening indigenous population . . . White Rhodesians thus see their nation as contingent upon Afrikaner commitment to them. In the end they do accept their quasi-fragment status, but with a South African orientation. If they are 'citizens', it is within a greater community of southern Africa in very much different terms than the colons of Algeria saw France . . . Unlike 'the Algerian conflict, the Rhodesian one points to an ultimate showdown (rather than agreement) even though South Africa now pushes Rhodesia to settle with nationalists.'

Another sample survey conducted in 1971 by Dr Morris Hirsch among members of the ruling Rhodesian Front Party, the multiracial Centre Party and independent opinion gave the following results:

Eighty eight per cent of RF claimed the racial position has not influenced their future plans or investment at all and 7% that their plans had been favourably influenced thereby. By contrast 23% of CP admitted that their future plans have been adversely affected by the racial position in Rhodesia. 42% of CP and 30% Independents would emigrate or were doubtful whether they would remain if they could take their assets out whereas only 1 in 5 of RF was of this mind. Black rule for Rhodesia would be disastrous for Whites under any circumstances of the changeover was the opinion of 77% of RF, 10% of the CP and 32% of the non-aligned. A surprising 21% of the RF and 62% of CP believed that the impact on the individual would depend on the timing and circumstances of the advent of Black control. Not one person of any group considered the change would be favourable and only 10% overall believe conditions would be tolerable although adverse. From this assessment the majority of all groups believed that they would not remain in Rhodesia under Black rule whenever it came or were doubtful – 77% of RF and 55% CP fell in these categories in which most RF were decisive and most CP in doubt.[15]

It is difficult to know how reliable an indicator of white opinion these surveys can be in the changed circumstances since 1968–9 and 1971 (i.e. before the adverse result of the Pearce

Commission when white confidence was high). Some of the beliefs expressed and tendencies revealed by the surveys may well have been reinforced by subsequent events. It would be surprising (given the time gap between the two surveys, the different sample groups and the inherent problems of conducting such attitudinal assessments) if there were not some discrepancies both within and between some of the implications revealed by the two surveys. The differences may only be apparent or they may reflect real contradictions and ambiguities in white attitudes. The salient points which emerge from both surveys suggest a number of relevant perspectives:

1. The most important common conclusion to emerge lies in the varying but high percentages of all the sample groups which indicated that respondents would leave Rhodesia or expressed doubt about staying with the advent of majority rule. As Shutz points out, this tendency is particularly strong among Whites with definite South African orientations.
2. However, as Hirsch mentions, 'a surprising 21% of the RF, and 62% of CP believed that the impact on the individual would depend on the timing and circumstances of the advent of Black control'. The means by which black rule is achieved in Rhodesia will obviously be the crucial factor in setting the final level of the white community's 'resistance threshold'. If there were to be a phased and controlled transition to a black parliamentary majority, even if this took only a few years, it is the opinion of the present writer that a not insubstantial number of Whites would remain. There are a number of reasons for this belief. There is a significant proportion of Whites who do not fit into the 'recent immigrant' category and some of them, for better or for worse, cannot envisage any other home – not even South Africa. Many Whites also do not have the educational or technical qualifications which would permit them to maintain the standards of living they would enjoy in Rhodesia (even under majority rule) if they were to emigrate to the more competitive conditions which obtain in Europe, the North Americas and Australasia. Many white families are tied by such factors

as mortgage commitments, young children and thei schooling and the lack of sources of financial support outside the country. As the Hirsch survey noted, income was entirely Rhodesian in origin for 82 per cent of the sample. Only 2 per cent received more than 25 per cent of their income from outside Rhodesia, while 11 per cent received amounts of less than 25 per cent. The advantages of staying put, despite fears about the possible consequences of black rule, may, when the time comes outweight the effort and uncertainty which would be involved in leaving. In this connection Hirsch's survey showed that while 77% of the RF sample felt that black rule would be disastrous for Whites under any circumstances only 10% of the CP and 32% of the non-aligned expressed this opinion.

3. Another significant observation from the Shutz survey is that

over one-fourth of the Salisbury sample indicated that they would remain in Rhodesia under *any conditions* in contrast to the 8·3% of the RF activists who were so committed. Those responding in this way usually identified their commitment in terms of 'staying and fighting'.

Also significant is that South African-born chairmen of the RF (13·5 per cent) expressed a greater inclination to 'stick it out at all costs' than those born elsewhere, including Rhodesia. This would suggest that there is a significant section of white Rhodesian society which is prepared to put up a strong resistance in defence of the white Rhodesian state with its attendant economic, political and social privileges. In the meantime the Rhodesian Government has made it increasingly difficult for people to emigrate. Exchange control regulations are very strict and in any case Rhodesian currency is virtually worthless outside the country. From October 1974 students, who had previously been able to obtain automatic deferment of their National Service, had to secure special permission to do so. In November, the new Defence Amendment Act bill stated that anyone who was eligible for National Service would have to get special permission to go out of the country for any reason. Alongside such measures to discourage or prevent people leaving, the Government has attempted to increase white immigration by its ambitious but unsuccessful Settlers '74 Campaign.

While a formal constitutional settlement (if this is possible) which provides for a controlled transition to majority rule may therefore not result in wholescale white emigration, a revolutionary take-over would be a different matter and the factors considered above (in 2) would have little relevance. A revolutionary take-over would probably be accompanied by panic flights, assisted evacuations and deportations of the remaining white settlers – all familiar features in such situations.

Political

Despite its record of survival so far, there nevertheless seem to be definite limitations, in economic and military terms at least, to white settler independence in Rhodesia. From a political viewpoint, appearances may be equally deceptive. The effect of economic sanctions and diplomatic isolation, far from securing the capitulation of the government or acting as an inducement to white reform, have effectively closed rather than split the ranks of white Rhodesians since 1965. In the general election of May 1965 prior to UDI, which was held under the legal 1961 Constitution, the Rhodesian Front won all 50 of the Higher Roll (and therefore effectively white) seats in the 65-seat Parliament. In the 28 contested Higher Roll constituencies, the RF secured just over 79 per cent of the votes, against a combined opposition total percentage of just under 21 per cent. Following the breakdown of the *Fearless* negotiations, the Rhodesian Front's 1969 Constitutional proposals were given overwhelming support by the electorate in a referendum on the issue: 73 per cent voted in favour and 27 per cent against. At the same time the electorate registered even greater support for making Rhodesia a republic: 81 to 19 per cent. It seems likely that the figure in support of the constitutional proposals, which was lower than that favouring a republic, may be accounted for by extreme right-wing opinion voting against even the symbolic inclusion of Blacks in Parliament.

Table 7a: Future Change in Rhodesia which would cause Departure

Future Changes in Rhodesia Which Would Cause Departure (by Frequency): R.F. Activists and Salisbury Urban Dwellers

Change	*R.F. Activists*		*Salisbury Sample*	
	Frequency	*Per cent*	*Frequency*	*Per cent*
White, liberal government and/or political instability	18	16·7	12	13·8
African government or the immediate threat of it	76	70·4	39	44·8
Other reasons concerning social and economic discontent	5	4·6	14	16·1
Nothing would cause departure	9	8·3	22	25·3
	N = 108	100·0	N = 87	100·0

Question: What changes in the country would cause you to leave?

Table 7b: Choice of Country if Leaving Rhodesia

Choice of Country if Leaving Rhodesia (by Frequency): R.F. Activists and Salisbury Urban Dwellers

Country	*R.F. Activists*		*Salisbury Sample*	
	Frequency	*Per cent*	*Frequency*	*Per cent*
South Africa	75	86·2	42	60·9
England	0	0·0	9	13·0
Australia	4	4·6	3	4·3
Canada	0	0·0	3	4·3
U.S.A.	2	2·3	2	2·9
New Zealand	1	1·1	1	1·5
Portuguese Africa	0	0·0	2	2·9
Portugal	1	1·1	1	1·5
France	1	1·1	0	0·0
Irish Republic	1	1·1	0	0·0
Greece	0	0·0	1	1·5
Italy	0	0·0	1	1·5
Cyprus	0	0·0	1	1·5
Europe (not specific)	1	1·1	1	1·5
Latin America	1	1·1	0	0·0
Not specific	0	0·0	2	2·9
	N = 87	100·0	N = 69	100·0

Source: Shutz, Barry Meyer, 'Homeward Bound? A Survey Study of the Limits of White Rhodesian Nationalism and Permanence', in *Ufahamu*, Journal of the African Activist Association Studies Centre, U.C.L.A., Vol. 15, No. 3, 1975.

In the April 1970 election, the first held under the new 1969 Constitution, the Rhodesian Front again made a clean sweep of all fifty 'white' seats in the new 66-member House of Assembly. In June 1974, the RF, repeated its success by winning 75 per cent of the votes in the 48 contested constituencies.

This overwhelming domination by the Rhodesian Front of white Rhodesian politics illustrates the assertion of settler independence. It also suggested that no effective initiative for significant change was likely to come from within the system of white supremacy. A recent analysis of the background to the 1974 election concluded:

> ... hoping for stability, the electorate may have opted for chaos – if it had any choice at all. Its near-fanatical support for the values which underpin Rhodesian settler colonialism may yet threaten the system itself. While the election results suggest that a prerequisite for constitutional change in Rhodesia is the abolition of the white electorate, they confirmed that the initiative for fundamental change in Rhodesia lies not with the whites but with the blacks.[16]

It would seem most improbable that white Rhodesia has the moral, human and material resources to sustain the luxury of racial privilege dependent on a system of political, social and economic discrimination. Rhodesia's segregationist policies, which tend to reinforce the comfortable but precarious illusions of an 'out of sight, out of mind' or 'sweep it under the carpet' mentality, well illustrate white Rhodesia's remarkable capacity for self-deception and the equally characteristic complacency of the man in the street. The uncomfortable reality of being outnumbered 22:1 by the black population is mitigated by the white community's propensity to live in the urban areas where the ratio is more favourable. In the two major towns, Salisbury and Bulawayo for example, this ratio falls to 4:1; and in the so-called 'European' land, which under the Land Tenure Act amounts to one half of the country, the ratio is 8:1. The role of rationalization and myth in Rhodesia has been examined by Peter Harris, who points out that:

> Myths serve a useful function to those who create them. They direct attention away from the more sensitive aspects of any existing prob-

lems . . . the difficulty with myths is that those who create them eventually come to believe them, and therefore resist change when change, painful as it may be, becomes inevitable.[17]

Even if the Rhodesian Government were to come under strong pressure from influential quarters in the security forces and the business community to negotiate a settlement with the black nationalists which would result in the lifting of sanctions and an end to the insurgency, the Government's room for manoeuvre would be cramped by an electorate which has been repeatedly told that there is no need for such a change. In a succinct assessment, Kenneth Good has argued:

> Myth and rigidity protects Rhodesia from a naked and possibly lonely reliance upon weak military power, in ultimate defence of its wealth . . . White dominance in Rhodesia is a brittle and fragile structure . . . This total inability to change – rather than to control change – and total concentration upon the politics of the white electorate, characterises Rhodesian settler colonialism and now, in changing internal and external circumstances, determines the downfall of white Rhodesia.[18]

This all suggests that the effective impetus for dismantling the existing structure probably had to come from external sources, principally: the widening and intensification of guerrilla activity; a more effective application of sanctions; and an about-turn in the South African Government's attitude to Rhodesia after the April 1974 Lisbon coup.

RHODESIA – AN EXTENSION OF SOUTH AFRICA?

The above analysis would suggest that neither the 'colony in trust' nor the 'independent settler power' perspectives provide adequate explanations of the Rhodesian experience; although the latter is certainly closer to reality than the former. The situation in Rhodesia, particularly as it has developed since 1956, can perhaps be more usefully understood in terms of the second classification described above: that Rhodesia is in some significant ways an 'extension' of a metropolitan power. In this case South Africa rather than Britain should be seen in this role. The links between a metropolitan authority and a dependent colony, where the latter is regarded as an extension of the former, are jealously preserved, the former Portuguese territories being a case in point. An even more extreme example of this kind of relationship is that between South Africa and South-West Africa which has been described as South Africa's 'fifth province'. John Sprack concludes in his aptly entitled pamphlet *Rhodesia: South Africa's Sixth Province*:

> ... the white minority in Rhodesia is heavily dependent for the maintenance of its domination on South Africa, in several crucial respects. It is also clear that the dominant white minority in South Africa is deeply attached by similar connections – military, strategic, economic, and cultural – to its Rhodesian counterpart. Indeed Rhodesia was historically and to a large extent still is essentially an extension north of the Limpopo river of the pattern of colonial conquest and racist rule for which South Africa is notorious. In the years since UDI this profound attachment has grown into concrete, extensive and apparently irreversible commitment by the rulers of South Africa to the maintenance of white rule in Rhodesia.[19]

Sprack shows very clearly how the birth and development of white Rhodesia has taken place in the context of close cultural, economic and military ties with South Africa.

In social and cultural terms the 'kith and kin' factor has always been important. Traditionally, the main source of growth in the white population has been immigration rather than birth. Although the percentage of white Rhodesians born in the country has risen steadily, from about 33 per cent in 1951 to 35 per cent in 1961 and 41 per cent in 1969, the immigrant component nevertheless remains substantial. In 1969, about 24 per cent of Rhodesian Whites had been born in the United Kingdom and 21 per cent in South Africa, a significant proportion of which is of Afrikaner extraction. Moreover, some of those born in the United Kingdom may have resided temporarily in South Africa before moving on to settle in Rhodesia. The number of those falling into this category, calculated from the discrepancy between emigrants reported in British statistics to be leaving for South Africa and those reported in South African statistics as having arrived from the United Kingdom, had risen from about 1,000 in the year following UDI to over 4,000 in 1971.[20]

The sympathy of South African Whites for their Rhodesian

Table 8: Migration between Rhodesia and South Africa, 1960–75

Migration between Rhodesia and South Africa

Year	*South Africa to Rhodesia*	*Percentage of total immigrants*	*Rhodesia to South Africa*	*Percentage of total emigrants*
1960	4,551	57	2,166	31
1961	4,635	58	5,760	58
1962	2,636	33	7,180	60
1963	2,214	32	15,414	86
1964	2,731	39	12,976	83
1965	2,764	25	3,494	39
1966	1,600	25	5,096	60
1967	2,617	27	4,115	54
1968	2,856	24	3,177	56
1969	2,639	24	3,441	58
1970	2,343	19	2,964	50
1971	3,073	21	2,585	48
1972	2,491	18	2,047	40
1973	1,580	17	2,706	35
1974	1,083	11	4,099	45
1975 Jan./March	424	15	1,933	83

Sources: South African Statistics, 1970, and the South African Quarterly Bulletin of Statistics.

cousins, particularly after UDI in 1965, was reflected by the spontaneous formation of such bodies as the 'Friends of Rhodesia' organization and the South Africa Rhodesia Association, which together gave money and equipment totalling more than Rh$500,000 to the Rhodesian government between 1965 and 1972. More recently a right-wing organization, the Southern African Solidarity Congress (SASCON) has been active in both Rhodesia and South Africa and has indicated that it would favour the incorporation of Rhodesia into South Africa. It is not surprising, then, that in times of uncertainty and crisis, spontaneous emigration of Whites is so often to South Africa. Whites who emigrate under more routine circumstances are more likely to have plans to settle elsewhere such as Europe, the North Americas, Australia and New Zealand. The above table shows the percentage of emigrants to South Africa rising significantly during periods of uncertainty (e.g. during the break-up of the Central African Federation, 1963–4) and after a particular crisis such as UDI in 1965.

Economically and financially, Rhodesia's dependence on South Africa inevitably increased after UDI with the imposition of international sanctions. There is a close relationship between the Reserve Banks of the two countries, which has been maintained since UDI. A United Nations Report in 1967 stated that 'since then, no statement has been made by the Ministry of Finance of South Africa on South Africa's financial relations with the Smith régime, although it has been reported that South Africa has become the main source of credit to Rhodesia'. South African financial involvement in the Rhodesian economy appears to have increased substantially, especially in mining and agriculture.

The collapse of the Central African Federation, and with it the high tariffs designed to protect the infant industries of Southern Rhodesia, and the effect of sanctions since 1966 have bound Rhodesian trade more closely to South Africa. Adrian Guelke has estimated (see Table 9) Rhodesia's increased dependence on South Africa for her imports (using United Nations and other sources).[21] Another study by Julian Burgess, also using UN, Rhodesian and other sources, states that the percentage of Rhodesian exports by value to South Africa was 10·2 in 1965, 25·2 in 1966, 33·6 in 1967, 27·8 in 1968, 28·6 in 1969, 27.4 in 1970, 23·7 in 1971, 21.1 in 1972 and 16·1 in 1973.[22] The secrecy surrounding sanctions evasion and the problems of allowing for re-imports and re-exports inevitably make any calculations or estimates extremely tentative. Since UDI there have been no detailed official Rhodesian trade figures and from 1973 the Rhodesian authorities even suspended the publication of total export and import figures for reasons of economic security. However, the Rhodesian Secretary for Commerce and Industry is on record as saying that manufacturing, mining and agriculture each accounted for about one-third of Rhodesia's exports, and export sales are believed to have risen by at least fifteen per cent to around Rh$ 375 million in 1973 according to an estimate by an economist at the University of Rhodesia,[23] a figure considerably lower than Burgess's estimate of about Rh$ 430 million. Whatever the correct figures, the general point is not in doubt – Rhodesia remains, despite the lower percentages in 1972 and

1973, dependent on South Africa for taking a significant proportion of her exports, especially now that Mozambique's independence has further undermined Rhodesia's economic and military security.

Table 9: Rhodesian Imports, 1964–73

Rhodesian Imports, 1964–73 (Rh$ million)

Year	*Total imports*	*Imports from South Africa*	*Increase over previous year*	*Percentage of South African imports*
1964	216·5	52·7	—	24·34
1965	239·6	54·9	2·2	22·91
1966	169·3	78·6	23·7	46·40
1967	187·1	96·4	17·8	51·52
1968	207·0	107·1	10·7	51·74
1969	199·4	110·7	3·6	55·52
1970	234·9	114·3	3·6	48·66
1971	282·3	121·5	7·2	43·02
1972	274·2	133·7	12·2	40·80
1973	322·6	121·0	12·7	37·50

As Adrian Guelke has argued, South Africa does not wholly welcome this heavy reliance by Rhodesia on her:

> . . . the stagnation of Rhodesia's total imports until 1971 – when for the first time the 1965 level was exceeded – has clearly been a limiting factor on the growth of South African exports to Rhodesia . . . Rhodesia's ability to pay for further substantial increases in imports while 'sanctions are in operation must be doubted, as the small decline in imports in 1972 suggests. In these circumstances the lifting of sanctions, opening the way to growth in Rhodesia's economy and her trade, would probably be in South Africa's best economic interests, even if her own imports declined as a proportion of the increased total. What is more, the liberal trade agreement between South Africa and Rhodesia in November 1974 – which replaced the restrictive 1960 agreement with the Federation – would help to safeguard South Africa's trading position. In short, the bitter political disappointment which the South African Government suffered when the settlement between Britain and Rhodesia was rejected by her African population in 1972 has its economic counterpart.'

South Africa had also been disappointed by the Rhodesian government's rejection of the *Tiger* and *Fearless* settlement proposals in 1966 and 1968.

Rhodesia's dependence on South Africa for circumventing sanctions has been further highlighted by the implications of the April 1974 Lisbon coup and Portugal's subsequent withdrawal from Africa, especially Mozambique. It is estimated that by the end of 1973 about three-quarters of Rhodesia's import–export traffic passed through the Mozambique ports of Beira and Lourenço Marques; and that between 500,000 and 600,000 tons of oil reached Rhodesia annually through Lourenço Marques. However, with the increased unreliability of the Mozambique ports since 1974, the volume of the traffic had probably fallen to about 40 to 50 per cent. An independent FRELIMO government is certain to observe sanctions more scrupulously than the former Portuguese authorities. Rhodesia therefore faces the prospect not only of severed oil supplies but also an end to the previous practice of falsifying certificates of origin for Rhodesian exports. If denied access to the Mozambique ports Rhodesia would be totally dependent on her road and rail links to South Africa – the traditional but circuitous and lengthy (2,100 km. from Bulawayo and 2,500 km. from Salisbury to Cape Town) route via Botswana and the newly-completed (October 1974) connection via Beitbridge between Rutenga and Messina in the Transvaal. It has been estimated that Rhodesia's export and import traffic amounted to about 20 per cent of the South African total. If the Rhodesian traffic were to be switched through to South African ports, the Republic's freight-handling capacity would probably have to be stepped up by a further 15 per cent, on top of the 15 per cent expansion already estimated for its own goods. Since the Rutenga link is not yet a 'heavy-weight' line, it has been estimated that it could bear only about 75 per cent of the total traffic load, (although it has been reported that the original 60 lb/yard truck is being replaced by 90 lb/yard truck needed for moving heavy ore).[24] A senior spokesman for South African Railways commented:

It all depends on what they are going to send us . . . We have improved the line between Pretoria and the Rhodesian border at Beitbridge for our own use, and we have a little spare capacity as a result. But to say we would be able to take all the goods Rhodesia would like us to send would be ludicrous. We would be faced with an insurmountable problem . . . I am afraid the Rhodesians themselves will have to draw up a priority list of what they want moved.

> He continued that, while he was sure that the government would not take steps which would be detrimental to South Africa's own economy, '. . . at the same time we would obviously not like to see them go under and we would help when we could . . . (but) . . . we certainly cannot be expected to provide an infra-structure just in case Rhodesia is hard pressed.'

With chronic congestion at her own ports and an already overloaded railway system, it seems therefore that South Africa is not likely to welcome the increased burden of Rhodesian traffic diverted from the Mozambique ports. In addition to the logistical problems, Rhodesia's rail lifelines to Mozambique and South Africa could also prove extremely vulnerable to sabotage by guerrillas, if the insurgency were to spread down the eastern border.

Rhodesia's comparatively secure position during the 1960s has changed almost overnight with the Portuguese withdrawal from Mozambique. As long as it seemed that the level of conflict could be contained to manageable proportions within Rhodesia, South Africa was prepared to provide the necessary degree of military assistance. However, the prospect since the Portuguese coup is of a rising level of violence in Rhodesia which could assume regional proportions and raise the spectre of external intervention in the area: a situation which South Africa is anxious to avoid at almost all costs. South Africa now sees a clear interest in attempting to defuse a potentially explosive situation by being prepared to countenance and assist in a controlled implementation of majority rule in Rhodesia. South African military assistance to Rhodesia has increased tenfold since 1967 and made an important psychological and material contribution to the Rhodesian counter-insurgency effort. In mid-1967 South Africa dispatched, according to the most reliable estimates, a company of paramilitary police to Rhodesia to combat the joint ZAPU/SAANC incursions in the Wankie Game Reserve area. A *Daily Telegraph* correspondent reported in September 1967 that four Alouette helicopters and two spotter aircraft had accompanied them. In 1968, the South African Government budgeted an additional £730,000 for its para-military force in Rhodesia: of which £250,000 was for subsistence, £467,000 for motor transport, and £8,000 for motor patrol boats on the Zambezi.[25] By the end of 1974 it is estimated that there was a para-military force of between 2,000 and 3,000 men and perhaps two squadrons of helicopters (operated under a contract with South Africa) in Rhodesia.

For the past ten years two strands have been evident in South Africa's attitude to the continuing Rhodesian problem: her own immediate security imperatives when threatened by infiltrating insurgents as in 1967 on the one hand; and her hopes for a normalization of relations with black Africa, particularly Zambia, on the other. The underlying tension between these contradictory tendencies has surfaced on a number of occasions: most notably at UDI in 1965, and in 1973 when Rhodesia unilaterally closed her border with Zambia. Prior to the Lisbon coup, the former tendency was more prominent, and South Africa felt constrained to provide moral and material support to the anti-insurgency campaigns in Rhodesia as well as in the Portuguese territories. Since then, however, faced with the unattractive prospect of an increasingly open-ended and uncertain military commitment which threatened to undermine regional stability, South Africa has placed the emphasis on diplomacy. Throughout 1974 there were signs that South Africa was taking steps to play down the military role of her forces in Rhodesia. In October it was announced that the South African police there were to be replaced gradually by a volunteer corps. In his speech at Nigel on 4 November 1974, the South African Prime Minister stressed that the police units had been sent to Rhodesia to 'protect South Africa's interests and not anybody else's' and expressed the hope that they would be brought home as soon as possible.

Rhodesia's dependence militarily, economically and politically on her more powerful neighbour suggests parallels with Portugal's relationship to her former colonies, although clearly the comparison cannot be pressed too far. The most obvious difference is that white Rhodesia has been capable of exercising a great deal more independent local power than the white settler communities in Angola and Mozambique. Indeed, since 1965 the settlers in Rhodesia have used this power in a way that has thwarted South Africa's own efforts to reach an understanding with black Africa, and, in particular, with Zambia. Another important difference from the Portuguese situation is that there has been no change of régime in Pretoria as there has in Lisbon. The South African Government is therefore subject to a variety of domestic political constraints which make it impossible for it to execute a complete about-turn in her attitude towards Rhodesia. However, when Sprack states that Rhodesia's close association with South Africa had grown into a 'concrete, extensive and apparently irreversible commitment by the rulers of South Africa to the maintenance of white rule in Rhodesia' he has arguably misunderstood the ambivalent nature of South Africa's commitment to Rhodesia, and overlooked the tendency of metropolitan powers to abandon their dependencies when they cease to serve a useful function or, worse still, become a positive liability.

7 Conclusion

During 1974 a variety of economic, military and political pressures and incentives arose in the sub-continent which resulted in a renewed attempt to explore the scope for reaching a measure of accommodation, within the framework of the 1969 Lusaka Manifesto, between the white- and black-ruled territories in the region. With the industrialized world preoccupied with the problems of inflation and economic recession there was a growing recognition in Southern Africa that the region's problems would have to be solved by local initiatives. The prospect of serious food shortages, declining prices for crucial export commodities like copper, soaring costs for vital import commodities like oil and fertilizer, and chronic transport difficulties gave impetus to the search for *détente*. Portugal's withdrawal from Africa, the other major factor in the situation, has profoundly altered the political and strategic balance in the region, threatening to undermine white rule in Rhodesia and to force South Africa into greater isolation. The two states most immediately concerned with initiating the *détente* exercise were Zambia and South Africa, and the main items on the *détente* 'agenda' emerged as: South Africa's response to the new régimes in the former Portuguese territories; the question of South Africa's continued economic and military support of the white régime in Rhodesia; South Africa's continued presence in Namibia in defiance of United Nations rulings that her administration of the territory is unlawful; and finally the fundamental issue of South Africa's internal policies.[1]

The longer-term, basic assumption behind South Africa's attempt to promote a policy of *rapprochement* with black Africa – that the natural economic interdependence of the territories in the sub-continent, and South Africa's overwhelming preeminence within the region, will ultimately lead to a workable political accommodation irrespective of ideological divisions – remains to be tested. In a more limited sense the search for *détente* could conceivably result in 'settlements' of the more immediate Rhodesian and South-West African problems. Temporarily at least, there is a coincidence of South African and Zambian interests in securing a controlled, constitutional transition to majority rule in Rhodesia. The behind-the-scenes manoeuvres leading up to, as well as the two-steps-forward-one-step-backward character of the negotiations subsequent to, the tentative Lusaka Agreement of early December 1974 on a basis for a cease-fire and constitutional conference, demonstrate very clearly the tension between the attempted assertion of independent settler power by Rhodesia on the one hand, and the degree to which Rhodesia is an *extension* of South Africa on the other. A few examples will help to illustrate the nature of this relationship.

During the Sinoia/Umvukwes by-election in February 1974 Allan Savory, a former Rhodesian Front M.P. but later co-founder of the opposition Rhodesia Party, called for an all-party constitutional conference, adding, 'I would go so far as to say that if all terrorist activity were to be stopped, ZAPU and ZANU representatives could also be invited to the conference table.' The Rhodesian Prime Minister, replying, asked:

> Is there no end to the irresponsibility of this man? – to his capacity for destroying the good name of Rhodesia? Were I thinking only of my own interests I would welcome the blunder because Mr Savory has successfully cut his own political throat. I do not believe any single Rhodesian worth his salt would be party to appeasement and abject surrender.

Yet, before the year was out, Mr Smith had, in line with the South African and Zambian initiatives, agreed to the very terms he had castigated his opponent for proposing. On 8 and 13 November and again in the first week of December the Rhodesian Government allowed several senior nationalists, including Joshua Nkomo and the Reverend Ndabaningi Sithole, to leave their places of detention and fly to Lusaka to take part in discussions about terms for a ceasefire and constitutional conference. According to apparently well-founded press reports some measure of agreement had been reached on a franchise for a common voters' roll which could provide for parliamentary parity between Black and White within the space of two or three years leading to a black parliamentary majority within a transitional period of a further three years or so.[2] If something along these lines had really been accepted as the basis for further constitutional negotiations it represented a considerable shift in the position of the Government, which had only a few months earlier been quite adamant that the fundamentals of the 1971 Settlement Proposals were not negotiable. Speaking at an election meeting on 22 July 1974, Ian Smith told his audience that he wanted to be 'practical and say that if someone suggests a little change here and there and it does not affect the principle and keeps the reins of government in responsible hands, I am prepared to listen to this sort of thing. But if people want basic changes, then the answer is no.' He made the point even more bluntly to the annual Rhodesian Front congress on 20 September: 'Our stand is clear and unambiguous. Settlement is desirable, but only on our terms. Fortunately, we speak from a position of strength and there is no need for any panic rush decisions.' The Rhodesian Prime Minister and his cabinet colleagues, let alone the white public, could hardly have imagined that within a few months 'yesterday's forgotten men', as the detained nationalists had been referred to, would be released; and that a preliminary agreement, however precarious and susceptible to widely differing interpretations, on the issues of a ceasefire and constitutional conference would be reached. Not surprisingly, these differences of interpretation immediately impeded further progress. On 7 December the Rhodesian Prime Minister accused President Nyerere, under pressure from nationalist militants and OAU quarters, of sabotaging the Lusaka Agreement by coming up with a last-minute demand that any constitutional negotiations should be based on an acceptance of 'the principle of immediate majority rule'. After a two-hour cabinet meeting Ian Smith announced the breakdown of the negotiations: 'Our representatives were informed that there would be no cessation of terrorism unless it was agreed that a pre-condition of the constitutional conference was that it would be on the basis of immediate majority rule. These proposals are not acceptable to the Rhodesian Government.' The South African Government, concerned at the early collapse of the Lusaka Agreement, particularly as the rival nationalist groups had agreed to form a united front under a reconstituted African National Council, moved swiftly in an attempt to reopen negotiations. A South African delegation headed by Brand Fourie, Secretary for Foreign Affairs, flew to Lusaka to ask President Kaunda to exercise his influence with the Zimbabwean nationalists. Mr Vorster, for his part, flew to Salisbury on 9 December to persuade the Rhodesian Prime Minister to resume the negotiations. He had described the prospect of their failure as 'too ghastly to contemplate', and appeared to have achieved his purpose when, on the evening of 10 December, Mr Smith went on radio and television to announce that in response to assurances he had received that there would be no pre-conditions to a constitutional conference and that 'terrorist activities' would cease immediately, he had agreed to release the African leaders and their followers from detention and restriction. On 20 December, restriction orders on twenty political prisoners at the Wha Wha restriction camp in the Midlands were lifted and on the following day a further batch of twenty were released. Officials indicated that the Government planned to release over 300 more 'soon'.

However, on 9 January, the Minister for Justice, Law and Order, Desmond Lardner-Burke, accused the nationalists of failing to make any real effort to bring about a ceasefire: 'Not only have terrorists failed to obey explicit instructions from their alleged leaders to cease hostilities, they have increased their activities in some areas. Under these circumstances I am definitely not letting out any more at the moment.' In his report commenting on the Minister's statement James MacManus suggested that it 'underlined the increasing intransigence of the Rhodesian régime during the run-up to a constitutional conference. The Government in Salisbury has been concerned to demonstrate its authority in face of events that have largely bypassed it in recent weeks.'[3] Whatever the Government's motives, the breakdown of the negotiations was hardly unexpected, given the widely differing interpretations of the Lusaka Agreement held by the Rhodesian Government and the ANC. The Government's version was given on 7 December in a statement issued from the Prime Minister's Office:

> Resulting from these discussions the Rhodesian Government agreed to mount a constitutional conference on certain conditions. First, that there should be a cessation of terrorism in accordance with the Prime Minister's frequently stated principle that he would only be prepared to discuss constitutional issues with those who undertook to work constitutionally and within the law. Secondly, that any constitutional conference would have to accept that there would be no lowering of standards.

On 20 December a security force communiqué referred to the Prime Minister's announcement that he had received assurances that 'terrorist activities would cease immediately' and that the detained African leaders and their followers would be released: 'The cessation of hostilities has not yet proved to be complete, and specific breaches had occurred' although it was recognized that 'it might take some time for this (the ceasefire) to be fully effective'. Continuing incidents, including the killing of four South African policemen on Christmas Eve, led up to the Minister of Law and Order's announcement of the decision to halt the release of detainees and restrictees.

Two days later the ANC announced its interpretation of what had been agreed in Lusaka. Dr Edson Sithole, Publicity Secretary of the ANC listed eight points to which the Government had allegedly agreed:

1. That the Rhodesian Government would release all political detainees and restrictees (which included people in protected villages) immediately.
2. That the Government would release all political prisoners as soon as possible.
3. That the Government would revoke the death sentences on political prisoners and release them.
4. That the Government would grant a general amnesty to all those considered to have committed political crimes, including those outside the country.

5. That the Government would lift the ban on ZANU and ZAPU
6. That the Government would create conditions to allow free political activity and expression in the country.
7. That the Government would halt political trials.
8. That the Government would lift the State of Emergency.

On the issue of a ceasefire the ANC statement said that it had been agreed that there would be an informal arrangement which would require both sides to inform their forces without an announcement. After the announcement of a specific date for a constitutional conference and the start of meaningful negotiations there would be a formal ceasefire. 'The Government has not fulfilled these conditions,' the statement continued. 'It has partially fulfilled only one condition in that it has released less than one third of all detainees.'[4] If the Government had indeed given such specific guarantees, which seems most unlikely, it certainly showed little inclination to meet them and concentrated instead on trying to reassert its authority. Pamphlets were distributed in the operational areas instructing guerrillas to hide their weapons and surrender to the nearest soldier, policeman or District Commissioner's office; or to return to Zambia and Mozambique. Anyone found in possession of arms would be regarded as an enemy. The ANC objected to the Government's interpretation of the informal ceasefire as tantamount to almost total surrender. A teenage guerrilla who had given himself up after reading the pamphlet was sentenced to five years' imprisonment on 8 January and on 26 January two tribesmen were hanged for their involvement in the killing of Africans suspected of working as Government informers. On 4 March Ndabaningi Sithole was re-detained on, according to the Government, 'reliable information' that the President of ZANU was planning the 'assassination of certain of his opponents whom he considers to be a challenge to his bid for leadership of the ANC'. The Reverend Sithole was to be tried *in camera*, not on any specific criminal charge, but to determine whether the detention order was justified.* In the previous week, three convicted guerrillas

*During the trial, the Rhodesian Solicitor-General was called to give evidence that ZANU, of which the Reverend Sithole was President, was

were hanged in Salisbury's Central Prison and on 3 April three members of the ANC were arrested in connection with alleged contraventions of the Law and Order (Maintenance) Act. One of them, Maurice Nyagumbo, was a senior ZANU official who had accompanied the ZANU President to Lusaka for the second set of talks in mid-November 1974. All these actions were intended to leave no one in any doubt that the Government was determined to maintain 'law and order'. The attitude of the Rhodesian Government and in particular the rearrest of Sithole, whether or not there was any substance in the assassination allegations, was interpreted in nationalist quarters in Rhodesia and by members of the OAU as an attempt to isolate, physically and politically, the most militant nationalists in the hope that a settlement might be arranged with the nationalist leaders thought to be the most moderate. This attempt to 'divide and rule', if this was in fact the Government's motive, backfired badly.

On 2 April the Acting Chief Justice ruled that the detention was 'fully warranted' on general grounds of security although no investigation or judgement was made on the specific allegations of plotting to assassinate his rivals. The judgement threatened to undermine South African efforts to reach even a limited understanding with black Africa. Accordingly, the South African Foreign Minister, Dr Hilgard Muller, flew to Salisbury on 3 April to express this concern to the Rhodesian Prime Minister. In a radio and television broadcast, on the following day, arranged at only three hours' notice, Ian Smith announced that Sithole would be released so that he could attend the OAU conference in Dar-es-Salaam. It was not a request to which he had readily agreed, he said, and had only been permitted because the Presidents of Zambia, Tanzania, Botswana, the ANC and the South African Foreign Minister had assured him it was in the interests of moves towards *détente*.

---

responsible for a whole range of atrocities in twenty specific areas of Rhodesia. The Commander of the Special Board of the BSAP also gave details of 202 incidents which had occurred between 12 December 1974 and 19 March 1975, during which time 38 people, including 32 unarmed tribesmen, had been killed by insurgents operating in Rhodesia. See *The Times*, 26 March and 3 April 1975.

The failure to achieve a ceasefire which would have facilitated a mutually satisfactory withdrawal of South Africa's para-military forces from Rhodesia, a move which the Zambian Foreign Minister had described as a 'minimum reponse' in return for Zambia's willingness to exercise her influence with the Zimbabwe nationalists to try and bring about a peaceful transition in Rhodesia, further complicated an already sensitive problem. Incidents such as that on Christmas Eve when four South African policemen were killed only served to underline South Africa's continued presence in the country. However, on 11 February it was announced that elements of the South African Police were withdrawing from certain forward positions on the border with Zambia. The move followed a visit to Zambia by Dr Muller, during which he held discussions with the Foreign Ministers of Zambia, Tanzania and Botswana. A step further was taken when on 10 March South Africa's Minister of Police announced in Cape Town that all South African policemen in Rhodesia were being confined to their camps so that they 'will not be involved in any way in any possible incidents and thereby embarrass the Rhodesian Government'. The statement emphasized the widening rift between the South African and Rhodesian Governments over the direction of the *détente* exercise. Significantly, the Commander of the Rhodesian Army warned South Africa in a speech at the time of the Minister of Police's announcement that South Africa had a moral obligation to support Rhodesia if *détente* broke down.[5] However, despite this warning and the fact that there had been no effective ceasefire, the South African Minister of Police and Justice announced in Pretoria on 1 August that

> the stage has now been reached where the slightly more than 200 men who are still in Rhodesia can be withdrawn to the Republic and such an order has now been issued . . . As has been repeatedly stated in Parliament and in public, the South African police were sent to Rhodesia to stop South African terrorists on their way to South Africa . . . Gradually, the original necessity for the South African police presence has grown less. It has always been felt that their presence should not become a disturbing factor in the process of negotiations.[6]

Although South African newspapers and officials have been expressing impatience over the Rhodesian Government's inability to come to terms with even moderate black opinion since before the Lisbon coup of April 1974, the South African Government cannot afford to be seen to be pressing too hard or moving too fast on Rhodesia for fear of provoking a backlash from various quarters within South Africa which would limit the South African Prime Minister's room for manoeuvre. The Rhodesian Government has attempted to exploit this situation on a number of occasions. Speaking at a Pretoria agricultural show in late August 1974 Mr Smith retaliated against newspapers and politicians in South Africa who had criticized Rhodesia for being an embarrassment to the South African Government and warned them 'you are next on the list'. In order to boost white Rhodesian morale, sympathetic South Africans have been invited to Rhodesia and delivered messages of assurance that South Africa would not abandon them. In February 1975, for instance, a leading member of the Dutch Reformed Church, Professor Adriaan Pont, told the annual congress of the Association of Afrikaans Rhodesians that they had the unqualified support of every Afrikaner from the Cape to the Zambezi. In another speech on the same occasion the Rhodesian Minister of Health and Labour, Rowan Cronjé, stressed that Rhodesia was not prepared to be the sacrificial lamb of *détente*.

The Rhodesian Government has amply demonstrated over the past decade its inability to come to terms with African nationalism of its own accord. It has essentially been preoccupied with repressing the symptoms rather than addressing itself to the underlying causes of black disaffection. It remains to be seen how successful South Africa's initiative will prove in moving white Rhodesia towards an acceptance of a controlled, constitutional transition to majority rule. It is difficult to see how the existing system in Rhodesia can stand up to the mounting internal and external pressures for more than a very few years if South Africa shows herself to be irrevocably committed to a 'Trojan Horse' role. There is very little chance of the Rhodesian Government agreeing to what would amount to an immediate handover of power in accordance with the demands of the most militant nationalists although it is conceivable that external pressures on both the Government and the nationalists will ultimately result in the emergence of a political settlement – which would not necessarily be the same thing as a durable solution – on the lines of the Zambian/South African proposals providing for a black parliamentary majority in between four to six years. However, it is still possible that whites in Rhodesia will choose to resist change outright rather than attempt to control its pace and direction by accepting a phased transition to majority rule. The threat of a regional conflagration which might follow could be used by Mr Smith or his successor as his ultimate card. The whole purpose of the *détente* exercise in South Africa's view is to avoid this very situation. It is quite possible that South Africa could once again become involved militarily in Rhodesia if attempts to secure a controlled transition to majority rule fail and result in a breakdown of law and order which was perceived by the South African Government to be a threat to its own political or the state's physical security. While South Africa is anxious to avoid becoming embroiled in Rhodesia, two possible situations could prompt South African intervention. The Government could be forced to respond to the inevitably strong reactions of the white South African public if an intensification of the guerrilla war resulted in the widespread killing of Rhodesian Whites. A semi-conventional invasion of Rhodesia by any outside power in support of the guerrillas could also lead to South African intervention.

Appendix

(Illustrating the increasingly retrogressive series of constitutional proposals from 1961 to 1971)

(A) 1961 Constitution

Main features:

1. A Declaration of Rights to protect individual rights with an ultimate right of appeal to the Privy Council in Britain. Its application was limited to legislation introduced after the 1961 Constitution and therefore was no protection against earlier legislation such as the Land Apportionment Act.
2. A Constitutional Council to reinforce the Declaration of Rights. This was also of limited utility as it could only draw attention to, but not initiate action against, discriminatory legislation.
3. A qualified franchise with two voters' rolls: a white-dominated 'A' roll based on high income, property and educational qualifications; and a 'B' roll based on lower qualifications and therefore black-dominated.
4. A House of Assembly of 65 seats comprised of members returned from 50 constituencies (dominated by the 'A' roll) and from 15 electoral districts (dominated by the 'B' roll) under a weighted cross-voting system specifically designed to favour 'middle-of-the-road' candidates, white and black.
5. Amendment of entrenched clauses (including the franchise qualifications, Constitutional Council, Declaration of Rights) required both a two-thirds majority in the Legislative Assembly and a referendum in which each of the four racial sections of the population voted separately or, alternatively, the approval of the British government.
6. On the assumption that the government in power in Rhodesia would abide by both the letter and spirit of the 1961 Constitution a black parliamentary majority was envisaged in twelve to twenty-five years.

(B) 1965 (U.D.I.) Constitution

1. Based on the 1961 Constitution but amended to the new situation created by the unilateral declaration of independence in November 1965. The amendment procedure for entrenched clauses was simplified requiring only a two-thirds majority on two occasions.
2. It was operated by a government which paid lip-service to the multi-racial principles of the 1961 Constitution although the working reality was far different.

(C) Tiger Proposals (December 1966)

These and subsequent negotiations were, according to the British government, based on six principles:

1. Unimpeded progress to majority rule.
2. Guarantees against retrogressive amendments to the constitution.
3. Immediate improvement in the political status of the Africans.
4. Progress towards ending racial discrimination.
5. The British government would have to be satisfied that any proposed basis for independence was acceptable to the people of Rhodesia as a whole.
6. That there would be no oppression of majority by minority or of minority by majority.

If the *Tiger* terms offered by the British Labour Government had been accepted and not rejected by the Rhodesian administration, they would have amounted to a recognition of Rhodesian independence under a modified version of the 1961 Constitution which had already been rejected as the basis for independence by the previous Conservative Government. Following the Rhodesian rejection of the *Tiger* terms the British Labour Government gave an undertaking that 'in future no grant of independence will be contemplated unless African majority rule is already an accomplished fact.' (The principle of NIBMAR – No Independence Before Majority African Rule.)

(D) Fearless Proposals (October 1968)

These represented an abandonment of the NIBMAR pledge and the resuscitation of the *Tiger* proposals with a British attempt to strengthen safeguards against retrogressive amendments to the constitution by the right of direct appeal to the Privy Council and by a 'blocking quarter' of elected African representatives. An important British concession was made over the procedures for the return to legality which under the *Fearless* terms ensured that the Rhodesian administration, rather than the Governor, would retain control if the constitutional proposals were found to be unacceptable to the people of Rhodesia as a whole. Detailed calculations show that, given the most favourable assumptions, majority rule would not have been attained until the year 1999 at the earliest (see Claire Palley, 'No Majority Rule before 1999', the *Guardian*, 14 November 1968).

(E) 1969 Constitution

This was introduced to replace the 1965 Constitution which the Rhodesian Front administration considered to be 'no longer acceptable to the people of Rhodesia because it contains a number of objectionable features, the principal one being that it provides for eventual majority rule and, inevitably, the domination of one race by another and that it does not guarantee that government will be retained in responsible hands'. (*Proposals for a New Constitution of Rhodesia*, Salisbury, CSR32 – 1969, p. I). The new constitution was based on the premise of separate racial development in all spheres and envisaged the attainment of political parity between Black and White in Parliament in the very distant future. As Hodder-Williams points out 'The rate of increase in African seats ... now depends upon the proportion of personal income tax paid by Africans. No further increases will be created until they pay more than 16/66ths of the country's total income tax contribution. In the year ending 30 June 1968, only 986 Africans out of a total of more than 70,000 personal income tax payers earned a high enough salary to qualify to be taxed and their contribution was less than 0·5 per cent' (Richard Hodder-Williams, 'Rhodesia's Search for a Constitution: or whatever happened to Whaley?', *African Affairs*, vol. 69, No. 276, July 1970). This concept of 'parity' for less than a quarter of a million Whites and nearly five million Blacks was also extended to the distribution of land. Under the Land Tenure Act, which replaced the existing Land Apportionment Act, 228,296 Whites were to have 44·9 million acres, 4,846,930 Blacks were allotted 45·2 million acres leaving 6·4 million acres as National Land.

(F) 1971 Settlement Proposals

These proposals state that the proposed 'Constitution of Rhodesia will be the Constitution adopted in Rhodesia in 1969' with certain additional features such as:

1. A Commission to inquire into and make recommendations concerning discriminatory legislation, and a justiciable Declaration of Rights. However, attempts to remove racial discrimination may be vetoed if the government considers that there are 'overriding considerations' and the Declaration of Rights (which is qualified by numerous exceptions and provisos) could be rendered largely in-

effectual simply by the suspension of rights after the declaration of a state of emergency.

2. The prospect of eventual political parity followed by a black parliamentary majority in the subsequent election.
3. Amendments to entrenched sections of the constitution would require, in addition to a two-thirds majority of all the members of the House of Assembly and the Senate voting separately the affirmative votes of a majority of the white representatives and a majority of the black representatives in the House of Assembly. These procedures, while guarding against possible future retrogressive measures, could also be used to block progressive legislation.
4. Detailed calculations suggest that majority rule under these proposals would not be attained until the year 2035 at the earliest (see Claire Palley, 'Rhodesia: The Time Scale, Blacks' Best Hope – a Majority in 2035', *Sunday Times*, 28 November 1971).

Notes

Introduction

1. Ernesto 'Che' Guevara, *Guerrilla Warfare*, Pelican, 1969, p. 14.

2. John S. Pustay, *Counter-Insurgency Warfare*, The Free Press, New York, 1969, p. 5.

3. François Chenu, 'La difficile naissance de la Guerrilla Rhodésienne', *Les Temps Modernes*, 27 November 1970, pp. 890–915. Chenu mentions that a senior Rhodesian Army officer estimated that perhaps 1 in 15 of infiltrating insurgents survived to become guerrillas operating among and hidden by the people.

Chapter 1: The Failure of Compromise Politics

1. Francis Nehwati, 'The Social and Communal Background to "zhii", the African riots in Bulawayo, Southern Rhodesia, in 1960', *African Affairs*, vol. 69, July 1970, pp. 250–66.

2. Press statement issued after the Conference, which appeared in several papers, including the *Daily News* (Rhodesia), 8 February 1961.

3. Quoted from Nathan Shamuyarira, *Crisis in Rhodesia*, André Deutsch, 1965, pp. 163–4.

4. See Stephen E. C. Hintz, 'The Political Transformation of Rhodesia, 1958–1965', *African Studies Review*, vol. XV, September 1972, pp. 173–83.

5. See A. J. A. Peck, *Rhodesia Accuses*, Three Sisters Books, Salisbury, 1966, and H. D. Sills, 'The Break-Up of the Central African Federation: Notes on the Validity of Assurances', *African Affairs*, vol. 73, no. 290, pp. 50–62.

6. J. Chikerema, *Reply to Observations on Our Struggle*, 17 March 1970. (One of three documents which appeared during the ZAPU leadership struggle in early 1970.) The other two were J. Z. Moyo, *Observations on Our Struggle*, 25 February 1970, and J. Z. Moyo et al., *On the Coup Crisis Precipitated by J. Chikerema*, 21 March 1970.

7. Hassan Chimutengwende, 'My Guerrilla Fight Against Smith',

Sunday Times, 24 March 1968. For further details of Soviet and Chinese Communist involvement in subversion during the first half of the 1960s, see *Nkrumah's Subversion in Africa: Documentary Evidence of Nkrumah's Interference in the Affairs of Other African States*, Ministry of Information, Accra, Ghana.

8. Shamuyarira, op. cit., pp. 202–3.

9. For detailed background to the ZAPU – ZANU split, see Shamuyarira, op. cit., pp. 173–93.

10. Peck, op. cit., p. 86.

11. *Zimbabwe Review*, p. 11. See also Moyo, *Observations on Our Struggle* (Introduction, note 6.) (op. cit.) Moyo reveals that the decision to set up a military organization was taken in 1964.

12. For a detailed background of Rhodesian intelligence activities, see Roy Christie, *For the President's Eyes Only*, Hugh Keartland Publishers, Johannesburg, 1971, especially pp. 49–54.

13. Peck, op. cit., pp. 100–102.

14. Davis M'Gabe, 'The Beginnings of Guerrilla Warfare', *Monthly Review*, March 1969, reprinted in W. Cartey and M. Kilson, eds., *The Africa Reader: Independent Africa*, Vintage Books, New York, 1970. From the evidence given in court M'Gabe's account seems to have been unreliable in several important respects.

15. R. Shay and C. Vermaak, *The Silent War*, The Galaxie Press, Salisbury, 1971, pp. 21–2.

16. W. D. Gale, 'The Castle Crumbles', *Rhodesia, 1890–1970: Eighty Years Onwards*, H. C. P. Anderson, Salisbury, 1970, p. 42.

17. M'Gabe, op. cit.

Chapter 2: Insurgency and Counter-Insurgency

1. *Chronicle* (Bulawayo), 10 June 1966.

2. Chimutengwende, op. cit.

3. For a detailed account of the Sinoia engagement see Shay and Vermaak, op. cit., pp. 34–8. The background of the insurgents involved in the Hartley attack is not clear from court statements and other accounts. It is possible that some of them might have entered Rhodesia as early as mid-1965. Others may have been local recruits.

4. For a detailed account of an efficient combined security force operation against a well-trained guerrilla unit see 'Jackal Hunt One' (Ministry of Information, Salisbury), reprinted from *Outpost*, the journal of the British South Africa Police.

5. Reported in the *Chronicle* (Bulawayo), 7 May 1971. The failure to infiltrate South Africa via Rhodesia in 1967 and 1968 caused the

SAANC to turn to other methods. April, a Coloured veteran of the 1967 operation, entered South Africa in December 1970 under a false name and attempted to establish contact with the Indian community, but he was arrested and sentenced to fifteen years' imprisonment. See *Sechaba*, 5 August 1971, pp. 4–5, for an account of his trial.

6. *Zimbabwe News*, 30 September 1967, published by ZANU in Lusaka.

7. *The Wankie Fiasco in Retrospect*, a mimeographed pamphlet issued by the Publicity and Information Secretariat of PAC, Dar-es-Salaam, January 1969, p. 9.

8. Joe Slovo, 'The Armed Struggle Spreads', in *Guerrilla Warfare*, a pamphlet issued by the ANC Publicity and Information Bureau, 1970.

9. Colin and Margaret Legum, *South Africa: Crisis for the West*, Praeger, New York, 1963, p. 4.

10. *Observer*, 18 June 1972.

11. Ben Turok, *Strategic Problems in South Africa's Liberation Struggle: A Critical Survey*, LSM Press, Canada, 1974, p. 51.

12. See my essay 'White Power in Southern Africa: A Comparative Assessment', in Godfrey Morrison (ed.), *Change in Southern Africa*, Africa Confidential Conference Papers, 12 December 1974.

13. *Guardian*, 14 May 1975 and *The Times*, 14 May 1975.

14. Matthew Nkoana, 'Southern Africa: Internal Problems of the New Phase', *The New African*, vol. VIII, p. 12.

15. Extract from the joint statement by Oliver Tambo and James Chikerema, announcing the formation of the ZAPU/ANC military alliance on 19 September 1967. Reprinted in *Guerrilla Warfare* (SAANC pamphlet, op. cit.), p. 3.

16. Author referred to as 'Umkhonto Guerrilla J.M.', 'On the Eastern Front', in *Guerrilla Warfare* (SAANC pamphlet, op. cit.), p. 73.

17. For a more detailed account of these confrontations, see Kees Maxey, *The Fight for Zimbabwe: The Armed Conflict in Southern Rhodesia Since U.D.I.*, Rex Collings, 1975, pp. 72–84.

18. 'Forward from Wankie' in *Sechaba*, reprinted in *Guerrilla Warfare* (SAANC pamphlet, op. cit.), p. 79.

19. For details of this operation see J. Bowyer Bell, 'The Frustration of Insurgency – the Rhodesian Example in the Sixties', *Military Affairs*, 35, 1971. Captured weapons included 3 RPD light machine-guns and 9 magazines; 3 bazookas and 24 projectiles; 19 AK-47 assault rifles; 6 SKS rifles; 6 automatic pistols; 112 offensive and defensive grenades; 150 slabs of explosive; 4 anti-personnel mines and 40,000 rounds of ammunition, mostly 7·62 calibre.

20. *Guerrilla Warfare* (SAANC pamphlet, op. cit.), p. 22 (italics in the original).

21. For a detailed account of these actions, see Michael Morris, *Terrorism: Southern Africa*, Howard Timmins, Cape Town, 1971, pp. 66–71; and, by the same author, *Armed Conflict in Southern Africa*, Jeremy Spence, Cape Town, 1974, pp. 42–3.

22. See Maxey, op. cit., pp. 95–100.

Chapter 3: Divisions Abroad: Solidarity at Home

1. For analyses of the problems which confront both the exiled nationalists and their host territories see J. A. Marcum, 'The Exile Condition and Revolutionary Effectiveness: South African Liberation Movements' in C. P. Potholm and R. Dale (eds.), *Southern Africa in Perspective: Essays in Regional Politics*, The Free Press, New York, 1972, pp. 272–5; and K. W. Grundy, 'Host Countries and the Southern African Liberation Struggle', *Africa Quarterly*, New Delhi, April/June 1970.

2. Press conference in Lusaka reported in the *Rhodesian Herald*, 17 August 1971.

3. *Chronicle* (Bulawayo), 24 July 1972.

4. For more detailed background see *Rhodesia: The Ousting of the Tangwena*, International Defence and Aid Fund booklet, January 1972.

5. *Rhodesia: Report of the Commission on Rhodesian Opinion under the Chairmanship of the Right Honourable the Lord Pearce*, Cmnd 4964, H.M.S.O., 1972.

6. ibid., p. 116.

7. *Guardian*, 23 November 1973.

8. *Rhodesia Herald*, 7 August 1974.

Chapter 4: The Zimbabwe Nationalists Take the Initiative

1. Interview in *Information*, published in Copenhagen and quoted in the *Rhodesia Herald*, 18 August 1971.

2. *Zimbabwe News*, No. 9, September 1973.

3. Maxey, op. cit., p. 21.

4. For a more detailed account see Maxey, op. cit., pp. 114–63.

5. Cited in Peter Janke, 'Southern Africa: End of Empire', *Institute for the Study of Conflict*, No. 52, December 1974, p. 10.

6. Quoted in the *Daily Telegraph*, 29 January 1973.

7. *Rhodesia Herald*, 8 March 1968.

8. Chimutengwende, op. cit.

9. *Zimbabwe News*, vol. 9, no. 1, January 1975, p. 7.

10. Information on these FROLIZI infiltrations has been drawn from much more detailed accounts by Tony Kirk, 'Politics and Violence in Rhodesia', *African Affairs*, vol. 74, no. 294, January 1975, pp. 3–38.

11. *Sunday Times*, 8 July 1973.

12. *Rhodesia Herald*, 23 November 1973 and 14 June 1974.

13. ibid., 21 August 1973.

14. ibid., 26 November 1974.

15. ibid., 26 March 1974.

16. ibid., 25 April 1973.

17. ibid., 16 August 1974.

18. Chimuranya communiqué, no. 9.

19. *Mozambique Revolution*, no. 59, April/June 1974.

20. Peter Niesewand, *In Camera: Secret Justice in Rhodesia*, Weidenfeld & Nicolson, 1973, p. 127.

21. *Evening Standard*, 20 August 1973.

22. *Guardian*, 23 April 1974.

23. *Observer*, 2 September 1973.

Chapter 5: Counter-Insurgency Measures

1. The information in this section is based on the International Defence and Aid Fund's detailed analysis of the implications of the border closure, *The Rhodesia–Zambia Border Closure*, January–February 1973.

2. *Rand Daily Mail*, 6 September 1972.

3. ibid., 22 January 1973.

4. *Rhodesia Herald*, 20 January 1973.

5. *Sunday Mail* (Rhodesia), 21 January 1973.

6. ibid., 4 February 1973.

7. *Rhodesia Herald*, 5 February 1973.

8. Interview with Otto Krause in *Rapport*, 4 February 1973 (translated from the Afrikaans and quoted by the International Defence and Aid Fund).

9. *Sunday Mail* (Rhodesia), 4 and 11 April 1971.

10. *Rhodesia Herald*, 12 February 1973.

11. *Guardian*, 6 April 1974.

12. *Rhodesia Herald*, 21 January 1973.

13. ibid., 13 December 1973.

14. ibid., 7 August 1974.

15. Extract from Appendix III, 'The Slaughter in Mucumbura: Report by Frs. Alfonso Valverde and Martin Hernandez', *Terror in*

Tete: A Documentary Report of Portuguese Atrocities in Tete District, Mozambique, 1971–1972, International Defence and Aid Fund Special Report No. 2, 1973. Confirmation of the accidental massacre of Chief Singa and his family or of a very similar occurrence came from a Rhodesian doctor who was fulfilling his National Service obligations as a medical officer with the Rhodesia Light Infantry. He told Peter Niesewand that the massacre of which he had first-hand knowledge took place during a ten-day operation in Mozambique in August–September 1971. An RLI unit, he said, had set an ambush at a deserted village where they had found weapons and food supplies, making them suspect that it was either a FRELIMO camp or a supply base. His account continued: 'In the middle of the night, several people were heard entering the village. They were allowed to enter and then the RLI opened fire. At first light they went in and discovered that they had killed 13 women and children, the youngest a babe in arms.' *Guardian*, 24 August 1974.

16. *Rhodesia Herald*, 28 July 1973.

17. This document was later published as Appendix A in *The Man in the Middle: Torture, Resettlement and Eviction*, a report compiled by the Catholic Commission for Justice and Peace in Rhodesia, Christian Institute for International Relations, 1975, p. 16. Two of the signatories, the Bishops of Mashonaland (the Right Reverend Paul Burrough) and of Matabeleland (the Right Reverend Mark Wood) had also previously taken a stand against acts of brutality committed by insurgents. In a second letter to the World Council of Churches, the two Bishops noted that no reply had been received to their first letter written in January 1973 and stated that, since then, events

> compel us to plead once more that WCC funds should not be sent to groups of people whose avowed intention and action is to bring naked violence and terror into the land where we serve as Bishops. Since that date in 1973, members of the ZANU and their willing, or forced, accomplices have killed eighty-seven civilians in this country . . . Far and away the majority of these have been Africans innocent of any offence and most have been killed with great brutality. Others have been abducted, raped, beaten and disfigured.

(Quoted from *The Times*, 22 May 1974.)

18. Maxey, op. cit., p. 141.

19. Peter Gibbs, *History of the British South Africa Police*, British South Africa Police, Salisbury, 1972, p. 205 (quoted by Kenneth Good, 'Settler Colonialism in Rhodesia', *African Affairs*, January 1974, p. 11).

20. Dr Morris I. Hirsch, *A Decade of Crisis: Ten Years of Rhodesian Front Rule*, Peter Dearlove, Salisbury, 1973, p. 155.

21. *Financial Times*, 26 September 1975.

Chapter 6: Comparative Perspectives

1. Colin Legum, *Congo Disaster*, Penguin, 1961, pp. 47, 52.

2. Gary Wasserman, 'European Settlers and Kenya Colony', *African Studies Review*, African Studies Association, January 1975, pp. 425–34.

3. 'The Years Behind Us', *Zimbabwe Review*, vol. 2, January–February 1970, p. 7.

4. Good, op. cit., pp. 10–36.

5. P. S. Harris, 'The Wage and Occupational Structure of the Rhodesian Economy', *Labour Research Seminar No. 5*, University of Rhodesia, 1973.

6. *Financial Mail* (South Africa), 20 December 1974.

7. *Rhodesia Herald*, 18 September 1971.

8. For details of the economic background see Rhodesia Party pre-1974 election document, *A Settlement Versus Maintenance of the Status Quo: The Economic Implications – A Preliminary Analysis;* the section on Rhodesia in *Africa 74–75*, Africa Journal Ltd; and the *Monthly Digest of Statistics*, Central Statistical Office, Salisbury.

9. *Rhodesian Realities I: The Population Explosion*, report issued by the Centre Group, Salisbury.

10. *Financial Times*, 29 April 1975.

11. *Guardian*, 11 July and 11 October 1974.

12. *Daily Telegraph*, 16 March 1975.

13. *Third World*, March 1974.

14. Barry Meyer Shutz, 'Homeward Bound? A Survey Study of the Limits of White RhodesianNationalism and Permanence', in *Ufahamu*, Journal of the African Activist Association Studies Centre, U.C.L.A., vol. 5, No. 3, 1975.

15. Hirsch, op. cit.

16. Tony Kirk and Chris Sherwell, 'Rhodesia and the 1974 General Election', *Journal of Commonwealth and Comparative Studies*, Vol. XIII, No. 1, March 1975.

17. Peter Harris, 'Ten Popular Myths Concerning the Employment of Labour in Rhodesia', *Rhodesian Journal of Economics*, March 1974.

18. Good, op. cit.

19. International Defence and Aid Fund publication, 1974, p. 81.

20. For an analysis of the nature and pattern of migration in Rho-

desia, see Kees Maxey, *European migration in and out of Southern Rhodesia* (mimeo), 1973.

21. Adrian Guelke, 'Africa as a Market for South African Goods', *Journal of Modern African Studies*, vol. 12, no. 1, 1974, pp. 69–88.

22. Julian Burgess, a study written for the Q.E.R. Special series of the Economist Intelligence Unit, provisionally entitled *Interdependence and Détente in Southern Africa.*

23. Anthony Hawkins, 'Rhodesian Economy Under Siege', in the *Bulletin of the Africa Institute of South Africa*, No. 1, 1975.

24. *International Star Weekly*, 14 June 1975, for other details mentioned, *To the Point*, 13 December 1974, p. 40, and the *Financial Mail* (South Africa), 23 May 1975.

25. *Rhodesia Herald*, 6 March 1968.

Chapter 7: Conclusion

1. For a more detailed account see A. R. Wilkinson, *Security and the Search for Détente in Southern Africa*, Adelphi Paper, International Institute for Strategic Studies (forthcoming).

2. *The Times* and the *Guardian*, 17 December 1974.

3. *Guardian*, 10 January 1975.

4. *The Times*, 12 January 1975.

5. *Guardian*, 10 March 1975.

6. *The Times*, 2 August 1975.

Index

Index

Che's Guerrilla War

Régis Debray

On 8 October 1967, less than a year after the beginning of his campaign in Bolivia, Che Guevara was killed by government troops at the gorge of *El Yuro*. His revolutionary struggle to liberate Latin America was defeated before it had seriously begun, as the guerrillas, cut off from the local population, and hampered by hunger and disease, were unable to fight effectively against the government.

In this book Régis Debray analyses the historical reasons for the failure in the field of one of the world's foremost theorists of guerrilla warfare. He shows that although Che's grandiose strategy for revolution throughout Latin America was intelligent, the tactical details were ill-conceived and out of touch with the actual situation in Bolivia.

Régis Debray was with Che in Bolivia, and his story gives us a useful insight into one of the greatest setbacks the Left has suffered in Latin America.

The Man on Horseback

S. E. Finer

The Man on Horseback received wide acclaim when it was first published and has proved itself as the definitive work on the role of the military in politics. Now brought up to date with a new chapter, a revised bibliography and tables setting out the number, distribution and provenance of military *coups* in the last fifteen years, it provides a lucid and coherent summary of one of the key political phenomena of our time.

Professor Finer examines 'political colonels' as a type, generalizing from numerous examples about the military as a political force and the factors which promote or inhibit the intervention of the armed forces in politics. As the discussion develops, a clear pattern emerges from which the author draws the conclusion that military *coups* are likely to increase in the future, as the new nations of Africa and Asia develop.

'The writer's discussion of the motives and situations which precipitate military intervention is as thorough as his examination of the historical reasons which make it possible in the first place' – David Rees in the *Spectator*

esia

acism and Imperial Response

Loney

late 1950s and early 1960s saw the rapid and, in
st cases, peaceful decolonization of Africa. But today
odesia remains colonized, no longer controlled by the
perial power, but still governed by white settlers.
artin Loney describes the history of the colony and of
he continuous African opposition to the invaders.

Central to his theme is the development of the power of the intransigent white rulers; in his words, 'this book is about the historical development of that power, the systematic use which has been made of it to build a prosperous white society in Africa, and the consequent impoverishment of the African population. It is also about the complicity of the British governments, Labour and Conservative, in this process.'

In its assessment of the British sell-out and of the growing sense of national identity on the part of the African population, this is a book which will upset many of the comfortable ideas held about Rhodesia in this country.

Libya

The Elusive Revolution

Ruth First

'By God I am confused', exclaimed Colonel Gadaffi at one Libyan popular conference. Where Libya is concerned, who isn't?

Ruth First's main emphasis falls on the causes and consequences of the 1969 revolution, in which a group of young officers ousted the monarchy. This thorough survey provides a wealth of information about the religious, economic and social springs of Libyan politics, the sudden explosion of oil revenues and the fanatical – often naïve – pursuit of Arab unity. She introduces the reader to a twentieth-century social revolution based on the Koran; to an oil-rich state determined not to copy Kuwait; to a new centre of pan-Arabism which has almost invited the hostility of other Arab states; and to a régime which exhorts the people to embrace its historic role but suffocates all independent action.

Nevertheless this nation of under two million inhabitants has struck giant postures in recent years. Its strengths and weaknesses become clearer in the light of Ruth First's able study.

A Short History of Africa

Roland Oliver and J. D. Fage

Fifth Edition – Revised

This concise history of Africa has been in constant demand since it first appeared in 1962. Much had already been written on different regions of the continent and different periods of its long development, including colonial histories of the European powers, ephemeral articles on the emergent countries, studies of Africa's pre-history, etc.: but there had previously been nothing that offered the general reader an overall view of African history from the earliest times to the establishment of the Organization of African Unity and the events of the late 1960s.

The authors, who are both professors of African history, have drawn on the whole range of literature about Africa and on the evidence provided by archaeology, oral traditions, language relationships, social institutions, and material cultures to write this volume. *A Short History of Africa* not only marshals the most authoritative views of African specialists into an absorbing narrative: it also puts forward original conclusions that take the study of Africa a stage further.

'Admirable in its quality, its balance, and its scholarship' – *Sunday Times*

Which Way Africa?

The Search for a New Society

Basil Davidson

A man would have to be very brave or very foolha[illegible] try to forecast precisely the pattern of Africa's futur[illegible] Where events outrun the printing-presses, discretion [illegible] better part of omniscience.

In *Which Way Africa?* Basil Davidson, the well-known writer on African affairs, has steered clear of political ju-ju. Instead – and definitely more to the purpose – he has made what is the only up-to-date and comprehensive analysis in English – and probably in any language – of the social, economic, and political motives, myths, ideas, and beliefs which underlie modern African nationalism.

Events in almost every corner of the continent have shown the world an Africa poised on the threshold of new ventures, an Africa in flux. Only such an analysis as the author has successfully achieved in this volume can help to delineate the kind of societies which will now tend to emerge there.

Rhode

White R

Martin

The
mo
Rh
in
N
t